The Great Alliance

The Great Alliance

Economic Recovery and the Problems of Power 1945–1951

Jim Phillips

Pluto Press

LONDON · EAST HAVEN, CONNECTICUT

First published 1996 by Pluto Press
345 Archway Road, London N6 5AA
and 140 Commerce Street
East Haven, Connecticut 06512, USA

British Library Cataloguing in Publication Data
A catalogue record for this book is available from the British Library

ISBN 0 7453 1038 9 hbk

Library of Congress Cataloging in Publication Data
Phillips, Jim, 1968–
    The great alliance : economic recovery and the problems of power,
1945–1951 / Jim Phillips.
      p.   cm.
    Includes bibliographical references (p.   ) and index.
    ISBN 0–7453–1038–9 (hbk.)
    1. Trade-unions—Great Britain—Political activity—History—20th
century. 2. Trade-unions—Government policy—Great Britain—
History—20th century. 3. Trades Union Congress—History.
4. Labour Party (Great Britain) —History. 5. Great Britain—
Economic policy—1945–   I. Title.
HD6667.P47   1996
322'.2'0941—dc20   95–38684
                                                                            CIP

Designed and produced for Pluto Press by
Chase Production Services, Chipping Norton, OX7 5QR
Typeset from disk by Stanford DTP Services, Milton Keynes
Printed in the EC by WSOY, Finland

Contents

List of Tables

Acknowledgements

In preparing this book I have become greatly indebted to a very great number of people and institutions. Starting closest to home, as it were, I would like to thank everyone associated with the Departmental Modern History Research Seminar at the University of Edinburgh. I gladly acknowledge the invaluable assistance given to me over the years at the National Library of Scotland, the University of Edinburgh Library and the Mitchell Library in Glasgow. Further afield, I am indebted to everyone at the Public Records Office at Kew, Mr Richard Storey and Ms Christine Woodland of the Modern Records Centre at Warwick University, and to Mr John Connolly of the Transport and General Workers' Union, who provided access to his Union's records, both at Warwick and at Transport House in London. Thanks are also due to Mr Bob Aspinall and his colleagues at the Museum of London Library in Limehouse. Bob Aspinall kindly provided me with access to the records of various port employers' organisations, and generously equipped me with numerous other invaluable references. In addition, I greatly appreciate the assistance of Mr Stephen Bird and Mr Andrew Flinn of the National Museum of Labour History in Manchester. Andrew Flinn, who has sorted the files of the National Amalgamated Stevedores and Dockers, was especially helpful. For access to materials in the Communist Party of Great Britain archive, I owe thanks to Francis King and George Matthews.

Back in Scotland, I am particularly grateful for the invaluable and sustained advice of Dr Paul Addison, and extend thanks to Mr Ian S. Wood and Dr Angus Calder. It gives me great pleasure also to acknowledge Mr Terry Brotherstone and Professor Paul Dukes of Aberdeen University. Without their encouragement in 1990 I would probably not have embarked on this project, and without the treasured support of my family – Rona, George and Donald Phillips – and Anna Robertson, I certainly would not have completed it. Further thanks are due to my oldest friends, Nev Laverack and Dave Whyte. But my deepest debt of all is owed to Dr John Brown of Edinburgh University. Having supervised my work as a postgraduate student with admirable patience and great perception, John has remained a tactful, humorous and wise counsellor. With enormous gratitude I dedicate this book to him.

Preface

This is a book, essentially, about the 1945–51 Labour governments. It draws attention to Labour's governing priorities, and reviews the historical significance of the 'Great Alliance' between the Labour Party and the Trades Union Congress (TUC) by examining the extent to which this alliance sustained and supported the Attlee administrations. In order to explore these two related questions, I focus on the docks, where the workforce was organised by the governments' closest union ally, the Transport and General Workers' Union (TGWU). At a time of great economic emergency, it was in the docks that the Labour Alliance was at its most important, but, for historical reasons, it was also at its most vulnerable.

Clement Attlee and his Ministers have enjoyed a chequered historical reputation. From the left they have been attacked for failing to respond adequately to the alleged wave of popular radicalism which had swept them into power. At a time when political and social conditions favoured major socialist advances in Britain, runs the argument separately forwarded by Ralph Miliband and John Saville, Labour introduced a bare minimum of economic and social reforms that left the capitalist system largely unreconstructed.[1] For all these alleged socialist – or 'labourist' – limitations, the Attlee governments have been even more vigorously assailed from historians on the political right. In accordance with the prevailing political culture, it became particularly fashionable in the 1980s to attribute Britain's ever-decreasing international status to Labour's period in office after 1945. To Correlli Barnett, for instance, Labour wilfully squandered the country's meagre economic resources on the 'New Jerusalem' of expensive welfare services and inefficient nationalised industries which sapped enterprise and decisively reduced Britain's long-term economic competitiveness.[2]

This book rejects each of these hostile frameworks of analysis. Developments in the docks certainly suggest that Labour was not in the business of ruthlessly betraying a radicalised working class. Guided by the dockers' former leader, Ernest Bevin, the governments provided the dock workforce with an unprecedented degree of economic security. But Ministers were not concentrating on social reform at the expense of economic reconstruction, as their response to industrial unrest in the docks indicates. Labour took an increasingly hard line on unofficial action, using thousands of troops to

replace striking dockers and accusing their unofficial leaders of deliberately causing trouble in order to disrupt British and European
economic recovery. This toughness indicated that, contrary to
Barnett's view, Labour's central priorities were economic recovery
and the international containment of communism.

Kenneth Morgan and Peter Hennessy have both justly argued
that the immense economic problems facing Labour in 1945 made
the governments' achievements in domestic reform all the more
impressive. Morgan and Hennessy also contend that Labour's
triumph in adversity was shaped by the unique solidarity of the period:
the Cabinet, Parliamentary Labour Party and trade union movement
were all strongly united. In Morgan's words, 'the dominant mood
was one of unity. This extended from Downing Street to the
humblest of party workers in the constituencies, down the pit and
on the shop floor.'[3] The trade union leadership certainly shared
the governments' central priorities, and Ministers enjoyed immensely
valuable support from their union partners in pursuing economic
recovery and resisting communism. But labour solidarity was by
no means complete, and certainly did not extend to the key area
of the docks. The unofficial strikes indicated the existence of a great
deal of tension between the TGWU and large numbers of its dock
members. They also led to a great deal of private strain between
the government and the TGWU leadership: events in the docks,
it will be revealed, sorely tested the solidarity of the 'Great Alliance'.

Finally, in reviewing the conventional picture of the party–union
link at a key moment in its history, and in reassessing what is
widely regarded as Labour's most successful period in office, the
book has an important contemporary as well as historical relevance.
In the mid-1990s 'New Labour' seems to be on the verge of
winning a General Election for the first time since 1974. Like the
1945 Labour government, a Labour government elected in 1996
or 1997 would inherit huge economic problems, but it would not
necessarily enjoy anything like the same support from the TUC,
for Labour's modernising process has exacted considerable strains
on relations with the unions. With Labour no longer committed
to public ownership of industries and services, embracing instead
the rigours and dynamism of the market, the party leadership has
courted the hostility of union leaders who have seen their members
suffer as a result of market forces. Moreover, the public ownership
debate was accompanied by less-publicised but equally important
disputes between Labour and the unions over the minimum wage,
trade union and employment law and full employment.[4] Unless
these difficult areas of conflict can be resolved before the coming
General Election, the next Labour government – should it arrive
– will risk open and damaging confrontation with its millions of
trade union supporters.

List of Abbreviations

AFL	American Federation of Labour
CGT	Confédération Générale du Traveil
CIA	Central Intelligence Agency
CIO	Congress of Industrial Organisations
CPGB	Communist Party of Great Britain
CSU	Canadian Seamen's Union
CTLC	Canadian Trades and Labour Congress
DWRGLU	Dock, Wharf, Riverside and General Labourers' Union
ERP	European Recovery Programme
ICFTU	International Confederation of Free Trade Unions
ITWF	International Transport Workers' Federation
ILP	Independent Labour Party
MLNS	Ministry of Labour and National Service
MoL	Ministry of Labour
MoT	Ministry of Transport
NAPE	National Association of Port Employers
NASD	National Amalgamated Stevedores and Dockers
NATO	North Atlantic Treaty Organisation
NDLB	National Dock Labour Board
NDLC	National Dock Labour Corporation
NEC	National Executive Committee (of the Labour Party)
NJC	National Joint Council of the Port Transport Industry
NMM	National Minority Movement
NUDL	National Union of Dock Labourers
PCF	Parti Communiste Francais
PCI	Partito Comunista Italiano
PLA	Port of London Authority
PLP	Parliamentary Labour Party
PSI	Partito Socialista Italiano
RCP	Revolutionary Communist Party of Great Britain
RIRO	Regional Industrial Relations Officer (MoL)
SDF	Social Democratic Federation
SIU	Seafarers' International Union
STGWU	Scottish Transport and General Workers' Union
STO	Supplies and Transport Organisation
TGWU	Transport and General Workers' Union
TUC	Trades Union Congress
WFTU	World Federation of Trade Unions

Labour in Power, 1945–50

The 'Great Alliance', 1900–45

For the British Labour Party and its supporters the summer of 1945 was a period of unprecedented triumph and optimism. Following a sequence of setbacks between the wars, the labour movement had gained considerable organisational and political strength from its participation in the defeat of Nazi Germany and Japan, and now seemed on the verge of formidable achievement at home. Michael Foot evokes the spirit aroused by these developments in the opening lines of his second volume of *Aneurin Bevan*. Veterans of the labour movement who had renewed their faith after each successive disaster – the collapse of the Triple Alliance in 1921, the General Strike in 1926 and the defection of Ramsay MacDonald in 1931 – had 'special cause for exultation' in 'the blissful dawn of July 1945'. With the European conflict over and the war in Asia reaching conclusion, 'Eyes were fixed on the promise of a new society. Suddenly the vision of the Socialist pioneers had been given substance and historic impetus by the radical political ferment of wartime.'[1]

The scale of Labour's victory was indeed stunning. With 393 seats the party had earned a Commons majority of 146 over the other parties combined, and office with power for the first time: 'LABOUR IN POWER!' proclaimed the *Daily Herald*. This unprecedented situation brought a stern response, however, from *The Times*, which warned Labour that its mandate was 'national' rather than 'sectional'. The editorial dwelt evasively on Labour's 'close and characteristic connexion with certain specialised groups within the community', and urged upon the new administration the 'decisive importance' of embracing 'only those aspirations which are commonly accepted by the millions of men and women who have voted for them'. In other words, Labour would have to govern in a 'national interest', unfettered by their trade union supporters.[2]

In implying that Labour's first instinct in office would be to satisfy the needs of trade unions, and in suggesting that these needs were somehow incompatible with the 'national interest', *The Times* projected the conventional wisdom about the relationship between the Labour Party and the trade unions. This conventional view remains a key article of right-wing propaganda in the mid-1990s, as the Conservative Party persists with the tactic of portraying Labour as the pawn of its union 'paymasters', and to some extent the Labour leadership has encouraged this view by seeking changes to the party–union link which, it was felt, had contributed to the fourth successive electoral defeat in April 1992. The idea that Labour has always been bound by its ties with the unions is, however, extremely misleading. Such is the conclusion of Professor Lewis Minkin's acclaimed and persuasive analysis of the relationship, *The Contentious Alliance*.

Minkin emphasises the inestimable historical significance of Labour's ties with trade unions, stating that, 'For over 80 years this relationship has shaped the structure and, in various ways, the character of the British Left. Every major group and party in British politics has had to take account of what Keir Hardie called "the great alliance", whether they regarded it as "great" or not.'[3] Critics of the alliance have objected to its apparently sectional trade union values and aspirations. Socialist critics – Marxist and non-Marxist – have argued that the influence of a defensive trade union culture has constrained the Labour Party, narrowing the potential for radical economic and social transformation.[4] On the right the alliance has been held to represent a dangerous political and industrial threat to the constitution and the economy, with Labour in office dispensing special favours to powerful but unaccountable trade union leaders.

Minkin dispels the hackneyed right-wing images of 'union barons' and 'fixers' in 'smoke-filled rooms'. Instead he offers a sturdy defence of the party–union linkage, denying that Labour's trade union origins obliged party leaders, whether in opposition or office, to observe a parity of strategy and vision with their trade union counterparts. In 1935, Minkin notes, the Transport and General Workers' leader Ernest Bevin 'colourfully' observed that the Labour Party had been produced 'out of the bowels' of the trade unions. Indeed the party had been established at the start of the century to pursue 'trade union principles and ideals'; but by the middle of the 1930s the original party–union relationship had undergone considerable changes. Minkin defines the sum of these changes as the establishment of 'separate spheres': a relationship had evolved between two separate but mutually compatible partners, each with their own recognisable and different interests and responsibilities. This is ascribed to a number of loosely related but mutually re-inforcing factors, the most important being the movement's ideological unity. Both partners shared a commitment to Parliamentary democracy and believed that as the state was politically neutral, it was of immense potential benefit to working people. From 1900 unions provided the financial and numerical support which made the party viable, and participated in selecting candidates and formulating policy, but they made little attempt to interfere in the daily running of the parliamentary organisation. Such abstention was encouraged as unions grew, through the First World War and after, and as the burdens of trade union leadership became more onerous. With a dwindling number of senior trade unionists on Labour's benches, the Parliamentary party become more diverse in its social composition. An increasing number of professionals and non-trade-unionist intellectuals reinforced the separation of the political and the industrial. This diversity reflected the party's changing political identity. After 1922, when Labour's vote out-stripped its affiliated union membership for the first time, the party was decreasingly dependent on the votes of trade union members and their families. As Minkin points out, these different bases of support required 'differing obligations and concerns' from the alliance's respective partners, with the party increasingly having to address the aspirations of those outside the organised industrial working class as it sought political power.[5]

This divergence did not, of course, imply division within the labour movement. Minkin contends that any tension between the industrial and political was defused by an informal system of rules which developed organically across the first three decades of the Party's existence. These 'rules' – never rigidly codified but implicitly recognised by the unions and the party nevertheless – were based on the core trade union values of freedom, unity and solidarity, and emphasised the partners' individual rights and collective obligations. 'Freedom' implied that in any dispute the union concerned was entitled to protect its members without interference from other unions or politicians; the unions' autonomous position in industrial matters was to be observed by the party, and in return the unions would leave politics to the 'politicians'. 'Unity' and 'solidarity' – the watchwords of strength in the labour movement – required trade unions to marshal support behind the Parliamentary leadership, and in the stormy interwar years to protect the disappointing Labour governments against criticism from the left.[6]

These values were determined by the historical essence of the TUC. Minkin argues that while generally adhering to a wide range of social, economic and political goals, the TUC's single over-riding priority at every stage of its development, its 'primary considera-tion', has been the 'defence of trade unionism'. Usually this priority has confined unions to a narrow 'economist' strategy of seeking improved working conditions, but where wider political develop-ments have intervened, the TUC has broadened its strategy. It was in order to defend trade unionism that the TUC supported estab-lishing the party at Westminster. And in the 1930s it was the realisation that fascism directly threatened trade unionism which motivated Bevin and Citrine in their successful efforts to commit the Labour Party to collective security and rearmament.

This fundamental issue, the defence of trade unionism, determined the unions' attitude to the 1924 and 1929 minority Labour administrations. The potential conflict between the movement's political and industrial wings was brought immediately to the fore in 1924. On 16 February Bevin, as TGWU leader, authorised a national dock strike in pursuit of a wage increase and a guaranteed working week. Ramsay MacDonald's government responded by threatening to operate the 1920 Emergency Powers Act and Bevin called the strike off, having won the wage claim but on decasualisation having to accept the compromise of a Court of Inquiry. In March, facing a strike by another group of TGWU workers, London tramwaymen, the government actually obtained the King's signature on an Emergency Powers Proclamation. Bevin backed down again but he was furious that the government had abused the trade union autonomy which the Labour Party had been created to protect by flouting his members' freedom to protect their individual rights via collective strike action. The episode indicated that Labour in power would not administer special favours to its trade union allies. It also showed unions that their industrial interests should not interfere with Labour's obligations to the wider community, and the outcome was a sharpened division between the movement's separate industrial and political spheres. Responding to criticism that the TGWU strikes were jeopardising the first Labour government and the future success of socialism, Bevin simply pointed out that, 'governments may come and governments may go, but the workers' fight for the betterment of conditions must go on all the time'.[7]

Bevin's pragmatic prescience was borne out by the subsequent five years of Conservative government, with the TUC and the Labour Party engaged in visibly separate spheres of activity, most notably during the General Strike. This process was of course encouraged by the Conservatives' 'revenge' for the General Strike, the 1927 Trade Unions and Trade Disputes Act. Introducing the principle of contracting 'in' rather than contracting 'out', the legislation physically loosened the relationship between the Labour Party and the unions.

The relationship between the 1929 Labour government and the trade unions further exemplified the governing 'rules' of behaviour and the strain which they could come under. TUC leaders, including left-wingers like the miners' secretary Arthur Cook, did much to deflect criticism of the minority administration's failure to attack unemployment effectively and abolish the 1927 trade union legislation.[8] However, with Bevin increasingly concerned about the wisdom of the government's priorities, as large-scale unemployment continued to undermine the size, strength and confidence of the labour movement, the TUC gradually withdrew its uncritical support. It was in order to defend trade unionism that the TUC mobilised internal Cabinet opposition to the unemployment benefit cuts in August 1931. The 'solidarity' of the alliance also ensured afterwards that the unions would provide what Bevin described as 'ballast' for the party. Labour's morale, which had been steadily eroding since 1929, was badly bruised by the government's downfall, MacDonald's defection and the crushing electoral defeat which followed. In the face of this collapse the TUC brought comfort to the movement by acting decisively on two important questions: insisting upon the expulsion of MacDonald and Snowden from the Labour Party on 28 September, and opposing the National government's record on unemployment after Labour's parliamentary strength had been reduced to just 46.

The unions' stabilising role at a moment of crisis was not, as Minkin records, 'without its clear quid pro quo'. After 1931 a number of important new 'rules' defining the nature of the partnership in the unions' favour were established, the most pertinent being that the political leadership would never again commit itself to a governing coalition or political alliance without first seeking the movement's approval.[9] Moreover, when Labour returned to office in 1945, the experiences of 1929–31, along with those of 1924, would not be forgotten. The Attlee governments were to avoid a great deal of trouble by observing the 'rules' of the alliance which MacDonald had ignored. In the meantime the role of the TUC was vital, holding the alliance and the party together until the outbreak of war in 1939.

In the twentieth century, according to one common view, war has been the great motor-force of economic, social and political change, by accelerating and bringing to fruition deep-set historical trends. In Britain the Second World War certainly shifted the balance of political and industrial power in favour of the labour movement. There were a number of reasons for this. The political character of the war was undeniably confusing, as Ernest Mandel's Marxist account testifies, with an array of conflicting and contradictory interests characterising the nations and colonies which stood together against Germany, Italy and Japan.[10] Yet in Britain the dominant public theme was the stated need to defeat Nazi Germany. Involving democratic anti-fascist rhetoric and common sacrifices, this venture promoted a much stronger sense of social cohesion than had been evident in interwar Britain. The rationing of 'fair shares' was apparent testimony to the organising powers of the community – a belief further encouraged by the wartime alliance with the Soviet Union. As the Soviet command economy sustained a victorious repulsion of the Nazi invasion, fresh credibility became attached to the notion of economic planning, but long before the Red Army's advance on Berlin began, large sections of the British public had begun to disassociate themselves from the Conservatives. The pre-war appeasers, the 'guilty men', had kept millions on the dole instead of rearming to resist Hitler and defeat fascism.[11]

These developments in Labour's favour were complemented by the shifting economic position of the working class. With manpower as the ultimate 'scarce resource' during the national emergency, and Bevin at the Ministry of Labour, the unions grew in size and confidence, attaining unprecedented political and economic power. In July 1945 the Labour Party duly won a stunning victory in the General Election and the first majority Labour government was formed. These were years, as Minkin puts it, of 'solid achievement',[12] but the war also revealed considerable tensions within the labour alliance. The informal rules which underwrote its existence were called into question along with many other political, economic and social relationships during the peculiar conditions of total war.

During the great national emergency, when the future of the British working class as much as the British Empire was at stake, the TUC gladly reordered its historical priorities. After Bevin had become Minister of Labour, union leaders freely made concessions on dilution and industrial conscription. They also accepted a ban on strikes, in the shape of the 1940 emergency regulation, Conditions of Employment and Compulsory Arbitration (Order 1305 as it was commonly called), and its 1944 amendment, Regulation 1AA. These concessions were rewarded with considerable privileges in return. Bevin inflated industrial morale and maximised productivity by improving working conditions and the social status of working people. To this end measures such as the 1943 Catering Wages Act, the 1944 Disabled Persons Act and the 1945 Wages Councils Act were brought forward. Reform also encompassed the partial decasualisation of labour in the dock industry. This was something to which Bevin had long been personally committed, and the industry's casual regime was particularly ill-suited to the requirements of war. Moreover, with the War Cabinet regarding manpower as the most valuable industrial commodity, the organisers of manpower – trade unions – were given a key role in planning and rallying support for industrial strategy. The TUC's historic claim 'to represent the working people in all matters affecting their conditions of life and labour' was formally conceded, along with the principle of equal status in a tripartite system of collective bargaining.[13]

The TUC's enhanced status disturbed the balance of the labour alliance. The TUC's determination to secure the 'best available outcome' for trade union members at all times has been noted. As trade unionists had benefited from their experiences under the wartime coalition, and with Labour not expecting to defeat the wartime hero Churchill in a post-war election, for trade unionists the war's best available political outcome appeared to be a continuation of the coalition. Bevin thought that he might serve in peacetime as Minister of Labour under Churchill, and may even have felt that the TUC could represent a political *alternative* to the Labour Party given its access to government, its representation in Cabinet and the clear gains which the direct relationship had won.[14] He was clearly ambivalent about his relations with the party, refusing to attend meetings of the Parliamentary Labour Party (PLP) after back-bench criticism of the government's response to the Beveridge Report in February 1943. Disparaging the purpose of 'playing the party game', he only resumed contacts with the PLP in April 1944 in order to present his position on Regulation 1AA to MPs. Throughout the war Bevin plainly shared the premier's belief that he was in the War Cabinet to represent the trade unions and not the Labour Party.[15]

These developments antagonised the Labour left. Aneurin Bevan felt that in strengthening the state's coercive powers against striking workers and apparently entertaining the idea of a peacetime Coalition, Bevin was endangering the Labour Party's long-term future.[16] Given Bevin's evident ambivalence towards Labour in 1943, this fear was not unfounded. Bevan and the left were also unhappy with the legal action taken by the authorities against striking workers since the imposition of the Emergency Regulations in 1940 – most notably against 1000 coal miners at Betteshanger Colliery in Kent in 1942 – and the strengthening of the government's emergency powers with the amended Regulation 1AA in 1944.

Regulation 1AA angered the left because of its draconian provisions – inciting strikes in essential services was to be punishable with five years' penal servitude – and the manner of its introduction. The crucible of industrial conflict in 1944 was the coal-mining industry, with 1.85 million days lost to strike action between 28 January and 11 April. Implying that strikes were being fomented by 'Trotskyites' and other 'anti-war people' intent on disrupting the allies' invasion preparations, Bevin introduced Regulation 1AA after talks with the TUC and employers, but without referring the matter to Parliament. Bevan attacked Bevin for by-passing Parliamentary democracy in this way, an action representing 'the enfranchisement of the corporate society and the disfranchisement of the individual'. In the same debate Sir Richard Acland, the Common Wealth MP, ridiculed Bevin's implication that the miners' action was politically-motivated. The Trotskyist organisation concerned – the Revolutionary Communist Party – had a membership of 500 and a head office with weekly expenses of

£10: it could not possibly have nurtured a strike involving tens of thousands of miners.[17]

The conflict between Bevin and the Labour left did not, of course, result in the TUC abandoning the party: the values of loyalty and solidarity were too ingrained, the respect for majority decision absolute, and Bevin conceded to the Party Conference's decision in December 1944 that Labour fight the 1945 General Election independently. Any trade union misgivings about abandoning the coalition might have been assuaged by the sentiment which Bevin himself had expressed in 1924: while governments would come and go, the struggle for improved workers' conditions would not. This struggle had certainly been hindered by the Conservative and National governments between the wars, but the unions had survived. A Labour victory at the election would be richly preferable, but with its new strength and confidence the unions did not question their ability to survive further periods of Conservative government.

A New Situation?

In reviewing Labour's history to 1945, one sees that the party was influenced, but by no means bound, by the values of its trade union partners. *The Times* leader published on the morning of Labour's arrival in office certainly underestimated the extent to which it had already cultivated a national rather than a sectional identity. Attlee had been keen to demonstrate this theme during the election campaign. In response to Churchill's notorious 'Gestapo' speech, which had equated democratic socialism with Nazism, Attlee condemned the Tories as a 'class' party, wedded to 'property and privilege'. In stark contrast he characterised Labour as the only representative political force in Britain, comprising 'all the main streams which flow into the river of our national life'.[18]

The Parliamentary Labour Party which assembled to hear the King's Speech on 15 August reflected this diversity and apparently indicated that as Labour's electoral support grew, so its dependence on trade union and working-class candidates and support diminished. Of 393 members 259 were new to the House; the 119 trade union sponsored members constituted 31 per cent of the total, as opposed to 51 per cent in 1935 and 76 per cent after the 1931 catastrophe. On the same theme Margaret Cole estimated on behalf of the Fabian Society that around 150 Labour MPs came from manual working-class occupations; of the numerous professional groups present in the PLP there were now 49 university lecturers or school teachers (outnumbering the ex-miners), 44 lawyers, 25 journalists, 15 doctors and, in the party opposed to the Conservatives' 'property and privilege' there was even room for 25 company directors.[19] One former schoolmaster, the new Home Secretary Chuter Ede, was greatly pleased by the PLP's transformation. On 28 July he noted that 'the new Party is a great change from the old. It teems with bright, vivacious servicemen. The superannuated Trade Union official seems hardly to be noticeable in the ranks.'[20]

While the proportion of trade unionists had dropped, Attlee acknowledged the tensions that had arisen in 1924 and 1931 within the alliance by giving former trade unionists a greater share of Cabinet seats than they had enjoyed in previous Labour governments. He took great care, he told his press secretary Francis Williams, to balance 'intelligentsia' with trade unionists. Thus nine of his 20 Cabinet Ministers were trade unionists.[21] To the surprise of contemporary observers, these included the veteran leader of the National Society of Operative Printers and Assistants, George Isaacs, who resigned his position as Chairman of the TUC's General Council to become Minister of Labour. The Cabinet's 'mixed constitution', along with Labour's victory at the polls, restored the equilibrium of the labour alliance. With the trade union movement's great linchpin, Ernie Bevin, centrally positioned as Foreign Secretary within a majority Labour government, and the channels of communication between the movement's industrial and political leaderships open as never before, the unions were content to devolve 'political' responsibility upon the politicians.

The restoration of good will between the party and the unions would prove to be of immeasurable importance to the government. Ostensibly an entirely new situation had been created by the electoral verdict, presenting Labour with unprecedented power and opportunity. Attlee's huge majority allowed the government to press on with its manifesto commitments, and the first three years of the 1945 Parliament witnessed a flurry of administrative and legislative activity. In due course a number of interwar labour movement demons were exorcised: the 1927 Trade Disputes and Trade Unions Act was repealed, and the Coal Mining Industry and the Bank of England nationalised, along with the railways and the water, gas and electricity services. A comprehensive system of social insurance was put into place; and the greatest post-war Labour monument of all, Aneurin Bevan's National Health Service, was erected on 5 July 1948.

Nonetheless, there were two central problems which the government could not legislate away. The war which had been central to Labour's victory also bequeathed the new administration two huge dilemmas: a troubling economic perspective and the question of the post-war international settlement. The latter proved to be particularly problematic as the tensions of the Cold War gathered and intensified, for the quest for agreement between Britain, the USA and the USSR was complicated by the urgent matter of restoring Europe's shattered economy. In seeking solutions to these problems Attlee and Bevin held secret cross-party discussions on foreign affairs with Churchill and Eden.[22] Of greater significance, however, was the help which the government received from its trade union partners, with the TUC marshalling vital support for Labour's economic and international strategies.

Dollars: Economic Perspectives

Britain lost approximately one quarter of its national wealth during the Second World War. This damage was largely due to the heavy loss of earnings on both visible and invisible trade. Due to the needs of war mobilisation, export industries were deliberately run down after 1939, so that in 1945 manufacturing exports were 30 per cent of their 1938 level. This deficiency was exacerbated by the significant diminution of Britain's invisible exports, a traditionally valuable source of national income. In terms of shipping tonnage the net loss arising from the war was 28 per cent; foreign assets had also been lost, the earnings on which had been equivalent to the sum typically spent on around one quarter of the nation's imports. Collectively these circumstances confronted the country with a trade deficit which would only be balanced, and imports of food and raw materials restored to pre-war levels, if Britain could increase its exports to between 50 and 75 per cent above the 1938 figure.[23]

These difficulties were severely compounded when, within six days of VJ Day, the USA terminated the Lend-Lease arrangements by which Britain had been meeting its import expenses. In order to finance the external deficit and maintain the economic life of its people, the government sent Keynes to Washington to negotiate a loan with the United States. An agreement was signed, largely on American terms, on 6 December.

Despite this extremely grim perspective, the government was not greatly deflected during its first year in office. Optimism naturally flowed from the spectacular electoral victory, and in office Labour was buoyed by its initial legislative achievements. An exuberant Chancellor of the Exchequer, Hugh Dalton, introduced his first Budget in November 1945 with, he told the House of Commons, 'a song in my heart'.[24] Dalton went cheerfully about his business throughout 1946, with the maintenance of rationing and a general shortage of consumer demand ensuring that exports boomed. In November they reached 111 per cent of the 1938 total, prompting Dalton to predict rashly: 'If we keep going together as we have since VJ Day, the shortages and frustrations which still afflict us will disappear like the snows of winter, and give place to the full promise of springtime.'[25]

The following year saw an enormous change in Britain's economic fortunes. According to Kenneth Morgan 1947 was 'a year of almost unrelieved disaster' for the government.[26] An immensely harsh winter maximised the effects of a coal crisis which caused massive economic disruption, leaving two million workers temporarily unemployed. An even more damaging summer financial storm followed, and in October the optimistic Dalton – the song extinguished from his heart – gave way to Sir Stafford Cripps – the harbinger of austerity – at the Treasury. The symbolism of the switch can perhaps be overstated, for Dalton had initially recognised Britain's contracting global capacity and forced the issue of withdrawing economic aid to Greece and Turkey in February 1947, and Cripps did not reverse the social welfare progress which Dalton had financed. Nevertheless, from the autumn of 1947 the government re-emphasised that recovery was contingent upon restricting imports and expanding exports – a conjunction requiring a great deal of public co-operation and restraint. With Cripps, the embodiment of 'a new morality and sense of public rectitude',[27] as Chancellor, the government was better equipped to appeal for such popular support than when served by the less prudent figure of Dalton.

The apparent recovery in 1946 had masked Britain's precarious economic position. Despite the export boom, the balance of payments deficit was still £344 million.[28] This fragility was exacerbated by the Anglo-American economic relationship's disequilibrium. Generally speaking, to pay for vital US imports Britain used up dollars which it could not recoup, as the bulk of British export markets lay outside the dollar trading area.[29] British weakness was illustrated during the summer of 1947, as the 1945 loan rapidly ebbed away. With uncertainty surrounding the outcome of Anglo-American negotiations on US Secretary of State Marshall's proposals for a European Recovery Programme, Treasury officials prepared a series of austerity measures. These included much lower imports, a 'famine' food plan with compulsory direction of labour to agriculture over the next three years, and a drastically reduced building programme to save timber, steel and manpower for export requirements. With no further dollars, officials estimated that the daily ration would be reduced to 1700 calories – 1000 less than the wartime minimum.[30] This position was cruelly exacerbated by the commencement of sterling convertibility, in accordance with the 1945 loan agreement, on 15 July 1947. A spectacular run on the pound ensued, the outflow of dollars and gold in 1947 increasing fourfold on 1946, $4100 million as opposed to $900 million.[31] On 17 August Dalton told the Cabinet that $150 million had been lost on 11 August alone,[32] and on 21 August the government was forced to suspend convertibility.

After Cripps became Chancellor on 13 November 1947, economic recovery was essentially based on producing enough exports to earn the dollars that guaranteed imports of food and the raw materials which maintained full employment. This placed great demands on manufacturing industry, but – as subsequent chapters of this book detail – the industrial sector most affected was the docks, through which the vital exports and imports had to pass. These enormous strains contributed to mounting tension in the docks, which resulted in a number of damaging unofficial strikes. To the increasing annoyance of the government, the TGWU was unable to prevent these strikes, and the labour alliance itself was put under enormous strain.

Broadly speaking, however, the government's long-term economic strategy was largely successful, but it required a good deal of outside support. Of primary assistance was the US Treasury. After contravening the 1945 loan agreement by abandoning convertibility in 1947, the government expended a great deal of diplomatic activity in smoothing relations with the USA. But as international tension sharpened considerably in 1947, the US administration could not afford to be too impatient with Britain. In Washington the view was crystallising that the best insurance against communist ascendancy in Western Europe would be for the US to guarantee financially the continent's economic recovery. This perception was given fresh credence by the communist coup in Czechoslovakia, which prompted a previously reluctant Senate to pass Truman's Economic Cooperation Act in March 1948. Signed by President Truman on 3 April 1948, this provided the dollars which formed a basis for British recovery until the end of 1950. On 25 June the first meeting between British and American officials on the European Recovery Programme took place, Leslie Rowan of the British Committee for European Economic Cooperation welcoming Thomas K. Finletter, Chief of the US European Cooperation Act mission in London, to the Treasury.

The British and the US Treasuries maintained close contact throughout the European Recovery Programme's 1948–50 period, most notably during the 1949 financial crisis, when the post-1947 economic advance was temporarily halted by a depression in export markets. This reinflated Britain's gold/dollar and trade deficits, precipitating another exchange crisis which led to the devaluation of sterling from $4.03 to $2.80 in September. In July US Treasury Secretary John Snyder discussed the disequilibrium between the dollar and sterling areas with Cripps in London. On 29 August Labour Ministers concluded that devaluation was a necessity, and in September Bevin and Cripps crossed the Atlantic to inform the US government. These latter talks, along with devaluation, diminished the disequilibrium between the dollar and sterling areas, and led to a remarkable reversal in Britain's economic fortunes. In 1947 the gold and dollar deficit totalled £1024 million, and the current account deficit £381 million. Through a shift in the pattern of external trade, with less imports from and more exports to North America, and through attaining the necessary increase in overall export activity, up to 80 per cent in excess of the 1938 level, by 1950 the government had converted these deficits into substantial surpluses: £308 million and £307 million with respective regard to gold/dollars and the current account. These restored balances enabled Britain to opt out of Marshall Aid at the end of 1950, two years earlier than planned.[33]

While US finance was clearly instrumental to this recovery, in minimising the costs of the export drive during the vital Marshall Aid period, the government also enjoyed crucial economic support from the Trades Union Congress. During Dalton's Chancellorship, the TUC's economic behaviour had hardly deviated since it had responded to the 1944 Employment White Paper by stating that the responsibility for maintaining employment belonged to the government, which should seek no sacrifices from trade unionists in pursuing this duty. A TUC 'Interim Report on Post-War Reconstruction' duly insisted that it 'would have at all times to consider whether it was, on balance, better that the objective [of full employment] should be modified rather than that methods incompatible with the rights of work people and the objectives of Trade Unionism should be used to achieve it'.[34]

Even with a Labour administration the TUC remained cautious about abandoning its traditional functions and accepting new obligations. The TUC was a member of the tripartite National Joint Advisory Council, but this was little more than an educative body. Indeed, prior to 1948 it is difficult to identify the type of mechanical links between the TUC and the state – implied, for instance, in Keith Middlemas's corporate triangle of union leaders, employers' representatives and Whitehall bureaucrats – which would have allowed the unions to influence directly government policy.[35] Certainly union leaders supported the efforts of their labour movement partners, but links were through the party rather than Whitehall, and union leaders' efforts in this direction were largely confined to reminding members that the economic situation was extremely serious. In September 1945 Bevin's successor at the TGWU, Arthur Deakin, warned members that without 'a flourishing export trade' it would be impossible to raise working-class living standards.[36]

Such exhortations undoubtedly helped the government, but the TUC's real economic contribution came after the 1947 convertibility crisis. In November 1947 Cripps informed Cabinet that the export drive would only succeed if accompanied by effective wage and price restraint. With a minimum of goods and services available on the market, general increases in money wages could not be justified. A wider availability of goods and services would not result, but a build up of inflationary pressure would take place, further jeopardising Britain's external deficit as the cost of exports rose and their marketable value declined. Although it was not the government's place to intervene directly in fixing individual incomes, it was essential that firm guidelines be laid down for those to whom this duty did fall.[37]

The TUC was informed of this developing strategy at a meeting with Attlee on 17 November and responded with an 'Interim Report on the Economic Situation'. This conceded the potential need for restraint, but insisted upon the unions' prerogative to police any regulations that were introduced: 'any attempt on the part of an outside body to regulate or directly control wage movements would have disastrous effects ... if there was to be greater restraint upon wage movements it could come only from within the trade union movement itself'.[38]

In February 1948 the government issued a White Paper entitled *Statement on Personal Incomes, Costs and Prices*, bringing the essence of Cripps's argument for an incomes standstill into the public sphere.[39] Ministers reassured the TUC that the standstill was voluntary and that steps would be taken to restrict prices and profits, and a special conference of union executive councils on 24 March took the unprecedented step of accepting, by over three million votes, a peacetime pay freeze. The TUC's co-operation on incomes lasted until September 1950 and was of immense benefit to the government. Between June 1945 and March 1948 wages advanced by 8–10 per cent. In the 18 months from March 1948 the increase was only 3 per cent. After devaluation the TUC position on wages became even more important. On 23 November 1949 the General Council recommended an extension of the freeze, and agreements that pegged wages to the cost of living were suspended, on the condition that the retail price index did not rise above 5 per cent. In the 12 months from September 1949 money wages increased by 1.4 per cent, and with retail prices rising by 3 per cent real wages were stationary or falling. This was all the more remarkable when unemployment was below 300,000, hourly wage rates increasing after March 1948 no more rapidly than between 1934 and 1938, when two million workers were unemployed.[40] The TUC complemented its action on wages by overseeing notable labour productivity improvements. This productivity increased by

1.6 per cent per annum from 1945 to 1951; by 2.5 per cent per annum from 1948 to 1951 and by 3.5 per cent per annum in the crucial manufacturing sector in these last three years.[41]

It is worth spelling out that, in adopting a more active economic role after 1947, the TUC to some extent qualified its traditional responsibilities and functions. Union leaders – most notably in the docks – paid for this departure in terms of growing rank and file dissatisfaction and unofficial industrial activity. Yet by marshalling mass support behind the government's economic strategy, the TUC was steadily affirming the labour alliance 'rules' of behaviour. To recap, these required union leaders to show 'solidarity' with their political comrades while at the same time securing the 'best available outcome' for their members. In abandoning the traditional pursuit of seeking an advance in wage labour's monetary value, the TUC was actively attempting to secure the best bargain for its affiliated members. Before 1947 Deakin – the dominant figure on the TUC General Council – was an unreconciled opponent of wage regulation. Shaken by the convertibility crisis, however, he changed his mind, fearing an impending economic and political catastrophe comparable to that of 1931. His General Council colleagues agreed that counter-inflationary mechanisms were essential lest working-class living standards be blown away in a whirlwind of rising prices and incomes that would lead to economic collapse and dislodge the Labour government. In this respect the timing of the wage freeze was all-important. By the middle of 1947 the government's main legislative work was either in place or well under way; its progress would stand or fall on the basis of the government's subsequent economic record – a perspective which presumably contributed to the ascendancy of Morrisonian 'consolidation' from the spring of 1948. With the government facing great international economic pressure in 1947, the TUC's rethink on wages reflected a desire to defend 'their' government. The repeal of the hostile 1927 legislation, the consultative avenues to Whitehall, nationalisation, the wider social and welfare benefits and, above all, the maintenance of full employment, represented a position of considerable material advance for trade union members. To defend the government and these advantages, the TUC was more than willing to concede its privileges on wages and productivity.

Labour's strategy for economic recovery, based on promoting exports with the assistance of Marshall dollars and TUC-policed wage moderation, had largely worked the trick by the end of 1950. With the outbreak of hostilities in Korea in June 1950, however, Labour's final year in office was characterised by renewed economic difficulties. Under immense pressure from the United States, the government adopted a massive rearmament programme. The package, enshrined in Hugh Gaitskell's controversial first – and only

– Budget in the spring of 1951, cost £4700 million over three years
and dramatically reversed Britain's economic progress. By the end
of 1951 Britain's trade and gold/dollar imbalances were again
soaring, and in 1952 the Churchill administration decided to phase
the defence estimates in over four years rather than three.[42]

Defending Democracy: International Perspectives

Long before the outbreak of war in Korea these two aspects of
political discourse, economic renewal and international friction, had
intersected in Attlee's Britain; the growth of ideological conflict,
particularly from 1947, constituted a definite framework within which
Labour sought to rebuild the domestic and wider European economy
with US dollars. Bevin and Dean Acheson, his favourite US
counterpart, shared an appreciation, albeit from slightly different
ideological perspectives, that communism would best be resisted
in Western Europe by a dual strategy. The first requirement was
to rebuild economic life and so restore popular faith in the political
and market institutions of liberal democracy. The second requirement was the political will and military capacity to defend liberal
democracy and allow it the opportunity to flourish. Bevin and his
American allies believed that it was in the political interests of
communism for economic recovery to be delayed; and from this
assumption it was readily concluded that communists were the active
enemies of recovery, saboteurs or 'wreckers' concerned with
promoting the economic dislocation that would act as fertile ground
for communism. This belief increasingly chequered the government's
view of events in the docks.

Bevin's initial assessment of communism's disruptive nature
was derived from his long trade union career. In accordance with
trade union values of democracy and loyalty, Bevin cherished
majority decisions and vilified those who refused to observe them:
the communist-instigated National Minority Movement's 'fractional'
industrial activity in the 1920s and 1930s had duly inspired his
loathing. However, in the protracted sessions of the Council for
Foreign Ministers which, mostly fruitlessly, sought to settle the array
of international questions arising out of the war, Bevin found
intransigent Soviet diplomats less easy to deal with than recalcitrant London busmen or Glaswegian dock workers. This exhausting
round of talks and negotiations consumed a total of about eight
working months, starting in London in September 1945 and closing
without resolution in Paris in June 1949. These gloomy gatherings
were punctuated in 1947 by the formal emergence of two potentially irreconcilable power blocs. Early in 1947 economic weakness
forced Britain to abandon its military commitments in Greece and

Turkey, the primary purpose of which since at least 1944 had been to forestall partisan communist movements. Determined that communism would not go unchallenged on the Aegean, Bevin asked the US to assume Britain's obligations in the area. This offer was famously taken up in Truman's speech to both Houses of Congress on 12 March. The 'Truman Doctrine', as it became known, committed the USA formally to the global containment of communism. The USA was cast as the guardian of all 'free peoples' who were seeking to choose between the two 'alternative ways of life': one being based on 'the will of the majority', and the other 'upon the will of a minority forcibly imposed upon the majority'.[43]

The Truman Doctrine was followed by Marshall's announcement, on 5 June, that the US was prepared to underwrite a comprehensive recovery programme for Europe. The Soviet response was hostile, *Pravda* declaring that the proposal was 'apparently intended to solve the American export problem' and, if American involvement in Greece and Turkey was anything to go by, it would 'amount to interference in the internal affairs of European states and an infringement of their sovereignty'.[44] The US extended the offer of Marshall Aid to the USSR on the clear understanding that it would be rejected. As Peter Hennessy has shown, Stalin and Molotov knew that if the US was able to finance an economic renaissance in Europe, Soviet economic and political domination in Eastern Europe would be over.[45] When European representatives, including Molotov, met to discuss their response to the Marshall offer in Paris on 27 June, Bevin and Georges Bidault, the French Foreign Secretary, were both keen to play down their opposition to Soviet participation. Bevin was anxious not to attract the charge of precipitating an anti-Soviet bloc, while Bidault was preoccupied with the Parti Communiste Francais's status as the largest single grouping in the National Assembly.[46] In private, however, they both felt that Soviet participation would obstruct Europe's economic recovery, and they were therefore relieved when Molotov abandoned the talks on 2 July, repeating *Pravda's* charge that the programme constituted unwarranted interference in European political and economic life. The implications of Molotov's walk-out were immediately evident, possibly because they had been anticipated: 'This really is the birth of the Western bloc', whispered Bevin to his senior official Piers Dixon, and the blame for splitting Europe and the world down the middle could now be attached to Stalin. A turning point, in Britain's economic recovery and the development of the Cold War, had been reached.[47]

The Soviet bloc's formal riposte came in September, with the establishment in Warsaw of the Communist Bureau of Information and Propaganda, or Cominform. Comprising the seven ruling parties in Bulgaria, Czechoslovakia, Hungary, Poland, Rumania, the Soviet Union and Yugoslavia, plus the French and Italian parties, the new international was activated by Stalin to unify communist activity in Eastern Europe and wring a fresh policy twist from communists in Western Europe. Delivering the Cominform's foundation speech, Soviet Politburo member Andrei Zhdanov said that the world now consisted of 'two camps': the 'imperialist and anti-democratic camp' which aimed to establish 'the world domination of American imperialism' and demolish democracy; and the 'anti-imperialist and democratic camp' which aimed to undermine imperialism and consolidate democracy. The 'Two Camps' thesis was published on 5 October and supplemented by a Moscow broadcast that revived the sectarian 'class against class' analysis of the Comintern's 1928–33 Third Period.[48] This drew attention to the 'special place in the imperialists' arsenal of tactical weapons' which was occupied by 'treacherous' Western European socialists, including Attlee and Bevin, who hid behind a socialist mask in order to deceive the working class.[49]

There were clear limitations to this initiative. Under Stalin the old Communist International had been bound by the requirements of Soviet foreign policy, operating as a counter-revolutionary instrument in China in the 1920s and in Spain from 1936. The Cominform was even more unambiguously devoted to Soviet foreign policy. 'So little', notes Isaac Deutscher,

> did Stalin think of turning the Cominform into any genuine instrument of international revolution that he did not ask the Chinese or other Asian parties to adhere to the new organisation. His chief concern, outside the Soviet 'sphere of influence', was to adjust the policies of the French and Italian Communists to the new needs of his diplomacy.[50]

Nevertheless, the west read much into the Cominform's vilification of French Socialists and British Labourites, along with the task which it set for Communist Parties in the 'imperialist camp': to 'head the resistance to the plans of imperialist expansion and aggression in all respects – State, political, economic and ideological'. Shorn of Stalinist verbiage, this implied firstly a desire to separate social democratic leaders from their working-class followers in the west; and secondly, a threat to disrupt the Marshall Aid-driven process of European recovery through reconstituted working-class movements.

The British trade union movement was fully alive to Cominform's apparent threat, and the guiding principle that had shaped its position on economic recovery – the defence of trade unionism – also ensured that the TUC would strongly support Bevin's anti-communist foreign policy. The TUC's support was especially valuable in the difficult two-year period following the establishment of Cominform and the collapse of the Council of Foreign Ministers in December 1947. In 1948 the Communists seized power in Czechoslovakia on 25 February, the anti-Marshall Aid PCI–PSI alliance was defeated in the Italian general election on 18 April, and the Soviet blockade of Berlin began on 24 June. In 1949 Bevin signed the NATO Pact on 4 April, and on 12 May the Berlin blockade was lifted and the NATO pact ratified in Parliament. As on economic questions, TUC support for the government on these international difficulties was organised through party rather than state mechanisms. At Labour Conferences, for instance, the block votes delivered by the General Council's 'big battalions' – Deakin of the Transport Workers, Charlie Dukes of the General and Municipal Workers and Will Lawther of the Mineworkers – lent massive weight to the defeat of Bevin's foreign policy dissentients.[51] This support was derived partly from the informal rules of the labour alliance, which required the General Council to demonstrate 'solidarity' with its political partner. But the TUC's anti-communism was equally prompted by its appraisal of the menace which communism – like fascism in the 1930s – posed to trade unionism.

There was also a long history of conflict between communists and their socialist and labourist opponents in the British labour movement, dating from the very foundation of the Communist Party of Great Britain (CPGB) in 1920. The new party had sought affiliation to the Labour Party, taking Lenin's advice that to work for a Labour government which would rapidly discredit reformist socialism – 'support Henderson in the same way as the rope supports a hanged man' – would readily equip communism with an avenue to the organised working class.[52] Once denied affiliation, the CP attempted to gain a foothold in trade unions. To this end, again reflecting communism's international tactics, the National Minority Movement (NMM) was established in 1924. In this initiative the Party enjoyed some success, the NMM sponsoring Arthur Cook's election as Secretary of the Miners Federation in 1924.[53] These activities antagonised the TUC, which saw the NMM's centrally controlled groups as a threat to trade union democracy, and its factional 'political' campaigns as jeopardising labour movement unity.

The wider labour movement was further repelled by the Comintern's 'class against class' analysis, adopted by the CP in 1928. Labour's industrial and political leaders were characterised as 'social fascists', with their attempts to reform capitalism making them the chief enemy of the working class. As the identity of the real threat to international workers, Nazism, revealed itself in the 1930s, the Comintern analysis was again transformed. In 1934 communists launched the Popular Front campaign for concerted working class and progressive resistance to fascism, but this was rebutted by the TUC's 'Black Circular', which barred communists from Trades Councils and urged unions to exclude communists from office. The labour movement's impatience with the CP was compounded in October 1939, after the Party's Central Committee had belatedly realigned its position on the war in accordance with the Nazi–Soviet Pact. Having proclaimed its full support for the anti-fascist war on 4 September in the *Daily Worker*, on 4 October the Central Committee denounced the war as 'imperialist'.[54] After the Nazi invasion of the USSR in June 1941, the CP recast itself as a vigorous advocate of increased industrial production and was the fiercest opponent of unofficial strike action.[55] The truce with the wider labour movement was an uneasy one, however, with the CP holding out for the maintenance of a coalition government long after Labour and the TUC had recognised the wisdom of fighting the 1945 election independently.

After the war this historical tension was given a fresh twist by the activities of the World Federation of Trade Unions (WFTU), of which the TUC was a founding member. Established in October 1945, the WFTU's attempt to unite trade unionists across international and ideological barriers was derailed by the onset of the Cold War.[56] The WFTU presidency was assumed in 1946 by Arthur Deakin, who ignored a warning from Bevin that a non-communist president would lend legitimacy to an organisation that was gradually becoming subordinate to Soviet demands.[57] Deakin came to share Bevin's view of the WFTU, seeing the spectre of ulterior communist motive in virtually every sphere of its activity, from demands that it support a trade embargo against fascist Spain – resisted by Deakin as the British government was opposed – to the sending of delegations to Asia and Africa. Meanwhile, communists on the body's Secretariat, notably Louis Saillant of the French CGT and the Soviet leader Kuznetsov, took equal ideological objection to Deakin's position on other matters, including Marshall Aid.

Indeed, it was the question of the WFTU's response to the European Recovery Programme (ERP) which led to the organisation's demise. In November 1947 Saillant and his allies resisted an attempt by the American Congress of Industrial Organisations (CIO) to pronounce formal WFTU support for the ERP. With an acrimonious Council of Foreign Ministers already under way in London, Deakin seized the initiative, warning that the TUC would open talks with other national labour organisations in favour of the Marshall Plan unless the WFTU discussed the programme by mid-February. Two days after the Foreign Ministers' meeting had adjourned without resolution on 15 December, Bevin told Marshall that the 'essential task was to create confidence in Western Europe that further communist inroads would be stopped', and that in this he was 'much fortified' by the TUC's initiative.[58]

Bevin disingenuously overlooked his own role in the development of TUC international strategy. After Saillant had responded to Deakin's ultimatum by stating that the Executive Bureau could not possibly meet before 1 April, the TUC pressed ahead and organised a conference of 26 organisations from 14 countries. Held in London on 9 and 10 March, within days of the coup in Czechoslovakia, this gathering established a Trade Union Advisory Committee to liaise with the Committee for European Economic Cooperation which was administering the Marshall Plan in London. Bevin had orchestrated the timing of the London conference, telling his labour attaché in Washington on 19 February: 'I had advocated early in March because this would have a steadying effect in Europe, and also show America before the US vote on the ERP where genuine trade unionists stood.'[59]

Bevin also ensured that the virulently anti-communist American Federation of Labour (AFL) came to London. The AFL had refused to join the WFTU because of its communist elements, and had eschewed any co-operation with its national rival, the CIO, on similar if clearly unjustifiable grounds. The Cold War brought the AFL new opportunities to pursue its intolerance of communism. In 1947 its European representative, Irving Brown, in concert with US security forces and using CIA funds, helped to establish a breakaway labour organisation in France, Force Ouvrière, to undermine the CGT. Brown then approached Bevin, asking him to push the TUC into an open breach with the WFTU. Bevin refused to do this, fearing that such a move would rouse the labour movement's embedded hostility to 'splitters', but he reassured Brown with the information that the TUC was being encouraged to organise the London conference.[60]

In September 1948 Deakin had obtained for the General Council plenary powers to proceed on the WFTU as it saw fit. This allowed the TUC to leave the WFTU without attracting accusations of arbitrarily splitting the international body. Along with the other anti-communist unions, the TUC duly seceded from the WFTU on 17 January 1949. The General Council then set about cultivating the international links which had been formally established at London in March 1948. As the WFTU prepared to transfer its organisational headquarters from Paris to Prague, the TUC arranged a paving meeting of a new international. This was held in London on 25 and 26 June 1949, and an International Confederation of Free Trade Unions was officially launched five months later.[61]

Domestic Communist Influence

The TUC's support for Bevin's foreign policy also involved important anti-communist activities on the home front, with Deakin

and his colleagues sternly resisting communism's progress within
their own organisations. In electoral terms, communism had made
very little headway in Britain. Within the context of Labour's 1945
landslide only two communists, Willie Gallacher in West Fife and
Phil Piratin in London's Mile End, had been elected. Nevertheless,
it did appear to be gaining industrial strength, and from 1947 the
General Council was increasingly concerned, given the course of
international and economic developments, that communists might
be able to disrupt seriously Britain's recovery.

In February 1948, as the wage freeze was launched, *The Times*
published details of communism's industrial progress.[62]
Communism's industrial base reputedly lay in the two large craft
unions, with party members contesting control of the Engineers'
Executive and occupying the presidency and secretaryship of the
Electricians. These represented two potentially significant holdings,
the Engineers carrying a membership of 723,000 and the Electricians
162,000. But the overall balance of forces within the TUC hindered
the prospect of any further communist advance. In the TGWU,
Britain's biggest union with 1,324,000 members, communists had
made some headway. They held eight seats on the 38-member
General Executive Council and three positions out of eight on the
Finance and General Purposes Committee: an advance sufficient
to place a single communist, Bert Papworth, on the TUC General
Council as a TGWU representative. Like Bevin before him,
however, Deakin was a skilful operator in by-passing left opposition,
and in 1948 enjoyed the further political advantage of there being
no Biennial Delegate Conference at which communist opponents
might have rallied opposition to the wage freeze and his support
for Bevin's 'warmongering' foreign policy. In the Miners' union a
communist, Arthur Horner, had been elected secretary in 1946,
but this ran against the overall complexion of the NUM, with only
six communists on the 28-strong executive. Moreover, the union's
two other dominant personalities, President Will Lawther and the
Northumbrian leader, Sam Watson, shared Deakin's assumptions
on the nature of communism and the unions' responsibilities to
the Labour government. The same was true of Tom Williamson,
leader of the General and Municipal Workers, which had never
departed from its 1920s position that CP membership was 'incon-
sistent with loyal attachment to the Union', effectively barring
communists from office.[63]

The combined weight of these three unions alone, three million
votes in an affiliated TUC membership of eight million, indicated
the strength of the TUC's anti-communist majority. Nevertheless,
with Deakin as its dominant figure, the General Council regarded
communist activity with intense vigilance. A communist General
Secretary of the TGWU was improbable,[64] but a communist

majority on either of the union's important committees could not necessarily be ruled out in the long term. Worryingly for the TUC, communists were still emerging with success in the spate of union elections which had accompanied, since the war, an unprecedented turnover in the personnel of trade union leadership. *The Times* pointed this out: 'In spite of the sharpening cleavage between Communist and non-Communist based on international divisions, Communists on the whole have held their ground in these national elections, and have maintained their disproportionate influence.'[65]

The General Council's position on the WFTU, ERP, wages and productivity was vindicated at the TUC's Margate gathering in September 1948. Its authority enhanced, the General Council confronted communism's role in the British labour movement. Writing to TUC General Secretary Vincent Tewson on 26 October, Deakin stated that, 'it was necessary for the General Council to give consideration to the continued interference by the Communist Party with the working of the Trades Councils and Trade Unions ... and to decide upon what action should be taken'.[66]

The General Council on 27 October duly approved the publication of a short statement, 'Trade Unions and Communism'. This accused the CP of attempting to 'sabotage' the Marshall Plan under Cominform instructions by promoting unobtainable industrial demands and staging disruptive unofficial strikes. Emphasising 'the malignant character of Communist agitation', the General Council statement urged loyal members to 'counteract every manifestation of Communist influences within their Unions; and to open the eyes of all workpeople to the dangerous subversive influences which are being engineered in opposition to the declared policy of the Trade Union Movement'.[67]

The statement was issued to the press, circulated among affiliated organisations and reappeared in November as part of an extended TUC pamphlet, *Defend Democracy*. Drafted by the TUC's Assistant Secretary, Victor Feather,[68] this strongly re-affirmed traditional trade union values, reminding trade unionists that it was their duty to observe decisions taken by a democratic majority. The need for democratic loyalty was contrasted with the fractious behaviour of the communist minority, which had not accepted the majority verdict passed by the Margate TUC on a number of issues. In defending political and trade union democracy against communism, the pamphlet crucially observed: 'It is a matter for consideration by the Unions whether it is consistent with the obligations of loyalty to the policy of the Union and to the Movement as a whole that any member should serve on the Communist Party industrial sub-committees or on the national committees of the Communist Party whilst holding executive or delegate office in the Union.'[69]

The statement thus enabled unions to exclude communists from official positions; but the initiative's significance transcended the General Council's desire to exclude communists from union office. The very fact of the anti-communist initiative emanating from within the labour movement was perceived by the TUC as indispensable to its success. Exhortations from the government, even a Labour government, would not have the same impact, and any intervention from employers would certainly prove counterproductive. The labour alliance 'rules' of behaviour had required the TUC 'voluntarily' to police the government's wages policy; these rules also determined that the industrial organisations of the working class would be the only effective instruments for marshalling wider ideological resistance to the communism which threatened the survival of these organisations. On 28 October Tewson was contacted by a London manufacturing employer who expressed pleasure at reading the General Council's 'forthright and realistic' declaration in the evening papers. The employer asked 'if you will provide us with a full copy of it, and allow us to reprint it and distribute it amongst our workpeople'. This request elicited a highly significant response. George Woodcock, the TUC's Assistant General Secretary, replied, 'I am very sorry but I do not think that we can give you permission to reprint the statement for distribution in this way. It would, I am sure, go a long way to destroy the value of the effect of the statement if it were to be reproduced and circulated by an employer.'[70]

The propaganda offensive was maintained in 1949. The TUC accompanied the break up of the WFTU with a second Feather pamphlet, *The Tactics of Disruption*, which restated the unscrupulous and fractious methods of the CP as it sought to capture strategic positions in unions and trades councils.[71] At the same time the TUC's largest affiliate, the TGWU, began an internal anti-communist campaign. In the union journal Deakin repeated the charges made against communism in the TUC pamphlets, and warned that international communism planned to disrupt Britain's economic recovery with a concerted campaign of strike action in the year ahead. On the eve of the union's Biennial Delegate Conference in July, Deakin heightened the temperature of the debate, claiming that an on-going unofficial strike in the London docks vindicated his January forecast.[72] At the July conference Deakin secured rule changes that excluded communists from union office. These rule changes, described by the *Daily Worker* as a 'cowardly decision',[73] took effect quickly. Within two months Bert Papworth was attending his final TUC General Council meeting. Without apparent irony, the minutes of this meeting record Tewson's reference, 'to the retirement from the General Council of Mr Cowley, Mr Wolstonecroft and Mr Burrows and to the termination of membership of the Council of Mr Papworth. He expressed on behalf of the Council the good wishes to those members. Mr Papworth suitably responded.'[74]

At the General Council in February 1950 consideration was given to the possible establishment of a National Anti-Communist Committee. Deakin rejected the notion out of hand, and with Tewson's support the matter was dropped.[75] Later in the year, as the Korean War reinflated international tension, Deakin would return to the question of communism's role in British trade unions, vainly pressing – along with the Archbishop of Canterbury – for the CP to be banned. These events are discussed in the final chapter of this book. In the spring of 1950 however, with economic recovery under way, international communism apparently contained and the Labour government re-elected – albeit with a drastically reduced majority – the General Council was happy that its contributions to the labour alliance had fully been paid.

This opening chapter has been concerned, essentially, with the development of two general, closely-related themes. The first concerns the historical nature of the often misunderstood relationship between the Labour Party and the trade unions, which has never prevented Labour from laying claim to protect interests beyond its original constituent basis. The other relates how the 1945 Labour government was occupied with perplexing economic and international questions as much as with the establishment of 'New Jerusalem', and enjoyed valuable support from the TUC in attempting to cultivate economic regeneration and international containment of communism. This assistance from the TUC – coming to its government's aid – on economic and international matters, represents the point at which the twin themes of the labour alliance's historical character and the nature of the particular Labour government intersect.

The chapters which follow have a more specific focus: the port transport industry and dock workers' unofficial strike action in the six years which followed the 1945 General Election. This discussion, paying due attention to the difficulties which the Labour governments experienced in a particular area of the industrial economy, will bring fresh understanding to the two themes referred to in the previous paragraph. First, the governments' pugnacious response to unofficial dock strikes, which was motivated by broader economic and international (or ideological) considerations, revealed Labour's national rather than sectional aspirations under Attlee and Bevin. Second, and more importantly, the docks provided a particularly stern test for the post-1945 Labour alliance. At a time of great economic emergency, TGWU officials in the docks were periodically unable to exert the sort of discipline among their members which the government demanded.

On the Waterfront

The Docks as a Special Case

The success of the 1945–51 Labour governments has been partly measured by some historians in terms of the relatively calm industrial scene. Kenneth Morgan contrasts the two post-war periods: 178 million working days were lost to strikes in the five calendar years 1919–23, and only 9.73 million from 1946–50. This phenomenon he ascribes to the 1945 emphasis on social spending and full employment. Moreover, a 'decisive commitment was made to removing the discredited managements of the coal and other industries, instead of returning to the follies of "decontrol" and private capitalism', as had happened after the First World War.[1] These observations provide an extremely valuable perspective on the situation at the docks. In the port transport industry 'private capitalism' had been partially fettered since the First World War. The process of regulation continued after 1918, and was consolidated by Ernest Bevin during the Second World War and by the 1947 Dock Labour Scheme. This measure was regarded by the government and the Transport and General Workers' Union as a particular triumph, involving significant and lasting benefit for the workforce. Nonetheless, during the 1945–51 period the industry witnessed a disproportionate level of strike activity, as the following comparative figures indicate. In crude terms, the average docker was on strike six times more often than the average coal miner.

Table 2.1: Days Lost to Strike Action, 1945–51[2]

	Days lost (millions)	Size of workforce
All Industry	14.27	
Coal-mining	3.97	700 000
Docks	2.89	80 000

The Labour governments were acutely sensitive to this relatively high level of strike action because the docks were of central importance to Britain's economic recovery. With imported food and raw materials and manufacturing exports – the trade essential to maintaining national economic life – passing through the ports, any dislocation was extremely unwelcome. When dockers went on strike the government sought to remind them of the economic consequences of their action: the price being paid by their comrades in the labour movement and fellow British citizens in lost imports arising from delays in the turn-round of shipping. Apart from Attlee's broadcast during the London dock strike of June 1948, however, these appeals were largely unsuccessful. With persuasion generally failing, the government used more active strike-breaking methods. Large numbers of troops were deployed in the docks on six separate occasions: during two strikes in 1945, and once each in 1947, 1948, 1949 and 1950. 'Join the army and see Smithfield', went one Cockney barb, as troops in and around the Port of London became a regular sight. Conscripts also saw action in other major docks – Avonmouth, Bristol, Glasgow, Liverpool and Southampton.[3] This book places these unofficial dock strikes in the context of the government's economic and international problems, chapter 3 examining three of the six disputes. These three centred around various ports in October 1945; in London in June 1948; and on the Avon, the Mersey and in London again between May and July 1949. The three are singled out, first, because they were the largest disputes of the period, and second, because of the significant contrast in the government's response to the strikes as the wider economic and international problems grew in intensity from 1947 onwards.

All of these strikes were unofficial. Under Order 1305, the wartime emergency regulation which remained in force until 1951, official strikes were expressly forbidden. In any event the main dockers' union, the TGWU, was implacably opposed to strike action. Among Labour's strongest union supporters, the TGWU felt that industrial disruption threatened the immense economic and social benefits which the government had brought to its members. Yet the willingness of dockers to strike – in defiance of the law, the government and their union leaders – sat readily with the often turbulent history of the industry since the late nineteenth century.

Fernand Braudel, the celebrated French historian, has emphasised the importance of interpreting history in as long a historical context as possible. A human being operates, he wrote, 'in a landscape in which the infinite perspectives of the long-term, *la longue dureé*, stretch into the distance both behind him and before'.[4] As for the Mediterranean in the Age of Philip II, so for the Avon, the Clyde, the Mersey and the Thames in the Age of Arthur Deakin. In order to bring out the full significance of the 1945–51 period, this chapter duly examines the 1947 Dock Labour Scheme's longer historical origins: the immediate impact of wartime developments and the more remote accumulation of events between the Edwardian era

and 1939. This discussion will bring out the intrinsic problems of
dock labour reform, and show that the Scheme did not fully resolve
these problems, which, left in abeyance, added to the government's long list of difficulties.

Dock Labour Before 1940

Britain's docks were transformed by the huge expansion of
commercial activity in the nineteenth century. The handful of port
cities that were central to economic life in 1945 – most notably
London and Liverpool – established their importance by the late
Victorian era. The nineteenth century's other significant legacy to
the industry was the system of casual labour relations, with the bulk
of the workforce recruited on a daily, or even half-daily basis. This
had endured Edwardian reformism, the First World War, the
TGWU's interwar efforts and Bevin's limited 'decasualisation'
legislation of 1940–41. Even the 1947 Dock Labour Scheme was
not designed to eliminate casualism, which was finally removed by
Harold Wilson's Labour government in 1967.

Fernand Braudel's assumptions about the nature of human
society's historical development, shaped centrally by imperceptibly
changing environmental factors, might plausibly be applied to the
longevity of casual recruitment in the docks. While casualism's
endurance may be attributed to the conservatism of employers and
dock workers alike, with each side of industry resistant to reform,
the employers' position was initially informed by the physical
geography of the British Isles. The majority of the islands' ports
were tidal, unlike many on Continental Europe, and the flow of
ships into British harbours was uneven as a result. With another
environmental variable being the speed and direction of wind,
employers believed that they ought only to recruit workers as and
when the presence of ships required.[5] With fluctuating international trade a further variable, employers defended casualism on
three other counts: first, regular workers were supposedly less
productive than casual employees because of their greater job
security; second, permanency would possibly prevent employers
from hand-picking their own workers; and third, decasualisation
would ultimately strengthen the position of organised labour.[6]

Port employers faced their first serious challenge towards the end
of the nineteenth century. The year 1889 might reasonably be
cited as an important watershed, containing the great strike of
August and September in the London docks, and the publication
of Charles Booth's preliminary research on social conditions in
London's East End. Although John Lovell has emphasised that
important developments in dock labour organisation had taken place

before 1889,[7] the conjunction of industrial upheaval and the revelation that serious economic hardship existed in the Empire's first city, prompted the beginnings of wider public interest in the docks industry.

Booth indicated that a body of steady and reliable men existed in the docks, but public attention was drawn to some of his other findings. Booth was concerned, among many other things, in maximising the employment opportunities for the reliable men. This involved demonstrating that the casual system allowed many people who were unwilling or unable to take up regular employment to use the docks as a refuge. Exclusion of these inefficient and rootless workers was an essential precondition to the eradication of under-employment and poverty in the dock communities. It was with these occupationally rootless and therefore demoralised elements that the public equated the dock labour force as a whole. To use Lovell's words, 'waterside work was regarded by the public less as a genuine industrial occupation than as a residual employment for the refuse and unemployed of society at large'.[8]

Identified as a source of economic inefficiency, casual industrial labour became a central concern of the 1905–14 Liberal governments. From 1908 the Board of Trade sought to eradicate under-employment in casual trades by instituting a national system of labour exchanges. The docks were acknowledged as a special case, and the Board of Trade opened discussions with the Port of London Authority, newly-established to govern the capital's docks and waterways, with a view to opening employer-sponsored dock agencies. These would move workers from one engagement to the next, requiring employers to forego independent recruitment and accept the exchanges as their sole source of labour. The scheme made little progress, foundering – according to the PLA – on its allegedly prohibitive cost, which the traditionally parsimonious employers were unwilling to bear, and the upsurge of industrial conflict in 1911 and 1912.[9]

The Liberals' approach to unemployment-related poverty also involved the social insurance schemes which were enacted in 1911. This presented difficulties in industries where casual employment was predominant. Although dockers were not covered for unemployment insurance until 1920, they were for health insurance from the start. This was important, because it led to the first experiment in decasualisation. Between 1911 and 1912 in Liverpool, the nation's second largest port, a registration scheme for dock labour was devised by the labour exchanges' divisional officer, with the co-operation of employers and the National Union of Dock Labourers. Designed to bring dockers under the health provisions of the 1911 insurance legislation, it also aimed to eliminate an estimated redundant surplus of 7000 from the 27,000 who normally sought work in the port.

The scheme did not alter the casual methods of hiring labour, but as a first step to decasualisation it was important, and indicated two further items of significance. First, it demonstrated that industrial relations in the docks were characterised by considerable regional diversity. The scheme would not have been launched in Liverpool had it not been for the relatively positive relationship between employers and union leaders. The Liverpool employers were primarily shipowners whose export cargoes depended on a stable industrial atmosphere, and after the 1911 strike they agreed to give preference of employment to NUDL members.[10] This contrasted greatly with the situation in London, where employers successfully forced a showdown over the Dock, Wharf, Riverside and General Labourers' Union's (DWRGLU) monopoly of the labour supply less than a year after the 1911 strike.[11] Secondly, the most serious obstacle to the registration scheme's success was the angry response it provoked from the workforce. Many dockers were naturally hostile to the threatened redundancies, and also resented the new discipline which registration would exert on their working lives. Facing widespread resistance in the docks, the scheme's sponsors diluted their proposals, easing the rules on registration. The scheme duly had only a limited impact on the size, attendance and productivity of the workforce.[12]

The attitude of the Liverpool men in 1912 reflected the national workforce's general ambivalence towards casual employment. Although dockers' living standards advanced throughout the first four decades of the twentieth century, under casualism they were exposed to an unusually high degree of economic insecurity. While a significant number of skilled workers were regularly engaged, the permanent men or 'perms', the vast majority of work was obtained in perilous and degrading circumstances. Dockers were obliged to gather at the numerous 'calling-on' points scattered around the nation's ports. In London alone there were 500 of these in 1914.[13] Calls were conducted twice-daily, with the port employers' various foremen choosing the 13 individuals that typically comprised the gang for a particular job. This recruitment was extremely competitive and with dockers struggling to gain the foremen's attention, physical violence 'on the stones' – the call-on stance – was not unusual. Once engaged the docker was not even guaranteed the security of a full day's work. As the foreman's own position was dependent on his recruits performing to the satisfaction of his employer, a gang worked for him rather than the employer. Bribery and corruption were fairly common in these circumstances, with dockers 'buying' the right to work from foremen who retained the power to dismiss morning recruits and re-engage labour at the mid-day call. With work over the docker would be paid off, generally from coins out of the foremen's pocket, usually in the street but often in a dockside pub.[14]

Despite these obvious disadvantages of work and life in dock communities under the casual regime, which included high levels of ill-health and poor housing,[15] there were a number of positive features which Edwardian and later reformers tended to overlook. For one thing, the workforce was far from being a wholly demoralised and rootless body. Lovell has convincingly argued that in London, 'although casually employed, this labour force was in fact a regular body. It was composed of men who regularly looked for work at the waterside, and who rarely sought, and even more rarely obtained, work anywhere else.' This observation is highly significant, contradicting the generally perceived nature of dock workers as an underclass – a 'motley horde of unfortunates'.[16] While a rootless element did exist, the sizeable majority followed regular employers and regular types of work. The regular accepted that a refusal to move around looking for work on a daily basis would involve under-employment, but immobility allowed him to specialise in a particular skill and cultivate a relationship with a particular employer. These two factors at least guaranteed some work, which might be unobtainable through hopping from one call-on point to another. The liking for specialisation partly informed the Liverpool men's hostility to registration, which they felt would imply a compulsion to accept alternative waterside tasks. In London dockers also opposed greater regulation, with the permanently employed labourer a figure to be despised. Lovell offers as characteristic a remark made in 1892 by a London docker, 'if you are made permanent you are made a white slave of directly; you are transferable from here to there and everywhere'.[17]

The sum of these observations is that for all its economic hardship, casualism generally gave dockers more control over patterns of work and leisure than most other groups of industrial workers enjoyed. A TUC review of dock labour's history in 1986 noted that prior to 1940, dockers held 'a genuine freedom to choose: to choose whether or not to try for work on a particular morning, and whether or not to accept or reject work which might be offered'.[18] Dockers were free from the constraint of the rigid six-day week. Skilled pieceworkers, for example, could often earn enough money in the first part of the week to cover the cost of a three-day rest at the end of the week. As Ross McKibbin puts it, in 'the docks "come day, go day" was elevated to an art-form'.[19]

The fear that a reformed regime would jeopardise this freedom was confirmed by the increased discipline which the First World War brought to the docks. To ease shipping congestion and counter labour shortages, from 1916 the government encouraged the extension of registration schemes to other ports. These varied in scope and size, but by 1920 Glasgow was the only major port without a register. Dockers generally resented this trend and, in London at least, registration was delayed until after the war because of its unpopularity. Traditional antipathy to regulation was bolstered in 1916 when the Board of Trade appointed port labour committees in 32 ports. Comprising representatives of employers and trade unions, a labour exchange official and military recruitment officers, these committees controlled the labour supply via employment registers and certificates which exempted registered dockers from military conscription. With the assistance of registers, port labour committees could punish absenteeism by withholding military exemption, and dockers attended the call-on far more assiduously as a result. These were new methods of controlling the supply of labour, but the casual system of recruitment remained intact. The vast majority of dockers still sought engagements on a daily basis, and their relationships with employers were unreconstructed.[20]

The workforce's ambivalence about the reform of the casual system represented a serious obstacle to the organisation of trade unions in the docks. Casualism had created a workforce that was riven by two intersecting conflicts: local versus national and sectional versus industrial. In London, for instance, the multiplicity of waterside trades defied pre-1914 attempts to organise the workforce fully. There were vast differences in occupational and material status between shipworkers and shoreworkers, tugmen and lightermen, meat porters and corn porters; and these differences guaranteed that a tradition of industrial militancy – with impressive outbursts in 1872, 1889 and 1911–12 – was not supported by a tradition of sturdy and continuous organisation. The rapid growth of unionisation which accompanied each of these waves of strike activity was transitory, and 'paper' members were not brought into a vigorous branch life. Without consolidating members in the culture of trade unionism, industrial unions withered as the favourable short-term conditions for organisation diminished. Only sectional societies, notably the Amalgamated Stevedores' Labour Protection League, enjoyed uninterrupted progress from the 1870s onwards. Equally frustrating for the leaders of the DWRGLU, established during the 1889 strike, was the absence of national unity, as unions on the Mersey and the Clyde retained their separate identities.[21] In 1920 London dockers refused to load the *Jolly George* with weapons bound for use against the Red Army in Poland in 1920. This event can be interpreted as a display of international working-class solidarity, but dockers were often reluctant to support even fellow British port workers. An obvious and noble exception was the 1911 national strike, but an attempt by the National Transport Workers' Federation

– established in 1910 – to repeat the trick in support of its London men in June 1912, was a failure.[22]

It is within this specific historical framework, low-level organisation punctuated by occasional outbursts of mass militancy, that the establishment of the Transport and General Workers' Union (TGWU) in 1922 must be interpreted. Clearly Ernest Bevin, first General Secretary of the new organisation, constructed the industrial union of port and transport workers on shaky historical foundations. The TGWU was unable fully to combat the weight of the industry's long history, either in the first two decades of its existence or indeed after the Second World War. Later chapters of this book place the post-1945 unofficial strikes firmly in the docklands' tradition which Bevin inherited in 1922.

Bevin had earned his nationwide reputation at the 1920 Shaw Court of Inquiry into dock labour. According to Alan Bullock his position as the 'Dockers' KC' gave him sufficient status amongst the dock labour force to secure the establishment of the TGWU.[23] It became immediately apparent, however, that his powerful reputation did not immunise the union from labour organisation's historical problems in the docks. In 1923 Bevin negotiated a wage reduction in order to protect jobs. This sparked a seven-week unofficial strike involving about 40,000 workers. With the union refusing to issue strike-pay, the men went back without regaining their previous pay levels. The new union's authority was further damaged – and its position in London permanently weakened – in the aftermath of the strike. In 1922 Bevin had failed to incorporate the Amalgamated Stevedores' Labour Protection League in the TGWU. After the 1923 strike several thousand dockers left the TGWU, forming a Dockers' Section of the Stevedores' League which duly reconstituted itself as the National Amalgamated Stevedores and Dockers (NASD). The NASD retained the old League's sectional claim to represent the interests of stevedores who loaded cargoes onto ships, but in seeking to gather in dock members, it stood in direct competition with the TGWU. At the same time the lightermen also withdrew from the general organisation, at first joining the NASD, but later (in 1927) establishing their own union, the Watermen, Lightermen, Tugmen and Bargemen's Union.[24]

The credibility of the national and industrial union was partly restored when, to the chagrin of Ramsay MacDonald who was trying to establish Labour's 'national' governing credentials, Bevin successfully led an official dock strike in 1924. This dispute indicated the potential for effective national waterside organisation and, as such, reflected the ambitions of the twentieth century's supreme union builder. From an initial membership of 297,460 in 1922 the TGWU rapidly expanded. Boosted by a series of amalgamations,

by 1937 it had outstripped the Miners' Federation. With a
membership of 645,510 it was the biggest trade union in the world.[25]

This union-building benefited workers in a multiplicity of trades,
but it was not without its trials. The very diversity of the new
organisation tested the leadership as respective trade groups began
to strain in different directions. In the 1930s, for example, Bevin
frequently encountered difficulties with London busmen and their
unofficial organisation, the Busmen's Rank and File Committee.
These struggles were not entirely due, as Bevin publicly claimed,
to the mischief of communists, such as Bert Papworth, who rose
to prominence as an unofficial busmen's leader and subsequently
served on the TGWU Executive and the TUC General Council.
When Bevin's trouble with the busmen began, after he had agreed
a wage reduction with the bus companies in 1932, the Rank and
File Committee's motivations were economic rather than ideological.
Bevin had to re-open negotiations and reclaim most of that which
had been forfeited. In view of later allegations about communist
membership and tactical industrial disruption, it is important to
note that Papworth – whose dissenting voice within the TGWU
leadership was silenced by Arthur Deakin's anti-communist rule
changes in 1949 – did not actually join the CP until 1937.[26]

Meanwhile, developments in the docks continued to trouble
Bevin. The breakaway of his Glasgow members in 1932 apparently
confirmed the difficulty of reconciling local with national interests
in an industrial union of port workers. The trouble began on the
question of decasualisation. The TGWU was a keen sponsor of decasualisation, which provided an opportunity to increase union
membership. In 1916 the 'best available outcome', to use Lewis
Minkin's phrase, had been secured through voluntary co-operation
over registration and industrial conscription. This had rewarded
the union with a larger membership and therefore a stronger
position at the negotiating table once international hostilities, and
the industrial truce, were over. A similar reasoning informed the
TGWU's approach to decasualisation. Bevin believed that by controlling admission to employment registers, the TGWU would
ensure that the decasualised workforce was fully unionised.[27] In
1930, when the Labour government initiated a fresh inquiry into
decasualisation, Glasgow remained the only major British port
not covered by a registration scheme. At the Inquiry Bevin argued
for a national decasualisation scheme with compulsory registration.
In return for attending the call-on stands twice daily, the registered
worker would receive a guaranteed weekly maintenance of 50
shillings. The scheme would be financed by the transfer of unemployment contributions from State, employers and workers to a
special fund which would be administered by the National Joint
Committee for Dock Labour.

The Glasgow docks branch of the TGWU strongly opposed national registration. On the Clyde the union was already strong enough to control completely the supply and deployment of dock labour. Adherence to a national scheme would oblige the Glasgow men to share this control with employers' representatives. In 1929, along with Aberdeen dockers, the Glasgow branch established the Anti-Registration League to protect its advantage, condemning registration as 'a mere instrument of discipline and coercion'.[28] The branch was also in dispute with Bevin over the position of its eight full-time officials. According to Bevin the eight were to be centrally appointed rather than locally elected, as the branch insisted was its right, and in 1931 he ignored a High Court decision in the Glasgow men's favour. The Clydesiders regarded the national leadership's position on both issues as an unwarranted assault on their authority, and the branch seceded in 1932 to form the Scottish Transport and General Workers' Union (STGWU). This was a further breach in the big union's authority, for Bevin could not loosen the new body's grip on the Glasgow docks, and the STGWU was eventually admitted to the National Joint Council for Dock Labour in 1944.[29]

The 'longue dureé' of the casual system had left an indelible mark on the docks: in attempting to organise on a national and industrial basis a workforce that was strongly characterised by local and sectional divisions, and a historical wariness of increased regulation, the TGWU was only partly successful. The full extent of the TGWU's difficulties and the workforce's resistance to change would be revealed after the 1945 Labour government concluded a process of decasualisation begun by Bevin during the war.

The Docks During Wartime, 1940–45

The Second World War brought the question of dock labour reform urgently to the fore. This was largely due to Bevin's arrival at the Ministry of Labour in May 1940, but the urgent circumstances of war were almost equally important. Bevin had to extract the nation's precious human resources as efficiently as possible, so some form of increased regulation in the vital docks industry was essential. As Angus Calder has suggested, however, it was typical of Bevin to make of such necessary materials the items of 'rough social justice'.[30]

Within weeks of assuming office, Bevin introduced the Dock Labour (Compulsory Registration) Order in June 1940. This required all dockers to register and be available for transfer, as it was becoming increasingly necessary to move shipping from south and east coast ports to the west. With congestion building up in

the ports of northwest England and the Clyde as London faced
prolonged aerial bombardment from September 1940 onwards, the
War Cabinet concluded that more stringent measures were required
to reverse the dangerous delays in the turn-round of shipping. In
December 1940 Bevin approved a decasualisation scheme for the
northwestern ports with Arthur Deakin, his successor at the TGWU,
and Dan Hillman of the union's Docks Group. Bevin then secured
support for this scheme from his erstwhile opponents, the STGWU.
From March 1941 all registered dockers on the Clyde and the North
Western Approaches became employees of the Ministry of War
Transport on a guaranteed weekly basis.[31]

In March 1941 Bevin also introduced the Essential Work Order,
which allowed the Ministry of Labour to designate factories and
other economic units as being engaged in essential national work.
Under the Order, no worker employed in a place duly designated
could resign or be sacked without permission from the Ministry.
In May 1941 Bevin notified the Port Transport Industry's National
Joint Council (NJC) – a body comprising representatives of port
employers and trade unions – that he intended to bring all dockers
outside the Ministry of War Transport scheme under the Essential
Work Order, and asked the NJC to provide its own decasualisation programme. This initiative was of great long-term significance,
for the scheme produced by the NJC was to frame the post-war
settlement in the docks. The 1941 scheme was national in character,
with a central organisation – the National Dock Labour Corporation
(NDLC) – established to finance and administer its provisions. The
NDLC comprised an equal number of representatives of employers
and labour, with Bevin appointing an independent Chair and
Financial Director. The NDLC set up local joint boards to regulate
the labour supply, offering dockers guaranteed maintenance on the
condition that they attended the eleven weekly calls and accepted
any work available. Those unable to find work 'on the stones'
would report to the local board's manager. He could allocate them
to an employer in a different part of the docks, or even in a different
port altogether. If they failed to comply with these conditions,
dockers were liable for financial penalties or suspension – and in
some cases even dismissal – from the scheme. This was a clear
mixture of casual and non-casual methods. Dockers received their
combined wages and maintenance payments once a week from the
Port Labour Manager. He in turn received each week from employers
the sums of money owed to the workers, whether they had been
casually engaged or centrally allocated. The scheme's costs were
met by registered employers who were levied according to the size
of their wage bills. The first local scheme, appropriately perhaps,
given Bevin's West Country origins, was introduced in Bristol in
December 1941. By February 1943 all but 1000 dockers in the

nation's smallest ports were part of either the NDLC or Ministry of War Transport programmes.[32]

It is worth re-emphasising that Bevin's Ministry of Labour was centrally concerned with the efficient deployment of the nation's scarce labour resources. When the government extended the Essential Work Order in December 1941, Bevin cited developments in the docks as an example of the Order's value to the war effort, telling Parliament that the Liverpool and Glasgow scheme had quickened the turn-round of shipping by an average 2.5 days per ship. He added that this was the equivalent of 1.5 million tons of new shipping.[33] Bevin's stress on the need for maximum efficiency in the workplace was supported by the TGWU. In October 1941 Deakin used the union journal to remind dockers that they had all worked on ships 'which are now lying at the bottom of the sea'. With available shipping tonnage ever-decreasing, it was 'urgently necessary that we make the best possible use of every ship coming into port, securing the quickest possible turn-round and discharging or loading'.[34]

Bevin's wartime efforts were not, of course, confined to maximising productivity. He also attained for working people a significant advance in their social and economic status. At the TUC Special Conference in May 1940, called to deliberate its position on participation in the wartime coalition, Bevin had said, 'if our class rise with all their energy and save the people, the country will always turn with confidence to the people who saved them'.[35] This hope was amply justified, at least so far as the trade unions were concerned. As Bevin had anticipated when devising his decasualisation strategy before the war, the wartime schemes gave trade union representatives a new position of power in the industry. This had significant longterm implications, for at an early stage the TGWU expressed the desirability of retaining its new-found strength once international hostilities had ceased. In October 1941 Deakin passed comment on the character of the NDLC: 'setting up as it does a form of workers' control, expressed through the trade union organisations acting jointly with representative employers, it may be regarded as a great experiment – the principle of which we may desire to retain'.[36] Bevin shared Deakin's view, arguing in Parliament that both sides of the industry should have to accept a jointly-administered decasualisation scheme as a permanent feature in the docks.[37]

Until the end of the war the TGWU tried to establish decasualisation on a permanent footing, but its efforts were blunted by the National Association of Port Employers. The association's position reflected the traditional parsimony of port employers, who were unwilling to increase their labour costs and also reluctant to share administrative powers with the unions. As a result of the

employers' intransigence, negotiations on the industry's long-term
future yielded no positive results before 1945. The remaining war
years also suggested, however, that decasualisation might not be
fully popular among the TGWU's dock members. Rumblings of
industrial unrest in the docks indicated that dockers had not lost
their historical ambivalence to the casual system of employment.
Under the wartime schemes the Ministry of Labour recorded 33
separate dock strikes.[38]

In May 1944 the nature of this discontent was discussed in
Parliament, after a junior Transport Minister, Philip Noel-Baker,
had restated decasualisation's invaluable contribution to the war
effort. The Labour MP for Whitechapel, Walter Edwards, who represented many dockers and their families, responded by observing
that dockers had disproportionately borne the brunt of industrial
transfers, and politely questioned whether all transfers had been
completely necessary. Serious grievances, he added, were arising
from the requirements of the new regime.[39] This potential for
conflict was realised in March 1945 when the largest dock strike
of the war took place in London. Involving 10,000 men for a week,
the strike was the subject of an official Ministry of Labour inquiry
which noted that while 'a small subversive political section' had
encouraged the strike to spread, the dispute had 'originated in the
men's feelings of resentment against the alleged harsh exercise of
discipline under the Port of London Dock Labour Scheme'. Matters
had been brought to a head, the report stated, when the London
Port Authority had attempted to move the control point from
outside the Victoria Dock gate to inside.[40] This was a highly
sensitive historical issue in the docks. In November 1890, for
example, employers had terminated the practice won during the
1889 strike where workers were recruited outside the dock gates.
This had caused great bitterness among the men and, in breaking
the monopoly of the dockers' union, the DWRGLU, had further
weakened the long-term success of industrial unionism in the
port.[41] In 1945 as much as 1890, the threatened transfer of the
control point's location seemed to witness a potential strengthening of the employers' position at the workers' expense.

The relationship between increased industrial discipline and
growing industrial unrest was partly conceded by Victor Allen,
Deakin's sympathetic biographer. Writing in 1957 Allen stated,
'the strike indicated that the wartime schemes in certain instances
might have been operating at the margin of the men's tolerance;
that the cost of decasualisation to dockers in terms of liberty of
action could outweigh the social and economic advantages'.[42]
The fact that serious tensions could arise under decasualisation
did not rest easily with Deakin's belief, which has already been
noted, that the Dock Corporation scheme was a 'form of workers'

control'. The outburst of these tensions in March 1945 was a warning that permanent peacetime decasualisation would involve considerable hazards for the TGWU and its political partners in the Labour Alliance.

Towards the Post-war Settlement, 1945–47

Throughout the protracted and tortuous post-war negotiations on the industry's long-term future it was evident that fundamental differences existed between the positions of the unions and the employers. The government, while maintaining a public position of non-intervention, privately exerted pressures consonant with its determination that a key industrial sector would not be surrendered to market forces at a time of immense national economic difficulty and international political instability.

The government communicated its intentions to the industry within two weeks of its election. George Isaacs, the new Minister of Labour and National Service, wrote to the Chairman of the National Dock Labour Corporation, Lord Ammon, and indicated that a Bill for the peacetime decasualisation of dock labour was being drafted.[43] The Dock Workers (Regulation of Employment) Bill was duly introduced, the object of which was 'to enable permanent schemes to be made for ensuring greater regularity of employment for dock workers and securing that an adequate number of dock workers is available for the efficient performance of their work'.[44] The 1940–41 schemes had been introduced as essential economic weapons during the war; similarly, the Labour government saw decasualisation as central to its strategy for economic recovery. Introducing the Bill's Second Reading on 12 November, Isaacs stated that if the wartime systems of decasualisation fell to the ground without being replaced, with the old casual order restored, 'the effect would be positively disastrous – disastrous to the industry, to the men and the country'. Clause 2 of the Bill allowed the Minister to introduce his own proposals for decasualisation if the industry itself failed to produce a scheme by 31 December 1946. Until new schemes had been introduced, the present ones would continue, with the Minister adamant that 'there shall be no period during which a port may be working without a scheme'. Lest the House was in any doubt as to the reasoning behind decasualisation, Isaacs's Parliamentary Secretary, Ness Edwards, reiterated in the same debate that the national interest required an end to casual employment in the docks. 'We cannot afford', Edwards said, 'inefficiency in the docks, we cannot afford irregularity of work, we cannot afford a wasteful use of manpower in the dock industry. Manpower is going to be the bottleneck in this country in the future, and so we are anxious that this industry shall be put upon an efficient basis, and shall give regular, continuous and well-paid employment to those engaged in it.'[45] In February 1946 the Bill passed on to the statute book. A permanent scheme for decasualisation – whether produced by the industry or the Ministry itself – would be put in place by Statutory Order by 30 June 1947.[46]

The legislation was intended as a fillip to negotiations on the industry's future which were being conducted by the National Joint Council (NJC). There were three recognisable phases in these talks. The first period began in September 1945 with the workpeople submitting a claim for improved pay and conditions and ended in December with the settlement of this claim and the Parliamentary passage of the decasualisation legislation. The second period comprised the calendar year 1946, in which the NJC failed to break its deadlock on negotiations with Isaacs consequently publishing his own draft scheme, in accordance with the Dock Workers Act. The closing phase covered the first half of 1947, during which the government considered the industry's response to this draft, before the Dock Labour Scheme was launched on 1 July.

The first period was dominated by the claim for improved pay and working conditions which the unions communicated to employers on 3 September. The unions' primary demand was an increase in the daily minimum wage from 16s to 25s. The employers were determined to resist this, or indeed any pay increase, so long as the future pattern of industrial relations remained unclear. When the unions expressed their desire at the NJC on 6 November to settle wages immediately and deal with other issues later, the employers refused. They insisted that 'the wages claim could not be dealt with in isolation, but must be related to the industrial conditions as these emerged from the proposals for decasualisation and reorganisation of the industry; only thus would it be possible to assess correctly the value of the standard basic rate of wages'.[47] This hard line was strongly influenced by the huge unofficial dock strike which had lasted for the entire month of October and cost the industry more than one million working days. The stoppage had made the employers cautious about making concessions to the workpeople's side of the NJC before the union leaders concerned had re-established authority within their own ranks.

Despite the employers' predictably adverse response, the strike positively affected the pattern and outcome of the 1945 negotiations. On the morning of the Dock Workers Bill's Second Reading, Bevin offered Isaacs his thoughts on the general situation. Following 'some discreet inquiries', presumably with his TGWU colleagues, Bevin advised Isaacs that the wages question was causing immense contention in the docks. If it could be settled and an instrument put in place to maintain the wartime schemes, then the government and the industry would enjoy a far more peaceful environment in which to consider permanent decasualisation, 'the more difficult side of the problem'.[48] That afternoon Isaacs duly indicated in Parliament that the existing schemes would not lapse until they had been replaced with permanent measures, and on 29 November he appointed Justice Evershed under the 1896 Conciliation Act to consider the merits of the port employees' official pay claim. Evershed's Committee recommended that the daily minimum be increased to 19s, 1s more than the employers' final offer and 6s less than the workpeople's original claim. A National Docks' Delegate Conference accepted the Evershed findings on 14 December, while four days earlier the executive of NAPE, the employers' association, endorsed them as the best available 'in the circumstances'.[49]

With the pay dispute settled, the second phase of negotiations began, the NJC concentrating on a permanent scheme for decasualisation. The 1946 talks, however, were largely fruitless, as the two sides held irreconcilable positions on two important issues. First, while employers demanded monopoly control over local schemes, the TGWU held out for a national scheme under joint administration. Second, the two sides could not agree upon the basis of the workforce's guaranteed maintenance.

The first point of divergence had been raised in the NJC on 18 October 1945 when Sir Douglas Ritchie, the NAPE chairman, insisted that the right of employers to sole control of the employment registers was a point of 'fundamental' importance.[50] Following several months of inconclusive debate, the NAPE secretary, D.F. Macdonald, indicated the sum of the employers' position on administration of the schemes in a letter to the TGWU Docks Secretary, Jack Donovan. Macdonald stated that a national controlling body was unnecessary as the NJC already provided central direction. More importantly, he added, employers were determined to resist the imposition of joint administrative control of schemes which they were to finance.[51]

The TGWU was not prepared to relinquish its share in the system of joint industrial control established in 1941. Donovan had stated as much in the NJC's Decasualisation Sub-Committee on 20 March 1946, before adding some remarks on the second point of controversy. Having visited the districts to gather the thoughts of members, he was convinced that the employers' proposals on the form of guarantee were also unacceptable.[52] The TGWU wanted dockers to be paid 6s for each half-day that they proved attendance but received no work. At the end of each week, the worker's attendance money and earnings from normal working hours would be made up to a minimum sum of £4 16s. The employers' position was that all earnings, including piece-work and overtime,

were to be reckoned against the guarantee, and that this maintenance would comprise a lunar monthly guarantee of £16.[53]

On 23 August the NJC formally acknowledged the insolubility
of these differences and informed Isaacs that it was unable to
produce a scheme of its own.[54] Isaacs responded cautiously,
appointing a Committee of Inquiry under Sir John Forster KC, which
heard evidence from each side of the NJC before publishing its conclusions in December. On the two points of contention Forster found
largely in favour of the TGWU's position: the scheme would be a
national one under joint administrative control; and dock workers
would be paid for each half-day that their attendance at the call
stand was not rewarded with work.[55]

The Character of the 1947 Dock Labour Scheme

The final phase of the approach to peacetime decasualisation began
in December 1946, with the Ministry of Labour preparing a draft
scheme along the lines drawn up by Forster. Overall administration of the scheme was to be vested in a National Dock Labour
Board which would appoint local Dock Labour Boards to oversee
affairs in each port or group of ports. These boards would, both
nationally and locally, be under joint jurisdiction. The National
Board was to consist of ten members, four from each side of
industry with an independent chair and vice-chair. The Local
Boards – on which there would be no such independent representation – were to be responsible for disciplinary matters and the
allocation of labour within ports. Those workers not assigned an
employer on each day comprised a reserve pool of labour, held to
be in the employ of the Board and paid an attendance fee on a half-
daily basis. Such provision, with the vast majority of workers still
likely to be casually engaged via foremen on the stones, represented
a significant qualification to the notion of a 'decasualisation'
scheme. Although the wartime 'continuity' regulations were
maintained, which required dockers to complete assigned jobs and
hence prevented foremen from hiring by the half-day alone, in a
real sense dock workers were still casual employees. Paradoxically,
while bound by the disciplinary requirements of regular employment,
dockers were not to enjoy the compensation of the full economic
security which regular employment would bring. Indeed, a later
official investigation into the docks industry asserted that it was
misleading to describe the 1947 measure as a 'decasualisation
scheme'.[56] At heart the Dock Labour Scheme was, as the TUC
recognised four decades later, 'like its (wartime) predecessors, primarily
concerned with the efficient operation of the labour force. To that end,
therefore, it was drawn up so that it could continue to impose upon

the dockers the disciplinary framework necessary to efficiency. In accepting this framework, the dockers surrendered something they greatly valued.'[57]

Although these problems were not immediately apparent in 1947, Isaacs's draft naturally elicited quite different responses from the respective sides of industry. For the TGWU its appearance was a fitting climax to its 25th anniversary celebrations in January 1947. The special glossy-covered Silver Jubilee issue of the *Transport and General Workers' Record*, complete with full page portraits of Bevin and Deakin, proclaimed, 'THE LONG FIGHT FOR DECASUALI-SATION ENDS IN VICTORY'.[58] The employers' reaction could not have been in greater contrast. With both sides of the industry invited to lodge their observations on and objections to the Isaacs draft with the Ministry of Labour, NAPE fought a bitter, rearguard struggle. Sending a copy of his organisation's objections to the National Dock Labour Corporation on 12 April, Macdonald wrote of the employers' 'profound disagreement with the intention that its [i.e. the Scheme's] administration should be entrusted to a national body, with local agencies, on which the Trade Unions would have equal representation with the Employers'. Macdonald and his colleagues were particularly concerned about the implications of union officials fulfilling 'certain of the functions which belong to management, and thus [imposing] on them duties which are alien to their office and must on occasion be irreconcilable with the natural demands of their constituents'.[59]

The employers' misgivings were rejected by two separate Committees of Inquiry which Isaacs appointed to hear the industry's objections to his draft measure. The Cameron Inquiry, which ran for six days from 14 May 1947, into the nature of the Scheme's administration, and the Hetherington Inquiry of 19 May 1947 into the amount and basis of calculation of the guarantee, both endorsed Isaacs's general principles. The Scheme was duly put into operation, as scheduled in the 1946 Dock Workers Act, by Statutory Order. With a veteran of the 1929 Labour government as its chairman, Lord Ammon, the National Dock Labour Board assumed its duties on 1 July. The Board posted large notices around the nation's ports informing the workforce of the impending changes, and placed adverts to the same effect in the national press on the days 27–30 June.[60]

The doubts raised by the employers' organisation were not the only objections to the draft scheme expressed in the opening months of 1947. In February an unsigned internal Ministry of Transport memorandum expressed doubts about the proposed form of administration. This was modelled on that of the National Dock Labour Corporation, a body characterised, according to the memo, by an unwillingness to take decisions 'unpalatable' to either side of the industry. The new Scheme offered 'no improvement' on this matter. What was required was 'an independent element as strong numerically as either of the other elements'.[61] Senior Transport Ministry civil servants pursued this line with the Ministry of Labour, requesting that the National Dock Labour Board's independent chair and vice-chair be bolstered by two other independent members in order to balance the four representatives from the respective sides of the industry. To the disgust of Aubrey Clark, Assistant Secretary at the Transport Ministry's Docks and Canals Division, the Ministry of Labour rejected this idea.[62]

This was not to be the last significant disagreement between the Ministries of Transport and Labour over the Dock Scheme. Two years later, following a series of unofficial strikes, Transport Ministry officials restated the opinion that their Ministry of Labour colleagues had been mistaken in allowing the unions to share control of the Scheme's administration. This position, which is discussed in chapter 4, implied that the Ministry of Labour had conceded too much ground to the TGWU. The young MP who became Parliamentary Private Secretary at the MoT in 1947, James Callaghan, has recorded in his memoirs that 'Shipowners had great influence with the Ministry of Transport shortly after the war,'[63] and Clark's frustration, just two weeks after the NDLB had begun going about its business, certainly illustrates the sympathies detected by the Parliamentary Secretary. 'I should have thought', Clark wrote, 'that the employers, at least, would have taken the view that a strong independent representation would help ensure that the dock labour scheme was administered with due regard to economic and commercial consideration.'[64] This theme, that union representatives on the NDLB, unlike independents and employers, were incapable of distinguishing what was in the best interests of the industry and the nation, would be restated in subsequent MoT observations on developments in the docks. On these occasions Clark and his colleagues would not seek support from employers in vain.

While exposing considerable tension within Whitehall, the Scheme's introduction also revealed organised labour's internal divisions. In the week preceding the start of the Cameron Inquiry on 14 May, a pamphlet was circulated in the London docks by an unofficial body of dock workers, the National Portworkers' Defence Committee. Predicting that the six-day Inquiry would be a 'farce in six acts', the Committee proclaimed its willingness to strike in favour of a seven-point programme which included the introduction of one daily call, the election of NDLB officials and the immediate nationalisation – without compensation – of the nation's docks, ports, harbours and canals.[65]

The existence of this unofficial committee reflected the historical problems of official organisation in the dock industry. Unofficial leadership, which had first challenged the TGWU as early as 1923, re-emerged after the war during the Dockers' Charter strike of October 1945. The committees then established in various ports around Britain were never formally constituted, remaining active only so long as a significant dispute in the docks existed, but they reflected the dockers' historical impatience with constitutional procedures and their consequent willingness to pursue problems through unofficial channels. The unofficial movement appeared in various guises between 1945 and 1951. Despite styling itself in May 1947 as a National Committee, its activities on this occasion appear to have been confined to the London. Within the vast docks of the capital, however, the unofficial movement's base was fairly broad. During the unofficial strike in 1948 – and there is little reason to suspect that the situation in 1947 would have been appreciably different – its representatives were drawn from all of the four main systems: London, Surrey, West and East India and Millwall, and the Royals. Moreover, while predominantly composed of TGWU members, the movement also included members of the National Amalgamated Stevedores and Dockers (NASD). Given the thorny relationship between the official leaders of the respective unions, this was a significant example of industrial cooperation. As such it was a source of tension within the NASD as well as the TGWU.

The NASD prized its separate identity, which it had protected by refusing to join the TGWU in 1922. The union's tiny membership – about 7000 as compared to a TGWU dock membership that exceeded 80,000 – was in some respects a source of strength, for it had a far more democratic reputation than its big rival. But it was also a source of weakness, for the NASD leadership constantly feared that it might be swallowed by the TGWU. In order to protect his union, General Secretary Richard Barrett duly required tight discipline from his members. Any contravention of the industry's constitutional machinery would diminish the NASD's position as a credible force in the docks.

Barrett's respect for constitutional propriety was evident during the Cameron Inquiry hearings. On 13 May at a meeting of the union's Stevedores' Sectional Committee, Barrett's attention was brought to the activities of Bert Aylward, one of his Dock Branch secretaries. On official branch notepaper Aylward had circulated a notice in the Surrey Dock which threatened to establish a strike committee in opposition to the mooted Scheme.[66] This mirrored the position of the National Portworkers' Defence Committee. Although Aylward's precise role in this committee in 1947 is uncertain, at the very least he must have liaised with its Surrey representatives. He was certainly active on the unofficial strike committee during the 'Zinc Oxide' dispute of June 1948,[67] and in 1947 he did try to present some form of unofficial reasoning to the

Cameron Inquiry. When Barrett arrived at the Ministry of Labour on 14 May for the hearing, he encountered Aylward on the steps outside. As the Inquiry began, with Aylward in attendance, Barrett informed Cameron that only he and Hern, his Dockers' Sectional Secretary, were entitled to represent the NASD. On the advice of the chair Aylward agreed to withdraw, and the Inquiry was thus prevented from officially recording the unofficial movement's views. It would appear, however, that Aylward lingered in Whitehall long enough to confront Barrett and Hern with verbal abuse outside the Ministry during the lunchtime recess, and at a subsequent meeting of the NASD's Joint Executive Council Aylward was officially cautioned as to his future behaviour. The episode indicated that the Scheme had generated considerable tension even within the compact confines of the smaller union.[68]

There were thus two very different critiques of the 1947 Scheme. On the one hand, employers had expressed 'profound disagreement' with its administrative mechanisms, an observation shared by senior figures in the Ministry of Transport. The shipowners' gazette, *Fairplay Weekly Shipping Journal*, frankly stated the type of views which Macdonald and Clark had been expressing, albeit more subtly, in private. 'Decasualisation', ran its editorial of 15 May, 'is a blessed word which, like Mesopotamia and democracy, can mean different things to different people, and thus add to the confusion'. For employers decasualisation implied continuity of employment for those qualified, provided there was a sufficient supply of trade. Some employees, however, interpreted the Scheme as guaranteeing continuity of payment with actual employment a secondary consideration. This latter assumption was held by the journal to exist 'largely because of a flood of sentimental twaddle about the "rights" of Man, which rights are represented as the workers' due by noisy folk whose jaws are their hardest working member and to whom unearned income is only to be reprobated in the "idle rich"'.[69]

On the other hand, there were the doubts and objections of the National Portworkers' Defence Committee, and individuals such as Bert Aylward. Their concerns indicated a degree of unofficial cross-union action that struck a clear contrast with the frosty official relations between the TGWU and the NASD. It might also be relevant to note that after the extremely harsh winter of 1947, many dockers needed little rousing from 'noisy' unofficial leaders: they had been working all winter in formidably arduous conditions, with cranes frozen in the docks and the thaw only recently completed by the middle of May.[70] Many may well have agreed with the unofficial leaders who believed that the Scheme did not go nearly far enough in eliminating the power of private enterprise, and who voiced a willingness to back this sentiment up with strike action.

These opposing views, and the bases of support from which they had sprung, would reappear on more than one occasion during the Dock Labour Scheme's difficult early years. However, the alliance of government Ministers and TGWU officials had few misgivings about the Scheme. They largely accepted that the structure of the National Dock Labour Board (NDLB) was consonant with Deakin's characterisation of its wartime predecessor, the National Dock Labour Corporation (NDLC), as 'a form of workers' control, expressed through the trade union organisations acting jointly with representative employers'. Of greater significance to both sides of the alliance was the economic lever which the Scheme bestowed on them at a time of immense economic difficulty. During the 1946 NJC negotiations Jack Donovan had emphasised the economic significance of decasualisation. If the casual order was restored, he argued, it would not be possible to obtain the increase in exports required for economic recovery.[71] Lord Ammon, who juxtaposed his NDLC and NDLB duties with his role as the government's chief whip in the House of Lords, frequently confirmed Labour's economic as well as social and political commitment to decasualisation. At the sixth Annual General Meeting of the NDLC in June 1946, he stated of the ports that such 'an important fact of our National Economy cannot be subject to the caprice of local enterprise'.[72] In 1947, the year of the Scheme's introduction, as a result of intensified economic pressure, the docks assumed an even greater strategic importance. On 5 June the NDLC held its final AGM, just four weeks before its functions were to be assumed by the new National Dock Labour Board. Two important speeches were made: the first by Ammon, who was to chair the NDLB as he had the NDLC, and the second by Ernest Bevin. Ammon observed, gratefully, that employers and employees had by now accepted the importance of turning shipping around as rapidly as possible, stating that he could not 'stress too heavily, how vitally urgent it is to see that our ships are at sea and not lying idle in the ports; that is absolutely essential if the flow of raw materials we so urgently need for our workshops is to be maintained, if sufficient exports are to reach overseas markets, and indeed if the national production programme is to be realised'. Bevin spoke of how the wartime schemes had succeeded in maintaining the labour supply, and now called upon the new Scheme, as Ammon had done, to speed the turn-round of North Atlantic shipping. 'What I am putting to you', he said, 'is really our national survival.' The audience of trade unionists and employers was also told: 'you dug for victory in the war; now dig for dollars'.[73] The theme was taken up by Bevin's old union in the wake of the autumn sterling crisis which precipitated the appointment of the new Chancellor. With Cripps arguing in Cabinet that recovery was dependent on increased

exports along with a counter-inflationary incomes policy, the
TGWU urged its dock members to 'help the country out of its
present difficulties' by doing everything possible to eliminate delays
in the turn-round of ships.[74]

It was against this background that the unofficial dock strikes of
October 1945, June 1948 and May–July 1949 took place. Each of
these disputes, which are examined in detail in the following chapter,
can be understood only in terms of the peculiar heritage which decasualisation between 1940 and 1947 failed to uproot. Dock
workers, while historically given to spontaneous outbursts of militant
strike action, had never been fully immersed in the culture of the
labour movement. The central pillars of this culture, loyalty to union
leaders and solidarity with other groups of trade unionists and the
Labour Party, did not always command the attention of dock
workers. Their loyalty and undoubted occupational solidarity were
instead expressed at a more immediate level, with neighbours and
work-mates in the dock communities. The TGWU, established on
shaky foundations in 1922, had not resolved the two outstanding
conflicts in the docks – local versus national and sectional versus
industrial. The quest for a solidly organised union, commanding
authority among dock workers nationally and industrially, was as
elusive to Arthur Deakin as it had been to Ernest Bevin.

The 1945 Government and Unofficial Dock Strikes

The opening chapters of this book explored the problems which Labour faced in power and the traditional difficulties of trade union organisation in the docks. This chapter brings out the collision between the long history of the docks and immediate post-war developments by examining the large unofficial dock strikes of 1945, 1948 and 1949. These three disputes are noteworthy because of their size, and more particularly because the 1948 and 1949 stoppages unfolded against an appreciably different background from that of 1945. In 1947 a number of factors had come together that would influence the Labour government's response to strike action in the docks. In the ports a Scheme had been introduced to honour the dignity of dock labour by guaranteeing its material maintenance, but which simultaneously sought economic rationalisation through increased discipline of the workforce. In maintaining on a permanent footing the loss of freedoms which dockers had enjoyed under casualism, decasualisation seemed in some respects to mark a deterioration in the quality of the dock workers' existence. Meanwhile, beyond the docks, Attlee and his Ministers, supported by the TUC General Council, were increasingly occupied by the central problems of domestic – and European – economic recovery, and the international – and domestic – resistance to communism. Events in the docks duly demonstrated that these were Labour's highest priorities in office, for the economic and international issues shaped the government's response to the strikes.

The Dockers' Charter strike of October 1945 was the largest single industrial dispute of the period. Lasting from 24 September to 4 November, it involved the majority of the national workforce and cost the industry 1,107,000 working days, but the government's response was relatively relaxed. Ministers certainly acted with far less restraint during the much smaller 1948 and 1949 strikes, which cost 200,000 and 406,000 days respectively.[1] Perhaps as a result, the 1945 strike has been paid little attention by historians of the Labour government, who have concentrated on the later disputes instead.[2] Yet this vast unofficial strike acutely highlighted the extreme pressures which were bearing down upon Keir Hardie's 'Great Alliance' within months of its supreme electoral triumph.

And it is essential to look at all three strikes together in order to understand each of them fully.

The Dockers' Charter Strike, October 1945

The strike in October 1945 was prefigured by a ten-week-old pay and conditions dispute which the Labour government inherited in July 1945. Since May dockers had been on strike at various times in Glasgow, in the Humber ports of Grimsby and Immingham, in Swansea and in Cardiff. At each port Churchill's caretaker administration had deployed troops to unload cargoes. In London throughout July dockers had been operating a go-slow, and on 25 July 600 troops were prepared for deployment in the Surrey Docks. On 31 July, only five days after the election of the first ever majority Labour government, Clement Attlee ordered these troops to unload several of the ships affected by the go-slow, and on 13 August the go-slow was called off.

The workforce's dissatisfaction with existing pay and conditions found further expression on 24 August, when the union held its National Docks Delegate Conference in London. The Conference adopted six proposals as a basis for forthcoming negotiations with the National Association of Port Employers. Earning the nickname, the 'Dockers' Charter', the package comprised:

1 An increased daily minimum from 16s to 25s.
2 Two weeks annual paid leave.
3 Payment for statutory holidays.
4 A reduced working week of 40 hours.
5 Retirement allowances for the aged and infirm.
6 The introduction of medical and other welfare services in all ports.

The first of these demands was particularly pressing, for dockers had received no formal increase in their daily guarantee since Bevin had secured the 16s minimum from the 1920 Shaw Inquiry. Publicly the Transport Workers' leadership regarded the adoption of the Charter as a great success, with the union journal describing the gathering as 'one of the best docks conferences we have had in the union'.[3] In private, however, the Docks Group Secretary, Jack Donovan, was unhappy with the proposals, especially the 25s minimum. This had been adopted against the advice of the Docks Group Committee and Donovan regarded it as a communist-inspired 'slogan'.[4]

The employers were notified of the Charter's contents on 3 September, but negotiations proceeded slowly. When the National

Joint Council met on 27 September, the NAPE representatives argued that the intervening 24 days had been an insufficient period in which to consider its response. The NJC was adjourned until 18 October, with the employers privately resolving to resist any advance on the 16s daily minimum.[5] This adjournment, combined with a serious local dispute on the Mersey, sparked the huge unofficial strike in October.

The Mersey trouble began on 24 September with a piece-rate dispute over a cargo of pit props in Birkenhead. The stoppage became general throughout the Mersey system because 360 Liverpool dockers, temporarily working in Birkenhead, were prevented by the Port Labour Superintendent from leaving the blockaded west bank in order to seek employment on the other side. By 3 October 13,000 of the area's 18,000 men were on strike.[6] On 5 October Donovan arrived in Liverpool, hoping to resolve the local grievances, but at this point the unofficial strike committee broadened the issues involved by attacking the union's alleged failure to pursue negotiations on the NJC with sufficient vigour. The committee pledged that the strike would continue, with the Charter's implementation as its aim.[7]

Evidently the strength of feeling among Merseyside dockers was reasonably representative of the mood of the national workforce, for within a week unofficial strike committees had been established in many dock areas, including London and Glasgow. Work was also disrupted at Dundee, Garston, Hull, Grimsby and Immingham, Leith, Manchester, Preston, Sunderland and West Hartlepool.[8] By 12 October, according to official Ministry of Labour returns, over 40,000 dockers were on strike. From then on the daily strike total exceeded 40,000 until the men returned on 4 November, excepting 18 October when it dipped only marginally, to 39,823. On 24 October the number of strikers peaked at 45,720.[9] The position adopted by the Mersey men, that existing pay and conditions could no longer be tolerated, was shared by the strike committees in these other ports. The London Central Strike Committee, for instance, issued a 'mandate' for a resumption of work that closely resembled the Charter, demanding a 25s daily minimum, a 40 hour week, adequate pensions and improved medical services.[10]

The strikers accompanied their demands for the Charter with attacks on the TGWU leadership. Reporting from Liverpool during the first week of the strike, the *Manchester Guardian*'s labour correspondent found that the majority of dockers were actively hostile to the presence of Jack Donovan in the port. At a rally attended by an estimated 10,000 men on 14 October Philip Callanan, secretary of the Liverpool committee, drew hostile attention to the salaries drawn by union officials: as General Secretary Bevin had received £1365, Deakin was receiving £1114 and Donovan £686. Callanan claimed that these officials were out of touch with the members who paid these salaries.[11] In London the strike committee mocked the official leadership's insistence that due attention to constitutional procedures would bear fruit, publishing a pamphlet which noted: 'We have pleaded and begged for the Union to fight for better conditions. The Unions have pledged us that they are going forward, that the official machinery has been set in motion. It has been set in motion, round and round, getting nowhere, nothing happening.'[12]

The besieged TGWU Docks Group Committee met to discuss the situation on 12 October, with Deakin in attendance. Disquiet was expressed firstly by the union's Manchester officer, who pointed out that 'it did appear in the minds of the members that the union did not mean to do anything except take their money'. Dissatisfaction was also voiced by the Scottish representatives, who stated that unofficial action – particularly in Leith, their area's largest port – had arisen because the union had failed to keep their members abreast of the 'facts' behind the Mersey dispute. Deakin noted that 'his thoughts were running with what had been said', but paid far more attention to the evidence of the Liverpool area representatives, who claimed that the marginal Trotskyist organisation, the Revolutionary Communist Party (RCP), had been 'a big factor in the trouble'.[13]

At a Transport House press conference held later that day by Deakin and Donovan, the union issued a statement which lent heavily on the information supplied by the Liverpool officials. It referred to unspecified 'definite evidence' that the Mersey dispute had, 'been seized upon by people connected with certain political organisations who had ready-prepared machinery at their disposal for encouraging and maintaining strike action'. In response to questions, Deakin confirmed that the organisation referred to was the Trotskyist RCP.[14]

With the only apparent connection between the RCP and the strike being its offer of a £40 grant-in-aid which the Merseyside committee had refused, the *Manchester Guardian* lamented the fact that Deakin had introduced the 'old and once fashionable distraction in the Communist "bogy"'.[15] A marginal organisation with only around 500 national members in 1945, the RCP was clearly in no position to sustain a strike of over 10,000 Liverpool dockers. Nevertheless, Deakin's reference to political motivation set a precedent. During the 1948 and 1949 dock strikes, however, when he repeated the charge that unrest in the docks was politically motivated, Deakin cited the role of the Trotskyists' sworn ideological enemies, the British Communist Party. As ever, in October 1945 the CP and the RCP presented entirely different political analyses. The RCP opposed the Labour government and welcomed the dock strike as a healthy expression of conscious working-class struggle. The CP, on the other hand, was still committed to the position of 'wholehearted support' for the Labour government which it had adopted in the aftermath of the July election result.[16] Arguing that the government was capable of beginning the socialist reconstruction of Britain, the CP took a cautious line on the docks. The party supported the dockers' claim for improved pay and conditions, but publicly opposed the unofficial strike, on the grounds that it was damaging the unity of the labour movement, and therefore weakening the government and delaying the emergence of a socialist Britain.[17]

With the Communist Party an unambiguous opponent of the strike in 1945, the TGWU leadership was duly denied an established 'bogy' on which to pin blame for the stoppage. This may explain Deakin's references to the RCP, which recalled Bevin's wartime attacks on the disruptive tactics of 'Trotskyites and other anti-war people', at a time when the Communist Party's insistence on tight industrial discipline had been absolute. The situation during the 1948 and 1949 strikes, and the nature of allegations concerning political motivation, would be entirely different.

With the TGWU press conference and statement of 12 October failing to weaken the strike, the mass defiance of union members prompted speculation that a rival trade union organisation might emerge. There was certainly inter-port collaboration. The Bristol port authorities recorded a 'propaganda' visit by Constable and Campbell, two unofficial leaders from London.[18] Three days earlier Merseysiders had spoken at an unofficial meeting in London, and Londoners had been received at a similar gathering in Liverpool. The London meeting on 16 October was also notable for its 'inter-denominationalism', one of the local speakers being Thomas Powell, a NASD member and chairman of the London strike committee. In cutting across union borders, the committee's composition was a reminder of the TGWU's failure to organise the entire port on an industrial basis, and Powell claimed that a new union could be formed at a moment's notice. But the London committee insisted that its real objective, despite the degree of inter-union and inter-port activity, was to 'clean up the union from within', in order that it would campaign more vigorously for the Charter.[19]

At this stage a resolution to the strike appeared some way off. Indeed, the stoppage still had some two weeks to run, but the TGWU leadership was gradually beginning to reassert itself. On 18 October it met the NAPE representatives at the NJC which had been adjourned on 27 September. The employers refused to talk about pay because of the strike, but agreed to a joint statement that negotiations would re-open within 24 hours of work resuming. This

was an extremely astute move. The strike's immediate cause had
been the original delay in negotiations, but the NJC's straightforward
statement now implied that the only impediment to talks was the
strike itself. The union also took a hugely significant private step,
endorsing a secret gathering in Liverpool over the weekend of
20–21 October between unofficial leaders and union officials. A
clear departure from the TGWU's usual position of refusing to
recognise 'self-chosen' leaders, this meeting apparently discussed
'ways and means of terminating the strike'. Attention was drawn
to the National Docks Delegate Conference that had been arranged
for 23 October, and the strike leaders 'were informed that it was
possible that the National Committee [i.e. the official Docks Group
Committee] would issue a direction to the members to resume and
allow negotiations to proceed, and if this were endorsed by the
Delegate Conference they [i.e. the strike leaders] would be able to
say that they could not hold up negotiations any longer'.[20]

The Delegate Conference indeed passed such a resolution on
23 October, observing the men's 'deep sense of grievance', pledging
that there would be no victimisation, and calling for an immediate
resumption of work so that talks could restart.[21] The leadership's
conciliatory approach was quickly rewarded. Although the London
unofficial movement was suspicious, in Liverpool – which the
union saw as the key area – the strike leaders were gladdened by
the Delegate Conference's decision. On 24 October Philip Callanan
spoke of the men's 'duty to try to find a sensible way out of this
deadlock. We do not wish to create wholesale chaos throughout
the country.'[22]

On 26 October the union balloted members at Liverpool,
Manchester and the two Humber ports. These postal ballots,
counted on 2 November, revealed substantial majorities in favour
of a return: at Liverpool 7177 were for immediate resumption
with 2846 against.[23] Perhaps anticipating the result of the ballot,
on 2 November the Liverpool strike committee held a mass meeting
which voted for a return to work on the following Monday, 5
November. On 31 October representatives from all the affected ports
had gathered in Liverpool, forming an unofficial 'national'
committee. This body apparently coordinated a general resumption,
with dockers in various ports around the country also voting on 2
November to go back on 5 November. After 41 days the 'national'
unofficial committee declared the strike over, although warning that
further strike action might be taken if the NJC failed to reach a satisfactory settlement within 30 days.[24]

Work restarted fully on 5 November, and although the question
of pay and conditions was not finally resolved until the middle of
December, the national committee's threat was not carried out. The
Charter was not secured in December, but the employers were forced

into significant concessions. The daily minimum rate was increased for time and piece-workers to 19s and the workforce awarded an annual paid holiday of one week.[25]

Throughout October the Labour government shared the TGWU's position that unofficial strike action was entirely unjustified and, in order to diminish the economic impact of the strike, the government used substantial numbers of military personnel to unload ships. Under the 1939 Emergency Powers (Defence) Act a total of 21,000 troops were deployed across the country in order, as the Ministry of War Transport saw it, 'to do the work the dockers should be doing'.[26]

Troops were introduced in the first instance to protect perishable food supplies at Liverpool. On 9 October George Isaacs, the Minister of Labour, told Cabinet colleagues that unless troops unloaded bacon from two blockaded vessels, a cut in the ration would be inevitable. Ministers agreed that military labour should discharge the bacon along with food cargoes on four other ships. When these troops arrived in the docks the strikers bore them little resentment. Said Philip Callanan, 'The Army are our friends, our brothers and our sons. Liverpool dockers have provided for the Army, the Navy and Merchant Navy throughout the war. We appreciate that, whatever they do, they have to do their job as an order.'[27] Nevertheless, as Keith Jeffery and Peter Hennessy have indicated, the government's decision was of immense historical significance:

> There it was. Less than three months after taking office for the first time with an overall majority, a Labour Government contemplated the use of troops to break a strike, apparently without any dissent from the ministers around the Cabinet table.[28]

Of course, the government did more than 'contemplate' using troops who had also unloaded ships in London during the August 'go slow', but the significance of this observation stands. Without reference to the ideological implications of their action, the government would send troops into the docks on five other occasions before 1951.

In deploying these troops the government took great care to remain within the 'rules' of the labour alliance. To recap, these informally bound Labour politicians to cede trade unionists the freedom to regulate industrial disputes and discipline trade union members. Indeed, it might be argued that the troops were used to defend the TGWU and the industry's constitutional machinery as well as food rations, for the government made no attempt to resolve the dispute and refrained from publicly attacking the strikers. In commenting on the dispute, Ministers simply urged dockers to resume work immediately so that pay talks could proceed and the process of post-war economic recovery be allowed to continue. In announcing the introduction of service labour on 10 October, Isaacs told the House of Commons that the strike was unjustified: the 'constitutional machinery of the industry' had a long record of success and it was in the dockers' interests 'that its authority be maintained'. When a Liverpool Labour MP asked Isaacs to meet constituents who were on strike, the Minister replied that the government had no intention of trying to resolve the dispute: 'the men should trust the machinery of the organisation. They would, I am sure, resent a Government official stepping in between them and the Union. They should trust the Union. I am sure the Union will see them through.'[29]

In private Ministers also sought to bolster the union's authority. On 15 October Isaacs – whose handling of the strike was being closely monitored by Bevin – secured Cabinet's agreement that no enquiry into the origins and nature of the strike would be held. This, he argued, would undermine the normal process of industrial negotiation which was set to resume with the NJC meeting three days later.[30] This anxiety to stiffen the battered integrity of the TGWU and the industry ensured that Isaacs continued to refuse requests for positive government intervention. Within hours of this latter Cabinet meeting, the Communist MP Willie Gallacher asked him to call a conference on the dispute involving 'representatives of the dock areas' as well as employers and trade union officials. Isaacs responded that it would be 'most unwise to let anything accrue to those who take unofficial action in this matter'.[31] A fortnight later, on 30 October, he rejected a similar – if more impassioned – plea from David Kirkwood, the veteran of Red Clydeside; on 31 October he also ignored a request from Bessie Braddock, the Liverpool MP on the right-wing of the Labour party, to pay closer attention to the situation.

The separate interventions of such disparate figures as Gallacher, Kirkwood and Braddock were an indication that throughout the labour movement there was a degree of unease over the government's handling of the dispute. On 31 October the *Daily Herald* responded to this unease, patiently explaining that the government's approach was in the interests of the working class. A leader column entitled 'Your Government' included the following significant passage:

This Government won the votes of the people with a programme which included a solemn pledge to uphold and advance the Trade Union Movement.

The Government will be faithful to trade unionists: but trade unionists must be faithful to their unions.

Dockers who remain on strike in defiance of their democratically elected leaders, must surely realise that they are weakening the authority of the unions, damaging the repute and complicating the task of the Labour Government, and undermining Democracy. If the constitutional machinery is deemed to be inadequate it must be reformed from within.

What is happening now at the docks is that constitutional methods are being repudiated and that an advantage is being conferred upon the enemies of working-class organisation.[32]

On 26 October the government did broaden its involvement in the dispute. With over 46,000 dockers on strike and 225 ships immobilised, Cabinet Ministers responded positively to a request from Alfred Barnes, the Minister of Transport, that military labour be extended to encompass vessels loading export cargoes. Troops would also clear the ships which supplied imports bought with sterling. This would save the precious dollars which were being rapidly consumed by imports.[33] Barnes's successful request indicated the manner in which the government's priorities were ordered. With Keynes in Washington negotiating a loan from the US Government, the primary consideration was not simply to supply people with regular, if meagre, amounts of bacon, eggs, oranges and cheese. The perilous economic position, with the dollar shortage already desperate, persuaded the government that the strike could not be allowed to delay the turn-round of shipping any longer.

Jeffery and Hennessy record that the 'hard line' adopted by the government was a success: a 41 day strike ended without a firm pay offer 'on the table'.[34] To some extent this was the case. The government had not intervened to resolve the dispute, and its use of troops was a stern warning to strikers that supplies of food and raw materials would not be interfered with. However, as the secret Liverpool meeting between union officials and strikers' representatives indicates, the stoppage was not brought to a close by the actions of the government. Moreover, six weeks after the strike dockers won their first daily minimum pay increase since 1922. In the face of the employers' determination to defend the old 16s guarantee, it might be suggested that the strike had influenced this outcome, which the unofficial movements regarded as a great victory.[35]

The extent to which the government had adopted a 'hard line' is also open to question. Troops were used on a massive scale, but they were not accompanied by the tactical smears which would characterise the government's response to the significantly smaller 1948 and 1949 disputes. In contrast to Deakin's outburst on 12

October, Ministers made no suggestion that political subversion was underpinning the strike.

Despite secretly negotiating an honourable settlement with the unofficial committee at Liverpool, in the immediate aftermath of the strike the TGWU leadership warned its dock members about the dangers of unofficial action. The union journal referred to 'certain elements who have made up their minds that they will do everything possible to destroy the constitutional machinery which has been built up over a long period of years, and embarrass the Labour Government by trying to force it to act as a substitute for trade unions'.[36] In private, Jack Donovan was extremely anxious about the longer-term implications of the Liverpool 'national strike committee' meeting on 31 October. He told colleagues on the Docks Group Committee that, 'so long as these unofficial disruptive elements are allowed to retain their membership of the Union and carry on their activities outside the constitution, it will be absolutely impossible for me ... or the Dock officers ... to function'.[37] As the men returned to work this theme was pursued in *The Times*, which re-emphasised that for an entire month the official union leadership had been supplanted in each main port area by unofficial bodies. This constituted 'a crisis in the internal affairs of the dockers' section of the Transport and General Workers' Union'.[38]

What *The Times* failed to add, however, was that unofficial organisation and activity were well-established features of the dock industry. The huge unofficial strike of October 1945 represented a continuation of the historical tradition which was discussed in chapter 2. From its origins in the latter decades of the nineteenth century, dock labour organisation was characterised by occasional outbursts of militant strike action without a solid basis of unionisation ever being established properly. In other words, Bevin had built the TGWU on foundations that were historically flimsy, and the 1945 strike was an indication that the Transport Workers had yet to harness the workforce's undoubted capacity for organisation and union activity.

In terms of the dilemmas facing Keir Hardie's 'Great Alliance' in the immediate wake of 1945's huge triumph, the strike had been no less illuminating. The government had used huge numbers of troops for two purposes. The first objective was to maintain the position of the TGWU and the joint negotiating machinery, thus enabling the trade unions to continue with their traditional role of determining the wages and conditions of workers. The second objective was to maintain Britain's economic life in extremely perilous conditions. Only through economic recovery could Labour fashion the type of Britain that it was pledged to realise: strike-breaking was thus presented as a move to protect rather than penalise the working class.

It is worth re-emphasising that the October 1945 strike was the largest single industrial dispute of the 1945–51 period. Yet the government's attitude towards the strikers was much more relaxed than during the later, and significantly smaller, strikes. This is clearly a paradox, but one which historians of the 1945 Labour government have curiously failed to recognise.

The 'Zinc Oxide' Strike, June 1948

The second large-scale unofficial dock strike which the Labour government encountered was the 'Zinc Oxide' dispute of June 1948. Having refused to handle a cargo of zinc oxide to the satisfaction of the London Dock Labour Board, a gang of eleven London dockers were penalised under the disciplinary regulations of the Dock Labour Scheme which had come into force one year earlier. The London Board suspended the men from work for seven days, and their rights to attendance money and guaranteed make-up were withdrawn for three months. Although the latter penalty was reduced on appeal to two weeks (the unpaid week-long suspension was upheld), workers throughout the port reacted angrily. Between 14 and 29 June more than half of the port's industrial workforce – stevedores, lightermen, cold storage workers and tally clerks as well as dockers – were on unofficial strike. Approximately 19,000 of London's 27,000 men were involved and, with sympathetic action taken by about 9000 Mersey dockers on 28 and 29 June, the dispute cost the industry more than 200,000 working days.[39]

As in October 1945, the trouble began with a piece-rate dispute. At issue was a cargo of zinc oxide which a gang of eleven men, led by J.R. Coe, were assigned to load onto a ship in Regent's Canal Dock on 28 May. Coe's gang objected that the cargo was unusually obnoxious, and regarded the rate negotiated by their union official, 3s 4d per ton, as insufficient. Contrary to instructions from the official, who had fixed the rate from his office without actually seeing the cargo, the men refused to handle the zinc oxide.[40] The London Board initiated disciplinary proceedings against the men a number of days later, releasing its findings against the gang on Wednesday 9 June. Within 24 hours an unofficial committee was established at Wapping in the London Docks section, calling for a sympathetic strike against the 'inhumanity' of the penalties, to begin on Monday 14 June.[41]

The following week opened with a stoppage of 1700 men which rapidly spread so that by 17 June, when the gang's punishment was

only partially commuted, 12,000 dockers had ceased work. Over
half of the Port's 230 ships were affected, with activity especially
disrupted in the Royals Group. The unofficial Port Workers' Strike
Committee appears to have been particularly influential in the
Royals, but its composition also drew on the port's three other
upstream sectors – the London, Surrey Commercial, West and East
India and Millwall – and it included, as had been the case in 1945,
members of the NASD as well as the TGWU. The reasoning
behind the stoppage was provided in a pamphlet issued by the
unofficial committee, entitled *The Men's Own Case*. This emphasised
the manner in which Platt, the union official in Regent's Canal Dock,
had compromised Coe's gang by conducting the piece-rate negotiations by telephone rather than in person, and characterised the
penalisation of the gang as a 'harsh and vicious punishment'.[42]

Like their TGWU brothers, the NASD members involved in the
unofficial movement courted the hostility of their official leaders.
Throughout the dispute Dickie Barrett, the union leader, tried to
secure a general resumption of work, appearing at a meeting in the
Surrey Commercial Docks with Deakin on 26 June and asking the
strikers to go back immediately. Moreover, once the strike was over
he rounded on Bert Aylward, one of the NASD members on the
unofficial committee, and who was also a member of the union's
Dockers' Sectional Committee and its Joint Executive Council. In
1947, it will be remembered, Aylward had been reprimanded by
the Executive Council for his role in unofficially opposing the
Dock Labour Scheme's introduction. After the 1948 strike Barrett
bluntly told the Executive that there would be no further meetings
until it had voted to exclude Aylward, which it did on 18 August.[43]

TGWU officials responded to events more swiftly than Barrett
and the NASD. On the eve of the Dock Labour Scheme's introduction in 1947 Jack Donovan had warned his dock members that
as the scheme was based on an Act of Parliament, 'a strike on this
issue would not be against the employers but against the
Government'.[44] The TGWU's reaction to the strike, which was
the first major dispute arising from the scheme's disciplinary
functions, reflected the gravity of this warning. But the union's
position was also determined by the deteriorating economic situation.
It is significant that the dispute was also the first of its kind since
the convertibility crisis had deepened the government's economic
difficulties. On 18 June the TGWU issued a press statement which
the *Daily Herald* summarised in its editorial column on the following
morning. Under the heading 'DOCKERS AND DOLLARS', the paper
stated that the strike posed a double-edged threat. In delaying 100
or so dollar-earning ships, the strikers were holding up the dollar
exports required to purchase rations, raw materials and machinery;
and in maintaining an unofficial strike against the Dock Labour

Scheme the men were attacking rather than upholding trade union principles.[45]

At a local level, TGWU officers were keen to effect a compromise with the unofficial movement. Reflecting the manner in which the 1945 strike was resolved, one of the officers told the London Board's Assistant Port Manager that he had met the strike leaders. Speaking of his belief that 'drastic all-round face-saving action' was necessary, he advocated a suspension of the penalties while the NJC discussed amendments to the Scheme.[46] At a national level, however, the union was not prepared to compromise. Speaking at an official TGWU meeting at the Albert Hall on 22 June, Deakin conceded that the Scheme's disciplinary mechanisms would be a subject for discussion at the union's National Docks Delegate Conference in August. But in order to defend the union and the Scheme which it jointly administered, the men had to accept the findings of the constitutional machinery on this occasion, and return to work.[47]

Deakin's decision to hold an official meeting in South Kensington, several miles away from the docks, was raised in Cabinet. The strike was apparently straining government–TGWU relations, Ministers noting 'evidence that the Union had not been sufficiently active in trying to persuade the men to abandon the strike, and [that] it was reported that the strikers had expressed resentment at being summoned to attend the Union meeting at the Albert Hall'.[48] Certainly Deakin's Albert Hall efforts were largely negated by a meeting which the unofficial committee organised at the same time – and much closer to the docks – in Hackney's Victoria Park. Addressed by a veteran of the 1945 strike, Harry Constable, this gathering of about 5000 dockers voted to maintain the stoppage.[49]

Despite expressing private misgivings about Deakin's handling of the dispute, in public the government unambiguously supported the TGWU's position that the strike imperilled collective bargaining and the economic life of the nation. With Isaacs attending an International Labour Organisation gathering in San Francisco, Attlee shouldered his Minister's Parliamentary responsibilities. On 23 June he mounted a vigorous defence of the TGWU in the House of Commons, re-emphasising the benefits which the Dock Scheme – jointly administered by the unions – had brought to the workforce. By remaining on strike the men endangered the union, the Scheme and therefore themselves: 'Unless the members of trade unions use the machinery which has been set up with their agreement, the whole Scheme, which is of immense value to the worker, may be jeopardised. Further, the position won for the trade unions by so much sacrifice in the past is endangered by action of this kind.'[50]

Attlee was speaking after service labour had been introduced in
the docks. Ministers had begun preparing for this development on
21 June after an inter-departmental gathering of senior civil servants
had assessed the economic damage arising from the stoppage.
Frank Newsam, Permanent Under-Secretary at the Home Office,
pointed out that unless Deakin's Albert Hall meeting secured a
resumption of work, troops would have to be deployed to unload
perishable food supplies, mainly eggs and tomatoes, which were
in danger of rotting. Newsam, who had acquired considerable
experience in breaking industrial disputes at the Home Office,
starting in 1926 with the General Strike,[51] also indicated that the
strike was costing a daily total of $170,000 in export earnings. This
led the officials to conclude that, once introduced, troops would
have to continue working until the strike was over.[52] Ministers on
the Cabinet Emergencies Committee wanted to give the union the
utmost opportunity to restore order in the docks, with Food
Minister John Strachey particularly concerned that the introduction of servicemen might precipitate sympathetic strike action
among the Smithfield meat porters. Nevertheless, they too concluded
that troops would have to be brought in if work did not resume
within 48 hours.[53] Following the Victoria Park meeting's resolution
to stay out on 22 June, 300 troops were sent to the West India Docks
in Poplar on 23 June, where they loaded civilian lorries with the
perishable food cargoes. On the same afternoon the Ministry of Food
issued a press statement which spelt out the strike's implications
for food supplies in London. Consumers would have to accept half
of their meat ration in canned form, as abundant supplies of fresh
meat were being held up in the refrigerated holds of blockaded
vessels. There was, however, no danger of these frozen carcasses
being lost.[54]

    In using troops once more the government demonstrated the seri-
ousness with which it regarded the situation. Yet the government's
public position – as summarised by Attlee's statement in the House
of Commons on 23 June – was relatively restrained, couching an
appeal for a resumption of work in terms of the damage which the
strike was causing to the economy, the union and the workforce.
As the strike entered its second week, however, government and
union leaders broadened attacks on the strike leaders to include
charges of political subversion. These charges were to carry a
particular resonance because of the political storm which was
gathering over another European capital, several hundred miles to
the east.

On 24 June, with the number of strikers exceeding 19,000, Deakin
issued a statement from Transport House asserting that the unofficial
committee was politically motivated. Of its 48 members, 37 were

said to be communists or 'fellow-travellers'.[55] Implying that the dispute had been hijacked by conspiratorial forces intent on maximising trade disruption and political instability, Deakin reinforced this allegation on 25 June by telling a gathering of dockers in Southwark Park, 'You cannot challenge the State and you cannot challenge the Government.' Deakin's allegations were partially supported on the same day with six well-publicised resignations from the unofficial committee. In a press statement two of these six, Bernard Duhig and Frank Palmer, claimed that the strike committee was intent on causing enough economic disruption 'to bring about the downfall of the Government'. The strike leaders responded by claiming that of the 42 men who remained on the committee, 27 of its members held no party affiliation, ten of them were Labour men and only five Communist.[56]

In private, few Ministers appear to have believed that the strike was politically-motivated. In deciding to send troops to the docks on 21 June, the Cabinet Emergencies Committee noted that Deakin's position was largely groundless : 'Scotland Yard was of opinion that the strike was not being fomented by Communists, but there was some indication that the Communist Party was beginning to take an interest in it for political purposes.'[57] Nevertheless, an emergency gathering of ministers late on 24 June did implicitly recognise that the strike was indirectly associated with the deepening ideological crisis in Europe. The main item on the agenda was the Soviet blockade of Berlin, which had begun that morning in response to the introduction by the three western powers of a reformed currency in the Berlin areas under their control. The meeting was dominated by Ernest Bevin, who had been taking a holiday on the English Channel during the first week of the dock strike.[58] With Bevin's holiday cut short by the crisis in Berlin (he returned with the aid of a Royal Navy torpedo boat), the government's position on the dock strike immediately hardened, for the meeting discussed developments in London as well as Berlin.

Bevin believed that the government had to act pugnaciously in each city in order to preserve its political authority. Arguing for a rapid escalation in the deployment of service labour in the docks, he dismissed Strachey's earlier fear about provoking wider unrest:

> there must be no sign of weakness on the part of the Government: they must show their determination to maintain the distribution of essential foodstuffs. They should not be deterred by threats that, if further troops were employed, the strike would spread to the meat markets. If the strikers got their way, the Government would be at the mercy of unofficial strikers for many years to come. Whether the strike continued for one week or five, no

concessions should be made by the Government until the men had returned to work.

For Bevin it was essential that events in Berlin were met with equal pugnacity. To abandon Berlin now would ultimately involve abandoning the whole of Germany, placing Western Europe and Britain in mortal danger: 'If we now showed signs of weakness, we were in danger of being forced out of Europe. If we took a strong line ... the Russians would in the end come to terms.'[59]

Did Clement Attlee really only ever read the births, marriages, deaths and cricket scores in *The Times*?[60] If so, then the Prime Minister would have missed a remarkable leader column which the paper carried five days after Bevin had implicitly compared the London and Berlin crises. According to *The Times*, striking dockers were 'seeking to blockade Britain as surely as the Russians on the other side of Europe are already besieging Berlin'. With the strike aiming a 'mortal blow' at food supplies and threatening to destroy the fragile economic recovery, it constituted 'a challenge to be resisted as resolutely as the threat of an attack by a foreign power'.[61] The government did not take its lead on industrial disputes and international strategy from *The Times*. This column does reinforce the point, however, that the 1948 dock strike was unfolding against an economic and international background which differed greatly from that of October 1945 and, as the strike entered a third week, Ministers responded with renewed vigour.

On the morning of Monday 28 June 1600 soldiers were sent to discharge food cargoes in Poplar. Later that morning the Cabinet discussed weekend developments which had seen an extension of the strike to Merseyside. On Sunday afternoon two of the London strike leaders, Constable and Saunders, addressed a meeting of 2000 Liverpool dockers which duly voted in favour of a sympathetic strike. Although Deakin insisted that this decision was unrepresentative of the mood locally,[62] 9000 dockers – approximately half of the Merseyside workforce – were supporting this action on the Monday morning. Ministers also heard reports that the strike was possibly about to spread to Glasgow and Southampton.

In these circumstances the Cabinet felt that it had to bring the London strike to a rapid conclusion. Ministers briefly considered a proposal from Ness Edwards, Parliamentary Secretary to the still-absent Isaacs, that the Dock Labour Scheme be temporarily suspended in the Port of London. This would allow employers to recruit volunteers to clear congested ships and also remind dockers that they had to accept the Scheme's obligations in order to reap its benefits.[63] As Keith Jeffery and Peter Hennessy have pointed out, no Cabinet which Ernest Bevin belonged to could countenance the suspension of the Scheme which he regarded as his own personal triumph, and the idea was rejected.[64] In seeking to defend Bevin's Scheme, however, the government did take the remarkable decision to declare a State of Emergency under the 1920 Emergency Powers Act. Thus did a Labour government bring into operation powers which not been used since they had helped to inflict the terrible defeat upon the labour movement of 1926.

The Labour government had privately decided to invoke the 1920 powers on one previous occasion, during an unofficial strike of road transport workers in January 1947.[65] However, before the measure could be implemented the strikers – who were TGWU members – had decided to go back to work. With every indication on 28 June being that the dockers' action was set to intensify, Ministers noted the 'desirable' nature of the 1920 powers which would 'give a firm legal basis for the use [and accommodation] of troops'.[66] This position was entirely disingenuous. In August 1945 the Cabinet had agreed to retain selected wartime Emergency Powers for five more years, with the Supplies and Services Act,[67] and under these provisions over 20,000 troops had been mobilised during the October 1945 strike. To invoke the 1920 Act was entirely symbolic.

The Cabinet Emergencies Committee met on the afternoon of 28 June to consider which provisions of the 1920 Act were to be utilised. The committee heard that, according to the Commissioner of Police, the temper of the strikers was good. With no animosity between dockers and servicemen regulations relating to public safety and order were unnecessary. On the initiative of Aneurin Bevan, Ministers rejected this advice. Bevan urged toughness, suggesting that it would be prudent to wield more wide-ranging powers, lest relations between the strikers and the military deteriorate. Sedition and the disaffection of servicemen were duly covered by the widely drawn regulations, which George VI signed that evening at Holyrood Palace, and which were to become law on Thursday 1 July.[68]

On the evening of 28 June Attlee explained to the nation, via a wireless broadcast, why the government had invoked Lloyd George's strike-breaking legislation. Having agreed the broad outlines of his talk with Bevin and the rest of the Cabinet,[69] Attlee mounted a vigorous defence of the British system of collective bargaining, where agreements *had* to be honoured on both sides of industry. He spoke also of the immeasurable benefits which dockers had gained as a result of the Dock Labour Scheme, and emphasised the key role of the TGWU in eliminating the insecurity and poverty which had characterised dock communities before the war. Appealing to the dockers' class solidarity, he asked them to support the government by resuming work:

This Government has decided on full employment. Full employment is the greatest benefit to all our people. Everybody in the country – whether docker or any other worker – must continue to give us the output. We depend on transport, shipping and the movement of goods to keep up this output. Therefore, this strike is not a strike against capitalists or employers. It is a strike against your mates, a strike against the housewife, a strike against the ordinary common people who have difficulties enough now to manage on their shilling's worth of meat and the other rationed commodities.

He spelt out the connection between the strike and the hazardous economic situation, pointing out that the stoppage was delaying imports of the raw materials which maintained full employment, and increased the pressure on the strikers by emphasising the conspiratorial nature of the stoppage. The unofficial leaders were people without genuine influence, 'just a small nucleus' of 'agitators' who for political reasons were interested in destroying the 'only agencies' which could enhance conditions in the docks, namely the trade unions and the Labour government. The ten minute broadcast, recently described by Anthony Howard as Attlee's 'straight talk to the lads',[70] concluded with a direct appeal to the men on strike: 'Your clear duty to yourselves, to your fellow citizens and to your country is to return to work.'[71]

On the following morning, 29 June, the strike committee convened a meeting of around 6000 dock workers in Victoria Park. Charles Riddell, a TGWU shop steward in the London Docks, read out a resolution calling for a resumption of work on the following morning, 30 June. Blessed by Coe's gang, the resolution was accepted almost unanimously on a show of union cards. It was a strong statement of future intent, however, condemning the 'complacent attitude of the responsible parties – that is, the employers, the higher trade union officials, and the Government', and calling for a revision of the Scheme's 'penal sanctions'.[72]

Discussing this sudden breakthrough, Cabinet concluded that the introduction of Emergency Powers and Attlee's broadcast had both been great successes. Satisfied with the outcome, Ministers accepted Bevin's assessment that no formal inquiry into the strike would be necessary, the Foreign Secretary judging that any official government investigation would undermine the Scheme and the union which the government had been steadily defending throughout the strike.[73] The belief that Attlee's broadcast had been decisive was generally shared by newspaper editors. The *Manchester Guardian* described the men's vote for a return to work on 29 June as a personal triumph for the premier, and the *Daily Telegraph* recorded that Attlee's prestige was high following the dispute's sudden resolution.

Only the *Daily Mail* was critical from a right-wing perspective, rejecting as nonsense the notion that Attlee's force of personality had been crucial: 'What mainly broke the strike was the Emergency Powers Act – and the dockers' fear of empty bellies.' Meanwhile the *Daily Worker*, which described the 1920 Emergency Powers Act as a 'handy weapon against the working class', spoke of the 'Unholy Alliance' of Labour Ministers, Tory Opposition and Trade Union leaders who had 'transformed the strike into a political issue and created a nationwide crisis'.[74]

The *Daily Worker* was not all that far off the mark in its suggestion that the strike had been transformed into a political issue. In November 1945 the *Transport and General Workers' Record* discussed the 'Facts About the Dock Strike' in the Docks Group section, tucked away near the back of the journal. In July 1948 the *Record* relayed 'The Facts About the Unofficial Strike of London Dockers' much more prominently, in the General Secretary's monthly personal column which adorned the middle pages of the paper. Deakin stressed that the challenge facing the union in the docks was politically motivated, adding that the strike had been a tragedy, bringing great suffering down on 'our people' and damaging 'our Government'.[75] This last remark was of great significance, for many dockers – even those on strike – truly regarded the government as their 'own'. This much was evident during the unofficial meeting which voted for a resumption of work. When one of the speakers, Stan Smith, launched an attack on Attlee he was howled down.[76] In the words of a Ministry of Labour official, J.G. Whitlock, Smith's words drew, 'a murmur of disapproval which quickly spread through the whole assembly. Unwisely continuing Smith was finally howled down and disappeared, none too gracefully, from the platform.'[77]

Although indicating that many dockers supported the government, the strike also demonstrated that the traditional, introverted patterns of loyalty and solidarity had survived within the docks. As John Lovell points out, dock workers primarily expressed these values within their own communities, rather than within the wider labour movement;[78] and the workforce's commitment to the local men who comprised the unofficial committee was incontestable. With the men going back to work, Ministry of Labour officials recognised that the unofficial committee was 'still in control', especially in the Royal Docks.[79]

Strikes in Support of Canadian Seamen, May–July 1949

The third big docks dispute which the 1945 government faced was more widespread than the 1948 strike, but although involving a number of ports, it still cost the industry less than half the days which had been lost in October 1945. The 1949 trouble was caused by the presence in British ports of ships which were subject to an industrial dispute between the Canadian Seamen's Union and their Canadian employers. Contrary to instructions from the TGWU, the government and employers, dockers in five port areas refused to work these ships. At Leith and Southampton no working days were actually lost as a result of this action, but there were general stoppages elsewhere. At a cost of 142,000 working days, between 16 May and 14 June approximately 12,000 workers stopped work in Liverpool and the Bristol Channel ports of Newport, Avonmouth, Portishead and Bristol. In London a strike involving 15,000 men from 23 June to 22 July cost a further 264,000 working days.[80]

These were the most controversial strikes of the 1945–51 period. According to Ministers and the TGWU leadership, the stoppages were a communist-inspired attempt to weaken the union and destabilise the economy at a time of increasing international tension. Historians have tended to support the contention that these strikes were an episode in the Cold War, along with the assumption that they were more damaging in economic and industrial terms than the much larger strike in 1945.[81] This interpretation is readily explicable, for Labour's response to industrial unrest was clearly entangled with wider economic, ideological and international problems and these problems were more pressing in 1949 than in 1945. As a perceived Cold War episode – with helpings of Transatlantic conspiracy and ideological conflict – the latter dispute invokes much spicier historical associations. Nevertheless, such an interpretation is almost completely mistaken.

Historical literature on the 1949 dispute is also weakened by its inadequate discussion of events outside London. As unpublished official records indicate, the London strike cannot possibly be understood fully without examining 'provincial' developments. During the Avon and Mersey strikes attitudes were formed on all sides that largely determined the pattern of events in London. But London is still the starting point, for the Canadian dispute was prefaced by further evidence of industrial tension and unofficial activity in the nation's largest port system.

In February 1949 the TGWU called 17 members of the 1948 unofficial strike committee before a special five-man inquiry, headed by Arthur Deakin. The men gave an assurance that their unofficial organisation was no longer in existence,[82] but within six weeks a number of them were involved in further unofficial strike action, in support of 33 unfit and elderly men deemed 'ineffective' by the National Dock Labour Board and removed from the London register. Four of the 'ineffective' men belonged to the NASD. The union's leadership had opposed the unofficial strike in 1948, but in response to these dismissals on 11 April declared the first official strike since the emergency regulation Order 1305 – which prohibited strikes and was still in force – had been passed in 1940.[83] This official protest was supported by an unofficial strike of TGWU members, so that on 13 April a total of 15,021 dockers and stevedores, along with 1550 lightermen, were on strike.[84]

Believing that the 'communist dominated' NASD had mounted the strike to disrupt essential services and Marshall Aid, and concerned that the official strike might set a damaging precedent, the government prepared to prosecute its leaders under Order 1305.[85] Before this became necessary, however, Ministry of Labour officials warned Dickie Barrett that Order 1305 would be invoked. On 14 April Barrett backed down, persuading his members to resume work. This they did, together with the TGWU men, on Saturday 16 April. Nevertheless, many dock workers had been greatly antagonised by the brief episode, understandably fearing that the 'ineffective' dismissals had established a dangerous precedent for further redundancies. Indeed, the NDLB privately conceded that its long-term strategy was to reduce its 'load' of registered workers.[86] Of equal significance, the affair had also stirred the government's suspicion that political subversion was afoot in the docks.

It was against this background of underlying tension that the strikes in support of Canadian seamen unfolded between May and July. These stoppages centred on eight ships, docked in Britain, that were subject to a bitter dispute involving Canadian shipowners and two rival unions, the Canadian Seamen's Union (CSU) and the Seafarers' International Union (SIU). The contentious vessels were as follows:

Table 3.1: Disputed Canadian Ships in British Ports, 1949[87]

Ship	Port	Arrival Date	Union Crew
Seaboard Ranger	Liverpool	27 March	CSU
Gulfside	Avonmouth	28 March	CSU
Ivor Rita	London (Royals)	2 April	British articles
Beaverbrae	London (Royals)	4 April	CSU
Argomont	London (Surrey)	9 April	CSU
Seaboard Trader	Southampton	29 April	CSU
Montreal City	Newport	5 May	SIU
Seaboard Queen	Leith	17 May	SIU

The Canadian dispute began in October 1948, when an agreement on pay and conditions between the CSU and Canadian East Coast (Deep-Sea) Shipowners expired. With talks on a replacement deal deadlocked, Humphrey Mitchell, the Canadian Minister of Labour, appointed a three-member Conciliation Board which suggested that both sides prolong the terms of the lapsed agreement for 12 months. The shipowners agreed to this in February, but in search of better terms on 21 March the union organised a strike on East Coast vessels. The dispute escalated seriously at this point, with the shipowners signing an agreement with the Seafarers' International Union. The SIU was affiliated to the aggressively anti-communist American Federation of Labour (AFL), which in 1947 had covertly established the break-away French labour organisation, Fource Ouvrière, in order to undermine the communist-dominated CGT. The AFL appears to have been involved in a similar operation in Canada, exploiting the impasse between the communist-led CSU and the East Coast owners to pitch an anti-communist affiliate – hitherto without Canadian membership – into the Canadian shipping labour market.

With the CSU striking from 31 March on all East Coast ships in protest at the employers' pact with the SIU, the dispute had immediate repercussions in Britain. CSU crews in Liverpool and London dissuaded local dockers from unloading their cargoes in the first week of April, while employers in these two ports – and in Southampton when a Canadian ship docked on 29 April – made no attempt to requisition labour for the disputed vessels. The embargo of Canadian ships placed the TGWU in a difficult position. Like the CSU, the TGWU was affiliated to the International Transport Workers' Federation (ITWF). If it obliged members to work on the disputed vessels – in accordance with its duty as joint administrator of the Dock Labour Scheme – the union would undermine its fraternal Canadian organisation. This difficulty was removed when the ITWF stated on 23 April that the dispute was not a strike but an inter-union conflict. There 'was no occasion for unions abroad to interfere in the dispute', and no question of dockers being asked to refuse work on the disputed Canadian vessels. On 6 May the TGWU extended the ITWF's strike-breaking operation by hosting a press conference jointly with the SIU. Arthur Bird, who had replaced Jack Donovan as the National Docks Trade Group Secretary at the start of 1948, reinforced the point that the ITWF was asking British dockers to work the Canadian ships.

Bird was responding to trouble that was brewing on the Bristol Channel. On 2 April the CSU crew of the *Gulfside*, which had docked and unloaded at Avonmouth on 29 March, had been sacked. On 1 May an SIU crew arrived to take the ship back to Canada but the CSU men, who had stayed in the port, dissuaded tugboatmen and lockgatemen from assisting the vessel's passage into the Bristol Channel. The *Gulfside*'s original crew also warned dockers that another Canadian ship, the SIU-crewed *Montreal City*, was set to arrive. At an unofficial meeting on 13 May dockers pledged not to work this ship, which docked on the following day. Trouble duly came to a head on 17 May, when Bristol port employers insisted that no labour would be requisitioned until the *Montreal City* was fully manned and working, precipitating a general stoppage at Avonmouth from 18 May.[88]

The precipitation of the Avonmouth stoppage can usefully be contrasted with the manner in which trouble was averted at Leith, where an SIU-crewed ship, the *Seaboard Queen*, arrived on 17 May. CSU representatives had gone to Edinburgh and spoke to the Leith men who refused to discharge the vessel on 18 May. Leith employers, unlike those at Avonmouth, made no attempt to direct labour to the disputed boat and this more relaxed attitude ensured that the only cargo lost in Scotland was the 1000 tons of wheat and 3000 tons of timber carried by the *Seaboard Queen*. The Canadian ship eventually sailed without unloading for Bremen on 3 June.[89] A similar situation arose at Southampton, after the CSU President, Harry Davis, had spoken outside the dock gates on 16 May. At this impromptu meeting the Southampton men reaffirmed their refusal to work the Canadian ship, the *Seaboard Trader*, which had been idle since docking on 29 April. The local Dock Board made no attempt to direct labour to this ship.[90]

In common with previous dock disputes, the government's initial response to the Avon stoppage was cautious. Influenced heavily by Bevin, whose industrial teeth had been cut on the Avon waterfront, on 23 May Ministers decided against any official intervention. This, it was felt, would cause the strike to spread and deny the TGWU an opportunity to reassert its authority in the docks.[91] The Ministerial Emergencies Committee was, however, instructed to keep an eye on developments. Convening on 25 May, it made two highly significant observations. First, military resources were extremely limited: if the stoppage spread to other ports troops would be unable to maintain essential supplies. Secondly, if the strikers succeeded in isolating the Canadian ships, 'they would have established *de facto* the right to refuse to work certain ships'. The government duly deployed 1200 servicemen to defend the Dock Labour Scheme on the Avon. On 27 May the strikers requested that troops clear the *Montreal City* immediately so that it could leave the port, but Ministers insisted that other ships first be despatched. To do otherwise would have been 'impolitic', allowing the men to resume work without handling the *Montreal City*, by-passing their obligations under the Scheme and claiming this dereliction of duty as a victory.[92]

With the limited number of available troops committed on the Avon, the government's problems were greatly exacerbated when the Canadian dispute spread to the much larger Mersey system after a British ship, the *Dromore*, arrived in Liverpool from Avonmouth.

Liverpool dockers were unwilling to unload the ship because it had come from a strike-bound port. When the local dock board announced that no labour would be requisitioned until work on the *Dromore* began, an unofficial strike began on 27 May. This was supported by a steadily increasing portion of the workforce, so that by 8 June about 10,000 men had ceased work.[93]

Aware that the services could do nothing to relieve the strike, the government reversed the position which it had taken on the Avon and unsuccessfully asked the Liverpool employers to isolate the *Dromore* from normal operations.[94] This overture alarmed the chairman of the NDLB, Lord Ammon, who told Attlee on 7 June that isolating the *Dromore* would have vindicated 'the recalcitrant and sabotaging elements'. He urged the need for a 'showdown' by enforcing the Scheme in all the ports where the Canadian ships had been isolated.[95] Crucial support for firmer action came two days later from Bevin, who informed Attlee that 'it would be disastrous' if the workforce were allowed to isolate ships from the Scheme.[96] The government finally lost its patience after a substantial export cargo of cars was lost at Liverpool. The scheduled vessel for the cars' transportation to South Africa had been blockaded for a fortnight at Avonmouth, during which time the South African government had introduced new restrictions on car imports.[97]

Without the troops to break the Mersey strike, the government tried to repeat the trick which had worked successfully in June 1948, namely a national Ministerial broadcast. Responsibility for the 11 June broadcast was given to George Isaacs who told listeners that a communist conspiracy afoot in the docks was disrupting Britain's economy recovery. As Attlee had done in 1948, he also warned that the strike was jeopardising the TGWU's hard-won gains over the years.[98] The impact of Isaacs's statement appears to have been almost immediate. On 13 June unofficial leaders on the Avon recommended a resumption of normal work, including the *Montreal City*. This took effect on 15 June, ending the 27-day strike. In Liverpool the strike ended even more quickly, with all work resuming on 13 June. At Southampton on 18 June local TGWU officials secured a start of work on the *Seaboard Trader*, a task completed on 12 July, when the CSU crew agreed to take the vessel back to Canada.[99]

With the resolution of the Avon and Mersey strikes, on 13 June the National Dock Labour Board turned its attention to the situation in London, where two Canadian ships had been idle since 4 April. Lord Ammon told the Board that the time to direct labour to the Canadian ships had arrived. With the exception of Barrett, and Bird who was absent, the Board supported Ammon in this view and Isaacs was informed that workers would be sent to the disputed vessels.

The government raised no objection and on Monday 20 June members of the NASD were directed to the *Argomont* in the Surrey Docks. Barrett, as he had indicated to fellow Dock Board members, struck a temporary note of defiance, urging his members to refuse this allocation. As had happened during the 'ineffectives' dispute in April, however, following an appointment with senior Ministry of Labour officials, Barrett rapidly climbed down. With Order 1305 hanging over the NASD once again, on 21 June its executive advised members to accept work on the Canadian ships.[100]

Despite this official about-turn, on 22 June NASD members in the Surrey Docks – in all probability with Barrett's tacit approval – and TGWU men in the Royals refused to work on the Canadian ships. The London employers' organisation reacted by resolving to make no fresh engagements of labour until these vessels were manned.[101] After an attempt by the Canadian High Commissioner in London to broker a resolution to the Canadian dispute had failed, the London employers' initiative provoked a general unofficial stoppage in the Surrey and Royals on 27 June. The employers were supported by the London Board on 29 June, by which time work had completely stopped in the Surrey and Royal docks, and was considerably disrupted in the West India and Millwall areas.[102]

This action was concerted by an unofficial committee which once again drew strength from both main unions and all four sections of the port. This 'London Central Lock-out Committee' made its position clear on 30 June with a pamphlet entitled *We Want Work*. This made three claims. Firstly, the stoppage was not an extension of the CSU's campaign, but an expression of the dockers' determination to avoid taking sides in the Canadian dispute. Secondly, it was not a strike: in attempting to force the men to blackleg, the shipowners and the NDLB had locked them out. Thirdly, the men demanded the right to work on all ships apart from those involved in the Canadian dispute.[103]

The stoppage, predictably enough, drew the wrath of the TGWU leadership. In the union journal on 1 July Deakin warned that the great benefits won by the TGWU over the years 'must not be imperilled by ill-considered action'.[104] Nevertheless, the number of men on strike continued to grow steadily: 8209 on 2 July, more than 10,000 on 8 July, 13,000 on 12 July and over 15,000 on 18 July. Support for the strike remained above 15,000 until it was called off on 23 July.[105]

The government regarded the new stoppage as another threat to economic recovery and the trade union movement's authority. In public Ministers also saw it as a political issue, forced by communists in the CSU and the London docks. In terms that were now becoming extremely familiar, on 28 June Isaacs condemned the strike in the House of Commons. The damage to the economy was 'intolerable', the strike leaders were unrepresentative 'disruptive elements', and the strikers were collectively 'betraying the interests of the vast majority of their fellow trade unionists'.[106]

Developments were again monitored by the Cabinet Emergencies Committee which withheld an immediate introduction of troops on 4 July, feeling that this would cause the strike to spread.[107] But on 6 July the committee decided that the threat to food supplies and the increasing loss of export trade revenue were sufficiently serious to justify a State of Emergency. A decision on the 1920 legislation had to await the Cabinet meeting of 7 July, but troops were introduced immediately to move food. Meanwhile fresh urgency was given to the economic situation on the afternoon of 6 July, when Sir Stafford Cripps outlined Britain's escalating dollar deficit which had erupted from £93 million in the first quarter to £157 million in the second quarter of the year. He told journalists that, given this grim economic news, the country could ill-afford 'the ridiculous luxury of politically-inspired strikes' like the one in the docks.[108]

On 7 July the government decided to proclaim an Emergency under the 1920 legislation. According to Cabinet minutes, one unidentified Minister did suggest that the measure was excessive, given that only two ships were subject to dispute. Overall, however, Ministers were swayed by the 'grave economic crisis' and the threat to the Dock Labour Scheme, noting that there 'could be no compromise on the issue that the dockers must unload ships without discrimination'.[109] The decision was announced by Home Secretary Chuter Ede on Friday 8 July, with the powers to become effective unless the men resumed work on the following Monday, 11 July.

On 11 July an early-morning mass meeting of strikers in Victoria Park elected to ignore this threat and maintain the stoppage. According to the *Manchester Guardian*'s labour correspondent, the 5000-strong crowd generally agreed that to unload the Canadian ships would be 'against the collective conscience of the waterfront'.[110] The government duly invoked Emergency Powers for the second time in less than 13 months, establishing a small executive body to direct military and civilian labour in the docks for the duration of the Emergency.[111] The Port Emergency Committee, as it became known, was chaired by Sir Alexander Maxwell, who as Permanent Under Secretary at the Home Office from 1923 to 1948 had played a prominent part in directing strike-breaking troops during the General Strike. Before 11 July service labour was confined to food cargoes. Sir Alexander's committee directed a steadily increasing number of troops to work on all cargoes: from around 2500 on Tuesday 12 July to 5500 on Friday 15 July. During the fourth and final week of the dispute, the numbers rose from 7082 on Monday 18 July, to 10,821 on Thursday 21 July. When the strike ended on

Saturday 23 July, there were 12,792 troops working on a total of 130 ships throughout the docks.[112]

In declaring an Emergency the government was unable to emulate its quick success in 1948. It failed to secure a resumption, as had a Ministerial broadcast by Isaacs on 13 July. Invoking the authority of the Canadian Trades and Labour Congress (to which the CSU was affiliated), the International Transport Workers' Federation, the TGWU and the NASD, Isaacs had argued that the Canadian ships were not, as the lock-out committee insisted, 'black'. Thus, if the men went back to work, they would not be scabs or blacklegs, but defenders of the Scheme, their unions, their families and the country at a time of great economic danger.[113] A yet more graphic public attack was launched several days later by Nye Bevan. Addressing the Northumbrian miners' annual picnic, Bevan described the strike as 'a betrayal of the British labour movement'. The dockers were engaged, he added, in an undisciplined 'minority struggle' which jeopardised the government and 'the welfare of the nation as a whole'.[114]

While the government attempted to cow the men into a resumption, the TGWU also increased the pressure on the strikers. In the union journal on 1 July Deakin had given notice that TGWU members involved in politically-motivated strikes would receive 'their marching orders'. Deakin pursued this end at the TGWU's Biennial Delegate Conference which opened at Scarborough on 11 July, the day that Emergency Powers came into effect. The conference began by adopting an important constitutional change, proscribing communists – along with fascists – from holding any official position within the union. An extension of the TUC anti-communist campaign which Deakin had launched in 1948, in stating trade unionism's incompatibility with communism, the ban was also an indirect attack on the dockers' unofficial leadership, which contained several men who were communists as well as TGWU stewards. On 14 July the Conference also passed an emergency resolution, moved by Deakin, condemning the strike in customary terms. The stoppage, which prevented the union from fulfilling its obligations, was imposing 'a hardship and a burden on the community at a time when the country is struggling for its very existence'.[115]

Events at Scarborough failed to weaken the strikers' resolve. On Sunday 17 July the lock-out committee held a march from Canning Town to a rally in Trafalgar Square where the refusal to work the Canadian ships was reaffirmed. On 15 July the Board considered the idea of issuing each striker with a notice, specifying that if he failed to resume work by a particular date, he would be dismissed from the Scheme. The Port Emergency Committee rejected this proposal on Tuesday 19 July, Maxwell arguing that dismissal notices would transform the strike into an emotive defence of

victimised dockers.[116] Ammon promptly informed Attlee that
'"Emergency" as the name of the Committee seems a joke',[117] and
– despite the objections of Arthur Bird – the Board proceeded to
issue an ultimatum to the strikers. In the form of a press release
broadcast on the evening of 19 July, this advised dockers that
unless they resumed work at 7.45 a.m. on Thursday 21 July, the
'very existence' of the dock labour scheme would be jeopardised.
Alarmed by this announcement, the government immediately
issued a rival statement which denied that steps were afoot to end
the scheme.[118]

Conflict between the government and the Board intensified on
the following morning, with Ammon attacking Attlee and other
'panicky' Ministers who had 'crabbed a real chance of getting a
resumption of work'. To a large extent Ammon's exasperation
was understandable, for Ministers themselves had frequently
remarked that unofficial action imperilled the Scheme's future.
Nevertheless, Ministers were furious that Ammon had been disloyal
to the government which he served as Chief Whip in the Lords.
In September 1945, when Ammon had been appointed to the
government, Bevin told him that the two roles were ultimately irreconcilable.[119] It had taken almost four years, but on 21 July Cabinet
reflected on Ammon's recent behaviour and agreed that Bevin
had been right. While allowing him to retain his position at the
NDLB, Attlee obtained Ammon's resignation from the government
that evening.[120]

An indication that the strike might be coming to an end had
actually arrived before the NDLB's ultimatum. On 19 July the lock-
out committee stated its intention to hold a public meeting in
Victoria Park on Friday morning, 22 July. Before this took place,
on 21 July an official TGWU meeting, attended by 1000 strikers
at the West India Dock, voted overwhelmingly to resume work on
Monday 25 July. The Victoria Park meeting attracted several
thousand strikers, and began with a sudden announcement from
the CSU president, Harry Davis, that the Canadian strike in Britain
was over. He falsely stated that the Canadian Deputy Minister of
Labour had offered fresh conciliation on the original dispute. This
offer had actually been made on 27 June and was no longer valid,[121]
which suggests that the CSU was tactically withdrawing while the
dockers' support remained intact. The lock-out committee duly recommended a resumption of work in victorious terms. With the CSU
no longer on strike, the *Beaverbrae* and the *Argomont* were no
longer 'black', and men could resume work on these ships without
violating 'trade union principles'. This was unanimously accepted

by the meeting, and the men resolved to resume all work on Monday morning, 25 July.[122]

Normal work resumed accordingly, but the Board and port employers were extremely unhappy that an unofficial stoppage had again ended with the men's faith in their unofficial leaders unshaken. In the Lords Ammon criticised the Government for failing to act against the 'fomenters' of the strike; in allowing these men to go unpunished Ministers were storing up problems for the future.[123] The London employers' organisation was also pessimistic about the future. Within hours of the strike coming to a close, it was privately expressing its intention to force 'known agitators' off the London Board's register.[124]

Arthur Deakin, whose union had the most to fear from the unofficial movement, was even angrier. With the TGWU's authority once more usurped in the docks, Deakin told his Docks Group that the presence of unofficial leaders would no longer be tolerated. There were, he said, 'certain people who would be dealt with and they would not be dealt with sympathetically, they must face the music'. Having seen these people bring discredit to the union and disruption to the industry, Deakin was now prepared to put them 'out of the Scheme, he would go this far if people would not act decently. We could not afford to throw away the hardwon gains that the Dock Employees enjoy at the moment.'[125]

The London strike had restated the fact made evident during the 1948 stoppage: in the docks there was a core of vigorous and determined unofficial leaders who commanded levels of trust and support which the TGWU palpably did not. The stoppages at Avonmouth and Liverpool had also confirmed the lesson of the huge strike in 1945: the TGWU was still unable to organise coherently a diverse national and industrial workforce. At the Biennial Delegate Conference Deakin had fulfilled his promise to give communist shop stewards their 'marching orders' by banishing them from union office. Now he was to turn the TGWU's organisational wrath against the dockers' unofficial movement in London. This important sequel to the 1949 dispute is discussed in the final chapter, which examines the strains which the 1945–49 strikes exerted on the labour alliance. This is preceded, however, by an analysis of the character of these strikes.

Communist Conspiracies? The Allegations and the Reality

Strikes as Political Subversion

The association between unofficial strike action and political subversion was initially made by Arthur Deakin, the TGWU General Secretary, when during the huge Dockers' Charter strike of October 1945 he accused the Trotskyist Revolutionary Communist Party of 'encouraging and maintaining the strike action'.[1] Responding to the London strike of June 1948, Deakin perceived an altogether different political conspiracy. He claimed that the vast majority of the unofficial committee were communists and hinted that the stoppage – in disrupting trade in Britain's busiest port – was part of international communism's attempt to undermine Britain's economic and international standing.[2] On this occasion, in contrast to 1945, his charges of subversion were publicly supported by the government. Broadcasting on the strike Attlee referred to 'a small nucleus' of 'agitators' who wanted to pull the TGWU apart and disrupt Britain's recovery.[3]

Allegations of communist involvement were made even more explicitly during the 1949 strikes. When the NASD threatened official strike action in April, George Isaacs told other ministers that the 'Communist-dominated' union was seeking to embarrass the government,[4] and the Cabinet believed that communists on the union's executive were seeking to disrupt essential services and impede the delivery of Marshall Aid.[5] The government discussed the communist conspiracy theme with particular persistence during the strikes in support of the Canadian Seamen's Union. On 23 May Isaacs told colleagues that the CSU's President, Harry Davis, was 'a known Communist' who 'had been extremely active' in promoting the original Avonmouth dock strike.[6] In the Cabinet on 26 May Chuter Ede suggested that the seamen's strike was designed to interfere with 'the shipment of supplies under the European Recovery Campaign'; it was agreed that the affair 'illustrated the need for a more general campaign to put the dockers and other workers in this country on their guard against this sort of Communist exploitation'.[7] Ministry of Labour officials believed that the Liverpool stoppage, which followed the arrival of a ship from Avonmouth, also stemmed from communist intervention. On 9 June a departmental memo recorded: 'It seems definite that the difficulties which are being created is a Communist Party affair planned at the highest level. (This is from TGWU and Dock Labour Board officials). Stated that Communist Party made plans and were on the job as soon as the *Dromore* difficulty arose [sic].'[8]

The TGWU also insisted that the London strike, beginning in the last week of June, was political in character. Bob Mellish, TGWU-sponsored MP for the docklands constituency of Rotherhithe, told journalists that the strike was 'riddled with Communist activity of so serious a nature that the facts should be investigated by MI5'.[9] John Platts-Mills, who had recently been expelled from the Labour Party amid unsubstantiated allegations that he was a secret Communist Party member, responded to this statement by referring to Mellish in the House of Commons as the 'special agent for Rotherhithe'.[10]

Allegations of communist involvement on the basis of these incidents were taken seriously by the government. On 4 July the Ministerial Emergencies Committee repeated Chuter Ede's earlier observation that dock strikes were part of a communist-inspired attack on Marshall Aid: 'The dockers were being deluded and exploited by the Communists, and to make this clear would be one step towards bringing the strike to an end.'[11] Chuter Ede spelt out this analysis when announcing the introduction of Emergency Powers on 8 July, emphasising that the communist attempt to disrupt British and European recovery was an unacceptable challenge to the State's authority.[12]

The government's belief in communist conspiracies led to the publication in December 1949 of a White Paper on the Canadian strikes.[13] This included a foreword from George Isaacs, stating that evidence existed of 'a cold and deliberate plan' executed by unofficial dock leaders and the communist-dominated Canadian Seamen's Union. Intended to alert the public to the dangers of communist disruption, the timing of the paper's release actually ensured that it received the minimum of publicity. On 16 December, the date of its appearance, Parliament rose until 24 January 1950 and actually reconvened only after the General Election of 23 February. Thus Parliament was denied the opportunity to debate the White Paper, which received only slightly more attention in the press. While *The Times* simply provided an unqualified summary of its contents, the *Manchester Guardian* made three criticisms of the White Paper: there was no reference to the row between Ammon and Attlee; the government's tacit acceptance for two months that the Canadian ships were 'black' was ignored; and it demonstrated little 'official understanding of the genuine loyalties of the dockers which were exploited during the strike'.[14]

The government attempted to reignite public interest in the strikes and the White Paper following the 1950 election. In a speech to the Labour League of Youth in March, Herbert Morrison referred to the Communist Party's disastrous electoral showing and argued that communists would now switch their efforts from 'the political field to the industrial field'. This would involve an emulation of 'the true and detailed story published as a White Paper just before Christmas, of the international conspiracy which led to last summer's dock strikes here and in other countries'. Morrison added a rather unedifying sales pitch: 'This amazing record is published by the Stationery Office. It only costs 9d. and anyone who wants to see how the Communist game is played could not do better than order it from a newsagent and read it.'[15]

This chapter reappraises the notion that unofficial dock strikes were a component of the 'Communist game'. First, the three major strikes are re-examined in order to deal more directly with the question of political subversion in the docks. Recapitulating and bringing together points made in the previous chapter illuminates the essentially industrial – as opposed to political – characteristics of the three disputes. Second, attention is directed to a number of general problems in the docks, which contributed to the industrial tension that was the real cause of the unofficial strikes.

Re-examining the 1945–49 Strikes

Arthur Deakin argued that the Revolutionary Communist Party (RCP) had been instrumental in maintaining the Liverpool strike which sparked the huge Docker's Charter Strike in October 1945. Formed in 1944 as a merger between the Workers' International League and the Revolutionary Socialist League, the RCP was so minuscule an organisation that a number of its 400 national members believed the appellation 'Party' to be ludicrous.[16] While a handful of Trotskyists did work in the Liverpool docks, the RCP clearly lacked the resources to support a general stoppage in the huge Mersey port system for a period of weeks. Indeed, this largest single industrial dispute of the 1945–51 period had nothing to do with political subversion, but arose from the workforce's dissatisfaction over wages and conditions of work. Dockers had not received a formal increase in their guaranteed minimum daily pay since 1921. Bevin told Isaacs that this was the real cause of the strike: 'if ever there was a case where the men were entitled to improvement it seems to me to be in the docks industry'.[17]

The TGWU publicly conceded that pay levels were unsatisfactory, the official National Docks Delegate Conference acknowledging the workforce's 'deep sense of grievance' on 23 October. Moreover,

Deakin and his colleagues also privately recognised the other main characteristic of the huge unofficial strike. Impatient with the leadership's conduct of pay negotiations, large numbers of dockers had temporarily transferred their allegiance to unofficial representatives. Realising this, and that a return would only be secured if recommended by these men, the union sanctioned highly unusual – and ultimately successful – secret negotiations between Liverpool Docks Group officials and unofficial leaders on 'ways and means of terminating the strike'.[18]

Given Deakin's awareness of the realities of the situation, some explanation must be offered for his remarks about political subversion. The only actual suggestion of Trotskyist involvement came from Liverpool officers reporting to the Union's Docks Group on 12 October,[19] but there was never any solid indication of how this involvement had determined the strike's development. In the absence of such evidence, it might reasonably be speculated that the Liverpool officers were offering an explanation for events which deflected criticism from themselves. They had, after all, reacted very slowly to the initial piece-rate dispute of 24 September, opening negotiations with employers only on 5 October. There is also the possibility that rumours about Trotskyist involvement might have been started by communists. It should be remembered that the CP had embarrassed itself in the early part of 1945 by arguing for a continuation of the wartime Coalition, and had attempted to regain lost ground in August 1945 by pledging its 'whole-hearted support' for the new government. The CP's support for the government influenced its strong opposition to the dock strike; it is possible that some communist dockers saw an opportunity to both undermine the strike and attack their Trotskyist rivals by linking the two together. This is speculation, but unless the non-communist Liverpool TGWU officers merely invented the story to protect themselves from criticism, and with the government and the union already greatly embarrassed by the strike, only the CP really stood to gain from rumours of political subversion. Did Arthur Deakin himself unconsciously participate in a communist conspiracy on this occasion, by branding the strike as a Trotskyist ramp?

The 1945 strike was a traditional industrial struggle for improved pay and conditions. The 'political' nature of the 1948 'Zinc Oxide' strike in London was even more overblown. Cabinet Ministers were privately aware that, whatever Deakin said, Scotland Yard believed there to be no evidence linking the strike with political subversion.[20] Nevertheless, in his broadcast of 28 June Attlee studiously ignored the specifically industrial causes of the strike, and asserted that it had been organised by a small core of agitators. To recap, the strike followed the London dock board's decision to discipline a gang of eleven men, led by J.R. Coe, who had disputed a piece-rate negotiated by their union official on the telephone from his office. The men were suspended without pay for a week, and their rights to attendance money and guaranteed make-up withdrawn for 13 weeks, with this second penalty reduced to two weeks on appeal.

An unofficial pamphlet attacked the officer concerned in the initial dispute on the grounds that, in agreeing 'a rate before seeing the job and without consulting the men', he had committed an 'outrage'.[21] This criticism suggested a gulf between the union and its London members which was further exposed during the strike when the TGWU tried to restore order with an official meeting in Victoria Park. A small crowd of about 300 strikers gathered, but deliberately moved off as a body when the London Docks Group officials arrived. The humiliated officials were left with only a small band of journalists to address.[22]

While maintaining that the strike was a political conspiracy, Deakin sensibly acknowledged that his members had been greatly antagonised by the length of the men's original 13 week punishment. He threw the union's weight behind a demand that the maximum period of disentitlement to the benefits of the Scheme be drastically cut, and in November 1948 the employers' representatives on the National Dock Labour Board agreed to reduce this to four weeks. This admission is further evidence that the 1948 strike, just like the 1945 one, was the result of two things: an industrial dispute between employers and workers, and the perception which many dockers held – partly for historical reasons – that they were inadequately represented in these disputes by their union officials.

In 1949 the charges of political subversion were made with far greater persistence and certainty. As a result, the Canadian strikes have a relatively high profile in the historiography of the 1945 government, with various historians characterising the dispute as an early domestic episode in the Cold War. In public Cabinet Ministers and Trade Union leaders expressed the strong belief that the Canadian strikes were a communist conspiracy, and their allegations were published as bald statements of fact in the White Paper of December 1949. Having read the paper, however, the Ministry of Labour's Solicitor, A.F. Harrison, issued a stern warning to the Ministry's Chief Industrial Commissioner, Sir Robert Gould. Harrison stated that opinions expressed in its foreword – about the Canadian Seamen's Union and the character of the stoppage – were both defamatory and legally dubious.[23] Gould duly sought advice from Sir Hartley Shawcross, the Attorney General, who expressed the opinion that the 'communist conspiracy' charge was unlikely to stand up in court if the dockers' unofficial leaders or the CSU decided to sue the government for libel. He suggested that the government would only evade inevitable legal and political embarrassment by publishing the report under the 1840 Parliamentary

Papers Act as a White Paper. By appearing as a White Paper, the report's contents – highly contentious as they were – received important and absolute legal immunity,[24] and this legal protection enabled the government to deflect public attention from the character of the British stoppages and the merits of the Canadian dispute.

Shawcross's private reservations about the character of the strike were widely shared within the government. These reservations thus need to be considered in detail if the nature of the strike, and the government's response to the strike, are to be completely understood. This is also necessary because of the prominent and largely inaccurate place given to the Canadian dispute in historical accounts of the 1945 government.

The Canadian Stoppages: Strikes or Lock-outs?

To recall events discussed in the previous chapter, the Canadian conflict essentially arose from the virulent anti-communism of the American Federation of Labour, which was engaged in displacing the communist-led Canadian Seamen's Union with its own affiliate, the Seafarers' International Union, as the chief organiser of Canadian East Coast seamen. At the first formal Ministerial discussion of the Canadian-related troubles, chaired by Attlee on 23 May, George Isaacs blamed much of the trouble at Avonmouth on the CSU's communist President, Harry Davis. Davis had persuaded local dockers not to unload a Canadian ship, the *Montreal City*, which was crewed by members of the SIU. However, Isaacs also pointed out that on 17 May Avonmouth employers had decided to engage no fresh labour until the *Montreal City* was manned. Thus, he added, in voting to go on strike the Avonmouth dockers had 'been influenced by the virtual "lock-out" declared by the employers'.[25]

Arthur Bird, National Secretary of the TGWU Docks Group, shared the Minister's view that the Avonmouth stoppage constituted an industrial dispute between workers and employers. Having publicly advised his members to disregard the 'row between two [North American] unions' and work on the Canadian ships,[26] Bird was privately furious with the Avonmouth employers for attempting to coerce his members into working the *Montreal City*. He told the employers that they had locked his members out, and – vainly, as it turned out – demanded a reversal of their position.[27]

Further anxiety among Labour leaders was expressed in the Emergencies Committee on 25 May, which noted that dockers had refused to work on the *Montreal City* and another Canadian vessel, the *Gulfside*, because they believed that the SIU crews of these ships were blacklegs. Ministers sympathised with this belief, acknowledging that Canadian shipowners had flown in SIU crews to man vessels whose CSU crews were on strike. With dockers willing to work on all ships apart from the Canadian ones, Ministers duly felt that 'it was the action of the two groups of employers which had exacerbated the situation and led to the present stoppage. If that action could be reversed, the port as a whole could be re-opened and negotiations about the *Montreal City* and the *Gulfside* could go on as a separate and minor issue in a much better atmosphere.'[28]

The meeting ultimately rejected this course of action, because in order to preserve the Dock Labour Scheme's credibility, the unofficial strike had to be defeated. The committee's chairman was Chuter Ede, who as a former schoolmaster had little industrial experience of the labour movement. It will be remembered from his comments on the composition of the 1945 PLP that he also had little patience with 'superannuated trade union officials'. With this background, Chuter Ede was more willing than most of his government colleagues to conclude that the dock unrest was a communist conspiracy, and his impatience with the movement's industrial leadership was duly compounded when Arthur Deakin – of all people – denied that the dispute was a straightforward communist plot. In a meeting with the Home Secretary on 30 May Deakin also contested Chuter Ede's assumption that the government could clear the matter up by explaining the full facts of the Canadian dispute to British dockers. As Deakin himself put it, the SIU's case was not entirely sound, since it had signed a deal with Canadian employers during a legal strike by the CSU.[29] This obviously contradicted the position which the TGWU and the government took in public, however, and, it should be re-emphasised, no criticism of the SIU, the Canadian shipowners or British port employers eventually found its way into the White Paper.

The White Paper also ignored evidence which contradicted the government's insistence that communists had spread the trouble to Liverpool. Ministry of Labour information on communist activity on the Mersey came from local Dock Board and TGWU officials, via its Regional Industrial Relations Officer, A.S. Andrews. Although he believed that communists had plotted the action, even Andrews did not accept the full details of the story: 'TGWU officials allege that the plotting takes place in Bessie Braddock's office at Liverpool, This is perhaps a libellous statement.'[30] From the same officials who had cooked up the Trotskyist conspiracy in 1945, this was more than libellous. It was, in fact, outside the realms of common sense, for no less unlikely communist conspirator against the TGWU and the Labour government could have been suggested than Braddock. This was the same arch right-wing Labour MP who later wrote of Aneurin Bevan: 'He made it fashionable to be a dissident. He weakened the National Executive to a point where it could no longer deal effectively with infiltrating Trotskyists and Communists.'[31] In questioning this particular TGWU allegation, Andrews drew attention to the general unreliability of his union sources. Nevertheless, he continued to accept their broad contention that the strike was a communist plot.

The government was, however, given an alternative perspective on the Mersey dispute by one of its own Cabinet Ministers, Harold Wilson, the President of the Board of Trade and a Liverpool constituency MP. Having met constituents who were on strike, Wilson told Isaacs on 13 June that the stoppage was not communist in origin, and only a 'very small minority' of the strike committee were communists. His constituents claimed that the employers had deliberately forced a confrontation by directing labour to a ship, the *Dromore*, which had sailed from Avonmouth: 'The strike was not based on any sympathy with, or alleged solidarity with Canadian strikers, but was based on what they regarded as a point of Union principle in connection with the working of a ship they regarded as "black" which had come from a strike-affected port.'[32]

This assessment, that the strikers were merely observing a time-honoured trade union principle, confirmed Isaacs's private conviction – shared with TGWU leaders – that the strikes primarily revealed industrial rather than political concerns. At a meeting chaired by Attlee on 10 June, Chuter Ede strongly criticised Deakin, who he suggested 'was keeping from the dockers the real issues in the case, and also attempting to obscure the fact that the strike, though not inspired by the communists, was being vigorously exploited by them'. Isaacs countered this criticism of Deakin, arguing that far from bringing the stoppages in Avonmouth and Liverpool to an end, 'an attempt to expose the fundamental issues might lead to a total stoppage of work in all the docks in the country'. If the TGWU or the government provided dockers with a full statement of facts, as Chuter Ede wanted, the SIU's intervention against the CSU would be revealed, confirming dockers: 'in their belief that members of the SIU manning Canadian ships were blacklegs. This was a fundamental Trade Union point and to stress it would only do harm.'[33]

Instructed by Attlee that he would have to broadcast a statement on the dispute in any case, Isaacs acted upon the understanding which he shared with Deakin that an exposition of the dispute's true facts would prolong the strike. Going on air on 11 June, he suppressed his views on the confrontational tactics adopted by Canadian and British employers. Instead he reiterated the line that the strike was a communist plot, designed to hamper economic recovery and cause embarrassment for the government and the TGWU. In referring to Canadian events, he stated only that the communist-dominated CSU had been disaffiliated by its parent body, the Canadian Trades and Labour Congress. He ignored the CTLC's equal condemnation of the SIU, and the SIU's intervention against the CSU in its dispute with the Canadian shipowners.[34] Keith Jeffery and Peter Hennessy have bestowed great credit on Isaacs's broadcast, pointing out that, 'Evidently he convinced the strikers.'[35] Indeed he convinced the men, for the strikes at Avonmouth and Liverpool ended almost immediately, but it is unlikely that he convinced himself. Chuter Ede had argued for a broadcast in order to clarify the details of the Canadian strike, and to persuade dockers that their own strike action was dangerous and illegitimate. In fact, Isaacs and other Ministers realised that the strike would only be brought to an end if its true origins were obscured rather than clarified.

The government's characterisation of Canadian-related developments in London was equally misleading. The London stoppage began after employers had repeated the tactics adopted by their Avonmouth counterparts, refusing to engage any new labour until two disputed Canadian ships – the *Argomont* in the Surrey Docks and the *Beaverbrae* in the Royal Docks – were manned and working. The employers knew these vessels were a potential source of trouble, and had avoided directing workers to them since their arrival in London at the beginning of April. The dockers' unofficial leadership cited the employers' decision, announced on 27 June, and supported two days later by the London dock board, as a lock-out, and the sole cause of the stoppage. The 'Central Lock-out Committee' explicitly dismissed charges of political motivation, stating: 'it is inevitable that someone sooner or later will discover that the refusal of the workers to *blackleg* or go hungry through low wages and high prices, are really Communist plots'.[36] The main body of dockers seemingly agreed that the employers had effected a lock-out. They were certainly unimpressed with all attempts to convince them that they had been tricked by communists into going on strike. On 2 July Bob Mellish organised a public meeting in Poplar with the intention of establishing that communist intrigue under-pinned the dispute, but the event was a flop. A local Ministry of Labour official reported to headquarters in Whitehall, 'the idea of a "red plot" does not make much impression on dockers'.[37]

There was little wonder in this. On 7 July Cabinet heard that the police had 'little evidence about the activities of the Communists in fomenting the various dock strikes, though strikers were being advised by persons with legal experience who had Communist sympathies'. Legal advice from Communist sympathisers certainly did not impute a conspiracy to undermine economic recovery. The government's public line was also dismissed by its own law officers and the Attorney General himself. Having held talks with the Director of Public Prosecutions, Sir Theobold Matthew, and the Ministry of Labour's Solicitor, on 7 July Sir Hartley Shawcross told the Cabinet of his belief that the stoppage constituted a lock-out on the part of the employers. Isaacs contradicted Shawcross by reminding colleagues of the Dock Labour Scheme's continuity rule, under which dockers who had declined to finish work on ships for which they had been engaged, definitely were on strike. Nevertheless, Shawcross's views on the character of the dispute, expressed with the full authority of the Director of Public Prosecutions and complemented by police evidence that communist involvement was negligible, possibly contributed to the uneasiness felt by some Ministers about the introduction of Emergency Powers.[38] Shawcross personally favoured using Emergency Powers, but the dissenting Ministers may well have agreed with him when he told Isaacs after this Cabinet meeting that the stoppage was, 'both a strike in relation to some ships and a lock-out in relation to others. The real point is, I think, that the men seem now anxious to work all ships other than the two Canadian ones.'[39]

Shawcross repeated this judgement on 8 July, confirming in Cabinet that the dispute represented a strike in the case of some ships, and a lock-out in the case of others. He concluded, 'It is therefore, not possible in law to give unqualified support to the view that the present stoppage is a strike.'[40] That afternoon, in the House of Commons, Chuter Ede announced the Government's intention to proclaim a State of Emergency under the 1920 regulations. In so doing he unashamedly misrepresented the character of the dispute:

> The only reason why we are having to deal with the trouble in this country is that the Communists see in it the chance of fomenting unrest, injuring our trade, and so hampering our recovery and with it the whole process of Marshall Aid on which the recovery of Europe depends. The issue with which we are faced is not one of a legitimate industrial dispute. We are faced with a challenge to the authority of the state and it must be met.[41]

This amounted to wilful distortion. By the admission of Shawcross, backed by the Director of Public Prosecutions and police evidence, the dispute's central feature was not a communist-inspired attack on the Marshall Plan or the British constitution, but 'a lock-out by the employers'. To the recalcitrant dockers, the only thing that mattered was their unwillingness to unload two Canadian ships which were subject to an industrial dispute. Once committed to Emergency Powers, however, the government's public position on the character of the dispute grew even more uncompromising. On Wednesday 13 July Isaacs took to the airwaves for a second time during the Canadian dispute. Setting Shawcross's private misgivings aside, Isaacs stiffly informed dockers that their stoppage was definitely not a lock-out: 'Your so-called unofficial strike leaders tried to change the nature of this dispute. To call it a lock-out instead of a strike is just playing with words. You know you walked off the job and said you would return only on the condition that you would not work certain ships.'[42] As an experienced trade unionist Isaacs ought to have known that to call a stoppage a lock-out rather than a strike was more than 'playing with words'; and while insisting that under the continuity rule many dockers were on strike, he had not himself dissented from Shawcross's position that the employers were attempting to force many others on to ships that were subject to a trade dispute. The basic injustice that dock workers perceived in this situation was spelt out to journalists by Albert Timothy, the Lock-out Committee's chairman, on 11 July after an unofficial mass meeting in Victoria Park had voted to continue the boycott of the Canadian ships. Re-emphasising the dispute's basic industrial dimensions, Timothy accused the government of failing to understand 'the position of a good trade unionist down where we live. We will never go and scab on another man, or blackleg on another man.'[43]

This assertion that dockers were simply defending their traditional industrial values bore a pointed similarity to Isaacs's position earlier in the Canadian dispute. During the Ministerial discussion of 10 June Isaacs had explained that the reluctance of Avon dockers to work on disputed Canadian ships touched upon a 'fundamental Trade Union point'. Isaacs surely understood that London dockers were equally determined to avoid 'black' or 'scab' vessels; he also knew, from police evidence and advice from his own Ministry's legal department, that the strike was not a communist conspiracy. Nevertheless, along with the rest of the government he continued to mislead the public by denying that employers had acted in an inflammatory manner, and by erroneously insisting that the dispute was a politically motivated strike.

General Post-war Problems

Each of the three large unofficial strikes revealed a serious difference of opinion between the TGWU and sections of its dock membership on a specifically *industrial* issue: in 1945 it was pay and conditions; in 1948 the alleged victimisation of eleven workers; and in 1949 the question of intervening in a trade dispute between Canadian seamen and Canadian employers. The government and the TGWU were particularly frustrated by the 1948 and 1949 strikes: Labour's political and industrial leaders were broadly bound by an unwillingness to concede that industrial tension – a historical feature of the docks – had survived the introduction of the 1947 Dock Labour Scheme. The first chapter of this book observed that the government enjoyed invaluable support from the trade unions in pursuing economic recovery; the second that the Dock Labour Scheme, which provided a vital strategic industry with a regular workforce, was seen by the government as instrumental to Britain's export-driven recovery. Furthermore, the TGWU's conception and administration of the Scheme was cited as a particular example of trade union cooperation in the vital task of economic recovery. Reliant on the Scheme and the TGWU, the government had to defend them both from the attacks which it perceived unofficial dock strikes to represent. During the 1945–49 strikes the government therefore invariably sought a course of action that would not compromise the TGWU's efforts to reassert authority in the docks. The deployment of troops was part of this strategy. While troops maintained short-term supplies of essential food and raw materials, they also served the government's longer-term interests in the docks by breaking strikes and undermining the unofficial movement. In so doing troop operations were used to defend the authority of the Scheme, and thereby the reputation of the TGWU.

Driven by its economic priorities, the government also sought to defend the union and the Scheme by disingenuously attacking the strikes as politically motivated. Nevertheless, the strikes illuminated a number of underlying problems in the docks – with the Scheme and the TGWU – which Ministers were unable to obscure entirely. It is to these industrial problems which the discussion now turns.

Welfare Amenities

Britain's straitened circumstances had stiffened the government's determination to introduce the Dock Labour Scheme in 1947. The perilous economic position also ensured that the industry was unable to equip its workforce with improved welfare conditions. The government was aware that such improvements were urgently required. On 5 August 1948 George Isaacs informed the National Dock Labour Board of Attlee's concern that unsatisfactory welfare conditions had been a contributory factor in the recent strike in London. For this reason, Isaacs invited the Board to undertake an inquiry into the state of existing conditions in all ports, and to offer relevant recommendations for their improvement. Material was compiled by local dock boards during the winter of 1948–49, and the National Board submitted its findings and recommendations to the Ministry of Labour on 25 February 1949.[44]

The report observed that existing welfare provisions were greatly stretched by recent social changes in the docks. There had been an increased tendency, during and since the war, for the workforce to live outside the immediate vicinity of the docks, which meant greater demand for catering and washing facilities. Fewer men could thus eat their midday meal at home, which was in any case a problem further complicated by rationing; and dockers from Glasgow, on the Tyne and in Liverpool had commented on the problems associated with travelling home in dirty clothes on public transport. The report added that the process of social change, greatly accelerated by the Scheme, had involved greatly improved living standards and expectations among dock workers. This was reflected in more widespread demands for better canteens, wash-places and toilets. Indeed, on the basis that every local board had commented on the inadequacy of their sanitary arrangements, the Board believed that the need for improved toilets was especially urgent. Dock areas were exempt from the sanitary regulations of existing factory and public health legislation, and hence the quality of provision was, to say the least, mixed. The typical toilet was a pale latrine which discharged directly into the dock, canal or river, was housed in an iron or wooden shanty without protection from the elements, and afforded no privacy to the user. 'It is not surprising', noted the report, 'that the men avoid the lavatories wherever possible and have a real fear of infection.' Where decent toilets had been provided, the Board recorded no evidence of serious misuse or vandalism, and felt that the vast majority of dockers would respond favourably if improved toilets, along with updated catering and washing facilities, were instituted on a national basis.[45]

Having read the report, Isaacs told Morrison, who as Lord President was to chair ministerial discussions on the subject, that it revealed 'a state of affairs which demands urgent action'.[46] And Isaacs reminded members of the Committee on 1 April that the report had been commissioned by Attlee, who was anxious that its recommendations be implemented as soon as possible. Nevertheless, the Lord President's Committee as a whole regarded it unfavourably, principally because it had neglected to identify the body respon-sible for effecting improvements which had not even been costed. Isaacs attempted to mollify colleagues by pointing out that financial costs would probably be borne by port users, but this was not strong enough an assurance for Cripps. He explicitly ruled out Treasury involvement, either in planning or financing the improvements, and Isaacs was left to establish an inter-departmental Working Party – without Treasury representation – to cost the proposals and identify the body responsible for implementing and financing them.[47]

The Committee's Working Party reported on 28 October 1949. The intervening period had witnessed the Canadian-related strikes and more pertinently, as it turned out, a serious financial crisis and the consequent devaluation of sterling on 18 September. The Working Party re-emphasised that radically improved facilities were required in most dock areas, and confirmed Isaacs's earlier suggestion that responsibility for improving the dock amenities rested with port users. But the recommended measures would cost around £1 million over three years, and Isaacs conceded that the 'present economic pressure' ruled out their immediate implementation. His conclusion, that the measures would have to be shelved on economic grounds, was supported by the Minister of Transport, Alfred Barnes, and the Financial Secretary to the Treasury, Glenvil Hall. The Committee meekly concurred with this assessment.[48]

This decision was further notice of Labour's preoccupation with economic recovery. Yet the failure to press the port users or the Treasury to finance the improvements rested uneasily with the government's often asserted view that economic recovery required an efficient performance from the docks industry. Attlee and Isaacs had both expressed concern that such a performance was being hampered by poor dock amenities, with Isaacs describing remedial action as a matter of urgency. As a proportion of public expenditure, which in 1949 exceeded £2000 million,[49] the required sum of £1 million represented a modest investment for a potentially high return. The National Dock Labour Board was understandably frustrated by the government's decision, informing Isaacs that the indefinite postponement of reform fitted uneasily with earlier government assertions about the urgency of improving welfare amenities.[50]

The debate about the relationship between tense industrial relations and poor amenities did not end in 1949. Following another unofficial dock strike in London, in May 1950 Isaacs appointed an official Inquiry into unofficial stoppages in the port. This later strike, the establishment of the Inquiry and the consequent pressure which was exerted upon the government's relationship with the TGWU, are all discussed in detail in the final chapter of this book. At this stage it is enough to note that the Inquiry – which was chaired by Sir Frederick Leggett, the former Chief Industrial Commissioner at the Ministry of Labour – paid close attention to welfare amenities. Leggett's report, published in May 1951, emphasised that throughout the nation's docks these were significantly poorer than in the rest of modern industry. In London facilities were particularly poor and had appreciably augmented 'the sourness of industrial relations in the port'. Leggett also criticised the government for failing to act on the NDLB survey which it had commissioned. This had aroused the workforce's interest in the issue, causing fresh impatience and antagonism when the anticipated improvements had been abandoned.[51]

As the NDLB had emphasised in its February 1949 report on dock amenities, the workforce's general expectations had been enhanced by the Dock Labour Scheme's introduction. Where outdated welfare provisions failed to live up to these expectations, dissatisfaction was indeed likely. The government and the TGWU often publicised the notion that the Scheme had been a massive breakthrough: this notion of progress was not necessarily shared by dockers who had to travel home in wet and filthy clothing and use some of the most insanitary toilets in British industry. The government continued to accept that the quality of amenities had contributed to the unrest in the docks. In May 1951 the Lord President's Committee endorsed a paper to this effect by the new Minister of Labour, Alfred Robens,[52] but there was still no commitment to financing the improvements which were deemed necessary.

Problems with the Scheme?

The survival of squalid amenities in the docks reflected the 1947 Scheme's general failure to dispense with the industry's historic problems. The central feature of this history had been casual employment, and – as chapter 2 indicated – neither Bevin's wartime initiatives nor the 1947 Scheme itself had eradicated this. The survival of the free call on a twice-daily basis, which ensured that a substantial amount of labour was recruited casually, caused the Leggett Inquiry to observe that the Scheme had instituted 'little change from the habits and practices of casual employment'.[53] A subsequent official inquiry into the Scheme's operation, appointed in 1955 by the Conservative Minister of Labour, Sir Walter Monckton, and chaired by Mr. Justice Devlin, emphasised that the free call was contrary to the spirit of the Scheme. It allowed employers – through their foremen – to exercise favouritism; it also promoted an undignified and sometimes physical competitive scramble among dockers for the more attractive and lucrative jobs. Devlin also highlighted the problems facing dockers who were not employed in the morning but were obliged to attend the afternoon call five hours later. This required either a long wait or double travel expenses for an often fruitless return journey. The report noted that casual recruitment and the problems associated with the two daily free calls had aroused considerable discontent among the workforce.[54]

Devlin's observations were soundly based. Prior to the Scheme's introduction in May 1947, the London unofficial movement had indeed demanded that there be a single daily call, held each morning.[55] On the wider consequences of casual recruitment, it should also be noted that work was paid largely by the piece, and the rate generally reflected a cargo's market value rather than the physical effort involved in shifting it. This naturally bred a great deal of resentment. In London's Royal Docks there was always immense competition to handle cargoes of imported meat. Although tough work, it paid much better than many cargoes of comparable difficulty such as cement. Of those who congregated at the call stands to work on the meat, foremen saw a natural advantage in recruiting the younger and fitter men – in one docker's words, 'all the ruckers' – who were duly regarded with jealousy by older and less fit men.[56] The word 'ruckers', it might be added, conveys something of the physical struggle for the foreman's attention which Devlin recognised as characterising the free call.

In addition to citing evidence that the free call was an important source of underlying tension, the Leggett Inquiry reported that the twice-daily calls significantly contributed to the manner in which strikes started. In gathering men together, the calls gave men who had a grievance and were spoiling for a strike a captive audience, and this occasionally allowed 'a few men to sway the rest'. During the Canadian dispute Bevin made this very point to Chuter Ede, in successfully pressing for a temporary suspension of the call stands in London's Royal Docks: 'It causes such a congestion and works up mass psychology. It also enables our opponents to carry out their tasks and keep the men out.'[57]

The longevity of the casual tradition, however, also was a source of trouble in another way. Chapter 2 acknowledged the broad historical consensus that under the pre-1940 casual system, dockers enjoyed a significant advantage which very few other groups of industrial workers shared: they were free to decide whether or not to try for work on any given day, and free to accept or reject any work which they were offered. Under the Dock Labour Scheme, these freedoms no longer existed. Workers had to attend each morning and afternoon, and had to accept the work which they were offered. Although the bulk of the workforce supported the Scheme, the loss of this historical privilege – and Leggett observed that 'dockers have long memories'[58] – was keenly felt. In 1986 a TUC review of the Scheme's history emphasised the significance of these freedoms, and the workforce's perceived sense of injustice under the post-1940 regime: 'That freedom ended with the wartime schemes, with their demands that the men report regularly every day for work, or face disciplinary action ... the 1947 Scheme made these features permanent, with the disciplinary code being in some ways more severe than the codes which ruled in other industries.'[59]

If not quite inevitable, it was surely always probable that great
tensions would arise as the workforce adapted from one of the
slackest disciplinary regimes in British industry to one of the
toughest. Central to the strike in the London docks in March
1945, according to Arthur Deakin's sympathetic biographer, was
the rigorous application of discipline under the wartime decasualisation scheme. This had been operating, 'at the margin of the
men's tolerance'.[60] The reaction of the unofficial movement to the
'Zinc Oxide' affair, which led to the strike of June 1948, is surely
also to be understood in terms of this awkward transition. A
workforce accustomed to casualism might well have agreed with
the unofficial movement's assertion that the disciplinary measures
taken by the London Board against Coe's gang were a 'harsh and
vicious punishment'.[61] The 1948 London strike committee
emphasised its support for the Scheme, but argued that suspending
men from seeking work or enjoying guaranteed maintenance was
an unacceptable reversion to pre-war conditions, a 'throwback to
the days of Casual Labour plus Poor Law Relief'.[62] While the
NDLB acknowledged the men's disquiet on this issue by reducing
to four weeks the maximum period of suspension from the Scheme's
benefits, the general antipathy with which the workforce regarded
the new disciplinary regime was not removed. More than 14 years
after Bevin's wartime regulations had been introduced, the 1955
Devlin Inquiry found that the dockers' collective resistance to the
Scheme's disciplinary mechanisms remained a significant source
of tension: 'the docker who has been brought up to casual work
valued his power of taking a day off if he wanted to – and still more,
no doubt, the sense of feeling that he was free to take a day off if
ever he wanted it – and at the end of a long and strenuous job running
over a weekend he sometimes needed it'.[63]

It would thus appear that although the Scheme had banished casualism's worst feature, namely the financial insecurity which stemmed
from unemployment and underemployment, it had also stripped
dockers of their former control over work and leisure patterns.
Informal holidays, such as the London dock worker's annual hop-
picking excursion to Kent, were forfeited under the Scheme which,
according to Leggett, deprived dockers of, 'the pleasant side of a
bad system'.[64] In addition, less savoury elements from the past,
the wretched welfare amenities and the lottery of the free call, had
not been dispensed with.

Significantly, Leggett and Devlin both also argued that the
resultant tension was aggravated by the actual manner in which the
workforce had attained its greater financial security. This had
nothing to do with the Scheme itself, but was essentially a result
of generally favourable post-war economic conditions, and full
employment in particular. Both reports suggested that these

conditions had indirectly undermined the men's confidence in the Scheme, for few dockers were actually reliant upon its benefits in terms of the guaranteed minimum income. The daily obligation to report at the docks and accept any available work appeared all the more onerous as a result.[65] Having to endure the downside of both casual recruitment and non-casual discipline, and essentially enjoying the benefits of neither of the two employment methods, dockers thus laboured under the worst of both worlds.

The unofficial strike of June 1948 directly confirmed that the workforce was unhappy with the Scheme's disciplinary framework. It attested also to a deeper problem, namely that the traditionally difficult relationship between the TGWU and its dock members had been complicated by the union's role in the administration of the Scheme, and that the union's authority had been particularly damaged by the participation of its officers in the exercise of the Scheme's unpopular disciplinary procedures.

Problems for the TGWU?

According to the National Dock Labour Board's own statistics, in addition to the large-scale unofficial strikes of 1948 and 1949, between July 1947 and October 1951 there were 42 stoppages which cost the industry at least 1000 working days. Significantly the National Board recorded that 31 of these strikes were prompted by industrial disputes. At issue were piece-rates, holiday bonuses, compulsory overtime, the dismissals of allegedly unfit men, working methods and gang sizes. Of the other eleven, two resulted from the TGWU's expulsion of three dock members in 1950, and nine were in protest against the trial of seven dockers at the Old Bailey in 1951.[66] (These latter episodes are both discussed in chapter 5.) All being unofficial, the 31 'industrial' strikes defied the industry's established machinery for the resolution of disputes. This machinery was not always successful. In fact, as Fred Lindop has shown, established procedures for dealing with disputes could inadvertently promote stoppages. The origins of the 1948 strike particularly illustrate his argument that the official arrangements involved, 'getting a full-time trade union official down to the ship, which might well take time. Most issues – over piece work or gang size or difficult conditions of work – required immediate action: going with procedure – which meant continuing to work – would necessarily weaken the men's argument, if only by removing the evidence'.[67]

Of course, in the case of Coe's gang on 28 May 1948, the relevant officer, Platt, compensated for his distance from the ship by immediately evaluating the situation by telephone. Without seeing the cargo of zinc oxide he sided with the employer rather than his members on the question of the appropriate piece-rate. But this episode reinforces Lindop's general point, that the TGWU's physical distance from its dock members made an unofficial strike the likely outcome of a small-scale industrial dispute.

While the unofficial movement sharply criticised Platt's handling of the zinc oxide dispute, it also drew hostile attention to the activities of union officials on the London Board's disciplinary tribunal. In an attempt to save their members from the sack, the outcome which employers on the tribunal sought, TGWU officials had apparently advocated the penalties which were ultimately imposed. In the gang's own words: 'When the London Board met, Mr. Parsons [the head of Hay's Wharf Group, acting as Chairman] apparently asked for our dismissal, but Mr. Condon and other Trade Union leaders on the Board (who after all are there to defend us) in their graciousness suggested we should receive this harsh and vicious punishment.'[68]

The unpopular repercussions of this initiative were felt by Arthur Deakin, when addressing an extremely restive crowd of dockers in Southwark Park on 25 June. One heckler apparently shouted at him, 'You come down to the docks and handle a cargo of zinc oxide. Do you good to get out of your armchair!'[69] The *Manchester Guardian*'s labour correspondent suggested that this tension was to be understood in terms of the TGWU's enhanced political status, which had distanced union leaders from their members. He also made this significant judgement on the mood of the Southwark Park meeting, during which Deakin had made a characteristic assault on communism:

> It was interesting that there was no outcry at this attack on Communism. The crowd did not seem to resent it, which suggests that this was not a Communist crowd. The hostility to Mr. Deakin seemed to derive from lack of confidence rather than political hostility. 'He is just the agent of the Government, that's all he is. That's all the Union is nowadays,' commented one docker to another during the meeting. It was a revealing comment, and it shows something of the problem that the trade unions have to face.[70]

In a subsequent bulletin from the docks the same correspondent developed his idea that the strike illuminated a general problem which faced trade unions in the new situation of a Labour government and full employment: 'One of the most serious things about the strike is the strength of feeling that the official leaders of big trade unions have joined a remote and potentially hostile "they" and are no longer among "us".'[71] John Lovell has demonstrated that an important characteristic of the industry's history had been the long-term failure of trade unions to organise thoroughly in the docks, and the national and industrial union of port and transport workers established in 1922 had been unable to overcome the weight of this tradition. However, the *Manchester Guardian* correspondent was surely correct in detecting a recent deterioration in relations between the TGWU and its dock members. To some extent this reflected an ongoing process of demographic change, begun during the Blitz when bomb damage had forced dockers and their families in many port cities to leave traditional dock communities. Under casualism the TGWU's branch structure had been organised geographically, so with these communities beginning to disperse the union's hold on its membership was weakening.[72] However, the 1948 strike indicated that the union's historical problems were being immediately exacerbated by its association with the Scheme's unpopular disciplinary functions. Harry Fairlie, a correspondent covering the 1949 strike for the *Observer*, drew a similar conclusion. Having asked a striking docker about the TGWU's insistence that members work the disputed Canadian ships, Fairlie was told, 'I tell you, mate, before the war Brother Deakin would have called these ships "black". It's he that's changed, not us.' Fairlie suggested that Deakin's attitudes had indeed changed as a result of the TGWU's new relationship with the government, and this close identification with State power had cost the union dearly in terms of declining authority in the docks.[73]

Neither the government – guided by the Scheme's principal architect, Ernest Bevin – nor the TGWU would admit that the union was too closely identified with the State; nor would either admit that the participation of union officers in the punishment of their own dock members was a potential source of conflict. This was perhaps natural enough, given Deakin's earlier description of the union's role in the joint administration of the Scheme as 'a great experiment' in 'workers' control'. On the other hand, the strikes were interpreted by port employers and the Ministry of Transport as evidence to support their 1947 fears that joint administration of the Scheme would cause trouble in the docks. In April 1947 the secretary of the National Association of Port Employers, D.F. Macdonald, had warned the National Dock Labour Corporation that the employers were in 'profound disagreement' with joint control. Macdonald had especially anticipated difficulty arising from union officers sharing responsibility for the exercise of discipline, such 'alien' managerial functions being 'irreconcilable with the natural demands of their constituents'.[74] In 1947 Ministry of Transport officials, most notably the Assistant Secretary at the Ministry's Docks and Canals Division, Aubrey Clark, had also expressed concern that union officials – unlike employers' representatives – could not combine efficient administration of the Scheme with their traditional responsibilities. He had demanded

a greater degree of independent representation to counter the
inevitably sectional motivations of the union men.[75]

Despite their formal obligations under the Scheme, port employers
were never fully reconciled to its existence, and they used the 1948
and 1949 strikes to open a counter-attack on the system of joint
administration. As the 1948 strike came to an end, London
employers established a special sub-committee to consider possible
modifications to the Scheme, were it to come under review. Sir
Douglas Ritchie, a member of the National Dock Labour Board
and therefore nominally committed to the status quo, was appointed
to chair this committee.[76] A few days later R.H. Senior, the London
employers' chairman, told colleagues on the National Association
that he 'considered the present practice of Trade Union representatives acting as advocates on appeal tribunals [i.e. serving a dual
function at disciplinary hearings] highly objectionable'.[77]

Although desisting from positive action in 1948, after the 1949
strike the port employers pressed the government to order the
various unions to withdraw from the Scheme's administration. The
intention of this approach was settled by Macdonald and one of
his most senior NAPE colleagues, the Liverpool shipowner J.R.
Hobhouse. Hobhouse was particularly ebullient about the opportunity created by the unofficial movement's attacks on Deakin,
suggesting that this 'may possibly create conditions under which
the Transport and General Union could admit they were wrong
in having gone onto the Board at all'.[78] On 11 August Hobhouse
wrote to Alfred Barnes, the Minister of Transport, emphasising
that joint control of the Scheme had been 'a great mistake'. The
unions, he continued, enjoyed ample scope for pursuing controversial issues on the National and Local Joint Councils, but as an
executive body the Board had to be freed from these sometimes
endless and often insoluble arguments. In illustrating this point
Hobhouse cited the straightforward division between unions and
employers on the Board over the question of directing labour to
the Canadian ships, which had been in Britain for more than two
months before the Board finally ordered their clearance. According
to Hobhouse, the role of the union representatives in ensuring this
delay had caused immense damage to the industry and the country,
allowing the workforce to believe that their action in 'blacking' the
Canadian ships was justified. 'If the men are allowed to get away
with this, they naturally think they can get away with anything and
discipline breaks down generally. One need not be surprised,' he
concluded, 'that a jointly constituted Executive body like the
NDLB finds it difficult to handle such a situation with determination and consistency.'[79]

There was nothing coincidental in the fact that the Employers'
Association addressed its complaint to the Ministry of Transport

rather than the Ministry of Labour. As has already been noted, Lord Callaghan believes that shipowners enjoyed great influence at the Ministry of Transport, where he served as Parliamentary Secretary from 1948 to 1950. This explains the congruence of the positions adopted by Ministry officials and the employers in 1947, and also provides a significant insight into the objections to the Scheme which Barnes himself expressed during the 1949 strikes. Hobhouse received a brief and non-committal response from Barnes: 'This is a difficult and complex matter to which I have given much thought and I very much welcome your views.'[80] Yet the Minister had indeed been considering the matter and had already advocated changes to the Scheme's administration in a paper presented to the Cabinet in July 1949. Arguing that joint administration was 'a serious weakness', he recommended – as his departmental officials had done in 1947 – increased independent representation on the National and local Boards. He contended that through becoming too closely identified with the National Dock Labour Board, the Ministry of Labour had compromised its functions as an objective conciliator, and therefore also recommended that the Ministry of Transport assume departmental responsibility for the Dock Labour Scheme. The Cabinet rejected these proposals after Bevin had informed colleagues of the likely outcome if it became known that the Scheme was under review: 'Grave disquiet was bound to be aroused among dock workers throughout the country, and encouragement would be given to all those unsettling elements which wished to bring an end to the Scheme and the benefits which it had conferred upon the Dock Workers generally.'[81]

Barnes continued to enjoy support, however, from his junior Minister, for Callaghan also attempted to encourage a reappraisal of the Scheme in July 1949, focusing on the TGWU's position in its administration and operation. Unlike Barnes, whose views on the Scheme were apparently influenced by his officials and, to some extent, by port employers, Callaghan's position was derived from his constituency experience in Cardiff and a recently conducted tour of all the major port areas.[82] In a letter to Attlee on 15 July, Callaghan identified a relationship between unofficial strike action and the TGWU's share in the unpopular disciplinary functions of management. Reminding the Prime Minister of his round-Britain tour, Callaghan said that everywhere he had seen the consequences of a disciplinary system in which the TGWU was both 'Judge and Advocate':

> The system has had the result that the Dockers no longer regard the Unions as springing from them and belonging to them. The 'Union' has become no more than an organisation that a man must join if he is to hold a 'Card' and get a job. Because of its

share in the disciplinary machine the 'Union' is not visibly on his side, and in some places the men stand in awe of the local Union official who wields so much power over them and can stop them from getting a job. But such a situation does not yield moral leadership. What is needed is to amend the disciplinary system so that the Union returns to its traditional role of acting as advocate, and ceases to be judge, leaving discipline to be imposed by a body independent of employers and men.[83]

Even from a relatively junior member of the government, this was a strong reminder that the Scheme had greatly complicated the TGWU's relationship with its dock members; it was also an important private refutation of the government's simplistic public position on the strikes. Attlee passed the letter to Bevin, who sent a rather confused reply to Callaghan on 19 July. Possibly Bevin had not read Callaghan's letter properly, for he concerned himself largely with demonstrating that in South Wales a local decasualisation scheme – established as early as 1918 – which involved joint administrative control of discipline, had worked very effectively. He did not acknowledge that Callaghan's intention was to question the validity of the disciplinary mechanisms on a national scale. With admirable boldness, Callaghan wrote to Bevin, emphasising that his argument was not based on the situation in South Wales alone, and nor was it based on opposition to the Scheme, which he called 'the best thing the Dockers have ever had'. But he added that despite the TGWU's huge achievement in winning the Scheme, its influence in the docks had genuinely declined, and concluded by restating the case for independent disciplinary control: 'The Union is such a vital element in our industrial life that I want to see it regain its influence in the Docks, and I believe that changes in the disciplinary machinery would help it to do so. I would like to see discipline effected by a neutral body of which the Port Authority could be the nucleus.'[84]

Bevin's various certainties – on the value of the TGWU, the Scheme and the wisdom of his personal judgements – were not shaken by Callaghan's approach. He might also have pointed out, as Victor Allen has done, that the port authorities which Callaghan wished to have invested with disciplinary powers were seldom 'neutral bodies', but reflected almost exclusively the interests of the port employers.[85] Callaghan still maintains 'that disciplinary features of the Scheme were not working well'. In a graceful concession to his former colleague, he also indicates the prime reason for the government's failure to recognise these defects: 'Ernest Bevin, as a senior heavyweight figure in the Government, obviously carried many more guns than I did and I know from conversation with him at the time and later that he regarded the introduction of the Dock Labour

Scheme as one of his great achievements. And almost certainly felt that his experience and judgement was both longer and better than mine. He may well have been right.'[86]

The Unofficial Movement: Communists and Fighters

Bevin's refusal to countenance even minor changes to the Scheme stemmed from his respect, as a responsible trade union leader, for agreements which had resulted from collective bargaining. He generally took a dim view of people who refused to observe agreements, such as the Dock Labour Scheme, which had been arrived at in this manner. When he spoke, in opposing Barnes's call for a review of the Scheme, of 'unsettling elements' on 18 July 1949, he referred not only to the port employers who sought a restoration of their former administrative powers, but to the unofficial movement and the strikes which clearly contravened the workforce's obligations under the Scheme. The unofficial movement was consistently charged with – to use the then favoured expression – 'fomenting' strikes in order to wreck the Dock Labour Scheme. This serious enough allegation was supplemented by accusations of political motivation, with communist dockers supposedly duping non-communist comrades into support for action that would damage the progress of Britain's economic recovery.

The first of these charges, that the unofficial movement wanted to destroy the Dock Labour Scheme, was largely groundless. While critical of the new discipline, the unofficial movement – in common with the vast majority of the workforce – welcomed the Scheme's benefits as a huge advance on pre-war casual conditions. After the 1948 strike the London movement explicitly stated of the 1947 programme, 'it is a good scheme and the majority of Port Workers welcome it'.[87]

The other premise is only slightly more difficult to assess. In most ports communist influence in the unofficial movement was negligible. On the Mersey, the second largest docks system in Britain, the vast majority of dockers were hostile to communism. Presumably this partially reflected the Roman Catholic Church's influence in Liverpool; but one account suggests that it also resulted from the unofficial movement's suspicion that the Communist Party generally subordinated 'dock issues and unofficial movements to political objectives and winning influence in the TGWU'.[88]

In London there was far more evidence to link unofficial action with political motivation. Just as on the Mersey in 1945 and 1949, however, much of this came from TGWU officials who helped the local board to compile lists of unofficial leaders during the 1948 and 1949 strikes. The second of these lists gave prominence to the

committee's political orientation, with 15 of its 32 members characterised as communist and three more as being of 'mixed parentage'
– Irish Catholics who were also communists or held communist
sympathies. It also made much of the fact that a number of the
communists, notably Ted Dickens, Harry Constable and Albert
Timothy (who was one of the three 'Catholic communists'), had
been repeatedly involved in leading unofficial action since 1945.[89]

The prominence of these individuals was duly portrayed – by the
government as well as the TGWU – as evidence that the London
unofficial committees were motivated by straightforward ideological devotion to Cominform. This was actually far from the truth,
for even in London the Communist Party's influence was limited.
Although reflecting with unwarranted sentimentality on 'The Lost
World of British Communism', Raphael Samuel has provided the
perceptive insight that for its adherents in the immediate post-war,
pre-1956 period, communism was 'a moral vocation as well as a
political practice'. Being a communist meant working on behalf of
others, and this moral commitment was central to a communist's
involvement in unofficial trade union activity.[90] For communist
dockers, this meant assuming unofficial leadership in order to
defend the interests of their work-mates, and the Communist Party
usually found that members in the docks were not prepared to subordinate these interests to Party discipline. It is worth noting that
Constable, Dickens and other communists were active in the 1945
strike despite the Party's opposition, and Party influence in the docks
was further minimised by the workforce's parochial outlook.
Ironically, perhaps, the occupational and local loyalties which
made dockers such a difficult workforce for the TGWU to organise,
also impeded the Communist Party; communist industrial organisers
complained that communist dockers also shared these loyalties.[91]
According to Cyril Smith, a contemporary Trotskyist activist, in
1952 Harry Constable and Albert Timothy both left the Communist
Party, such was their disillusion with its insistence that Party
interests should always take precedence over dock affairs.[92] And
Bert Aylward, the NASD member who was prominent in a number
of the unofficial disputes, broke with the CP after it failed to
support the Dockers' Charter strike in 1945.[93] The unofficial
movement was not interested, it would appear, in generalising the
CP's version of the class struggle, but in furthering industrial issues
which specifically affected dock workers.

A number of contemporary observers also argued that the
unofficial movement had, in any event, emerged from industrial
rather than political circumstances. Reporting from the London
docks during the 1948 strike, the *Manchester Guardian* labour correspondent lamented:

There is nostalgia for the fighting days of Ernest Bevin and Ben Tillett. At one meeting I heard a docker say of the official trade union speaker, 'Ernie smoked Woodbines. I bet he smokes Players.' The social gap between Woodbines and Players has narrowed, but it is still a psychological chasm. Losing faith in the official leaders, the dockers are still anxious to find men to lead them. There is a vacuum of leadership [which] is being filled temporarily by the strike committee.[94]

The premise that the unofficial movement was an industrial rather than a political force, performing traditional trade union duties which sections of the workforce perceived TGWU officials to have abandoned, was repeated in a report produced by the Field Survey Group of the British Institute of Management. This research, conducted largely in the London docks after the 1948 strike, noted that paid trade union officials were not subject to the same pressures as dock workers, sometimes causing them to reach agreements with employers that their members could not accept. The tension which this created was greatly exacerbated by the involvement of these officials in the management of the Scheme, because it further reinforced the workforce's sense of estrangement: 'many workers have lost confidence in their leaders and workers' leaders have emerged who perform the traditional function of fighting the employer, and if need be the trade union officials and the government as well'.[95] Not surprisingly, the report was condemned by the industry's National Joint Council, which jealously regarded it as unwarranted outside intervention, but Morrison and Attlee felt that it merited 'serious attention'.[96] As such, the BIM report quite possibly influenced the government's decision – discussed in the following chapter – to appoint the Leggett Committee of Inquiry in May 1950.

The Leggett report confirmed that the TGWU had damaged its standing in the docks by administering discipline,[97] and the 1955 Devlin Inquiry re-emphasised that it was this loss of standing which had instigated the unofficial movement's emergence. According to Devlin, the movement's political character was of secondary significance. Very few dockers were communists and indeed most had little time for communism; but they did not 'regard a vigorous leader as disqualified from expressing their grievances because he is a communist'. Devlin disputed the perceived wisdom that every docker who regularly assumed unofficial leadership in the docks – the 'persistent agitator' – was either a communist or an especially subversive or dangerous figure. Rather he was perhaps merely quick to spot a grievance and articulate it for others as well as himself: 'In short, he is the stuff out of which in the past many trade union leaders were made and he may be no more than what is called a militant trade unionist.'[98]

These various observations about the difficult and complex underlying situation in the docks reinforce the argument that essentially industrial issues were behind the three large unofficial strikes. These strikes were clearly not politically motivated. The unofficial movement was not consciously attempting to hamper British economic recovery; nor was it seeking to strengthen Stalinism's icy grip on the world by destabilising Europe through the disruption of Marshall Aid. To fuse Devlin's characterisation of the 'persistent agitator' with Lewis Minkin's analysis of labour movement culture, the unofficial strikes represented a specific defence of traditional 'trade union values'. Vast sums of loyalty and solidarity were evinced, not only throughout the remarkable and huge nationwide strike of 1945, but also in London and elsewhere during the 1948 and 1949 strikes. In 1948 large numbers of men indicated their determination to stand by the eleven suspended workers. In the more drawn-out affair of 1949, the motives of the workers involved in the stoppages were varied: some men probably wished to demonstrate positive solidarity with the Canadian seamen; others perhaps simply took the chance of an informal 'holiday' which they no longer enjoyed under the Dock Labour Scheme. In all ports, however, the over-riding issue was the unofficial defence of a near-sacred dockland principle, the right to avoid black-legging in a dispute between another group of workers, the Canadian seamen, and their employers.

Arthur Deakin and his TGWU colleagues had an entirely different understanding of these values: 'loyalty' was a quality which dockers owed to official union representatives; and 'solidarity' a quality to be demonstrated with the Labour government by refraining from the kind of irresponsible action which unofficial strikes represented. Deakin certainly had no sympathy with the notion that unofficial leaders were simply articulating grievances which they shared with their fellows in the docks. Following the 1949 strike, Deakin had told the TGWU's Docks Group that these men, 'had sought to bring this Union into discredit, they had sought to dishonour and disrupt'. He had also spoken of his determination that these activists would 'face the music' and be expelled from the Scheme.[99] Deakin fulfilled this promise by turning the full weight of his union against these men, but in so doing he inadvertently brought the underlying problems in the docks to the surface. This placed great strain on the Labour alliance during Attlee's second administration.

The Alliance Under Strain: The 1950–51 Labour Government and the Docks

Attlee's Second Administration, 1950–51

The Labour government elected in February 1950 carried nothing like the confidence or vitality of its 1945 predecessor. This was partly due to the party's reduced Parliamentary circumstances. The General Election gave Labour 315 seats, the Conservatives and their associates 298: of the other twelve opposition MPs, nine were Liberals. When the new Cabinet met for the first time on 25 February, Attlee told colleagues that with a majority of only five, there would be 'no question of attempting to carry through any of the major controversial legislation which had been promised in the Party's Election manifesto'.[1] While dogged by a range of international and economic problems, the 1945 government had maintained labour movement morale by establishing 'the welfare state' and taking several industries, utilities and the Bank of England into public ownership. In stark contrast, the decision to eschew further contentious legislation in 1950 ensured that Attlee's second administration was unable to offset international and economic difficulties – which if anything grew more acute in these two years – in the same manner. Even more than in the post-1947 years of Crippsian austerity and Morrisonian consolidation, it seemed that the government's task was simply to defend the gains of 1945. Indeed, having rejected the prospect of bringing 'controversial legislation' forward, by November 1950 the government was having difficulty in finding sufficient legislative business to consume the available Parliamentary time.[2]

The 1950 government's main difficulties, economic pressure and international tension, were intimately connected. Against the background of escalating international tension, in the spring of 1951 the new Chancellor of the Exchequer, Hugh Gaitskell, prepared a budget that allowed for a huge increase – £4.7 million for the three years 1951–54 – in defence spending. The budget also brought to a head a long-running internal government debate about the funding of the National Health Service (NHS). Gaitskell resolved this debate by introducing charges for dental and optical treatment, and prescriptions. These charges amounted to an annual saving of some £13 million, which was a sizeable fraction of the NHS's overall budget of approximately £400 million. They were also the occasion of a government split which was to have damaging long-term consequences for the Labour Party. As Minister of Health, Aneurin Bevan had accepted the principle of prescription charges in October 1949, but he had vigorously resisted pressure to introduce them – along with other charges – in practice for more than two years. On 22 April 1951, following the Third Reading of the Bill which enshrined the introduction of these charges, Bevan resigned from the government.[3]

Thus were the divisive internal party battle lines of the 1950s drawn. The 1951 Budget also jeopardised economic recovery and diminished the government's popularity, and so brought nearer the days of Parliamentary opposition in which these internal party divisions were manifested. Attention was drawn to the serious economic damage which the programme would cause by the other Cabinet Minister to resign, Harold Wilson. In his personal statement to the House of Commons, Wilson remarked that Gaitskell's rearmament programme was physically incompatible with the available raw material resources. The consequence of this was that, 'the basis of our economy is disrupted and the standard of living, including the social services of our people, is endangered'.[4] This pessimism proved to be amply justified, for in the course of 1951 a massive set-back to the country's economic recovery was indeed revealed. From its healthy surplus of £300 million at the close of 1950, by the end of 1951 the balance of payments was once again running a huge deficit, the total negative balance exceeding £400 million. Admittedly this was the consequence of several other factors, such as a sudden increase in import prices and increased dollar purchases by other sterling area countries.[5] Yet for Alec Cairncross, the fundamental cause of the balance of payments crisis was the stress placed on the British economy by the rearmament programme which the government adopted to fall in with American wishes.[6]

In its economic and international policies, the 1950 government continued to enjoy the trade union support which had kept the previous government on course after the 1947 financial crisis. However, in September 1950, with the immediate trade deficit problem apparently resolved, the TUC loosened formal economic support for the government by dropping its commitment to the wage freeze. This deprived ministers of important support when they embarked upon the rearmament programme in 1951. Between 1945 and 1950 the government had found no greater trade union supporter than Arthur Deakin and the Transport and General

Workers' Union. Deakin avidly maintained his loyalty to the government after 1950, remaining a committed advocate of the wage freeze until the last in September 1950. But he gave this support despite a considerable amount of private strain between ministers and the TGWU, caused by the government's growing reluctance to allow the TGWU sole responsibility for maintaining the workplace discipline of its dock members; and in disturbing the labour alliance's informal 'rules' of behaviour, the government inadvertently provoked tension with one of its most important supporters.

The Expulsions Strike, April 1950

After the prolonged 1949 dock strike in London Arthur Deakin had informed his TGWU colleagues that he was determined to take action against 'certain people' who were prominent in the unofficial movement.[7] This ambition clearly had some bearing on a resolution which was jointly put by the union's London Area and London Docks Group Committees to the TGWU General Executive Council on 15 December 1949. This called for an Inquiry into the involvement of eight dock members in the 1949 strike. The resolution was carried,[8] and the Inquiry took place at Transport House on 27 January 1950.

This was the union's second official examination of unofficial activity in the London docks, following the February 1949 investigation into the activities of 17 dockers during the zinc oxide strike of June 1948. This had concluded with the union's Executive Council warning that 'serious notice' would be taken of any individual who repeated his involvement in unofficial action. As with the 1949 investigation, the Inquiry of January 1950 was led by a special five-man committee, chaired by union President Fryer and including Arthur Deakin as an ex-officio member. The hearing was attended by members of the London Area and London Area Docks Group Committees, and eight London dockers whose unofficial activities had aroused the union's wrath: Blomberg, Constable, Cronin, Dash, Dickens, Kirby, Marney and Saunders. The London union officials' case against the eight consisted essentially of two points. First, the 1949 strikes had breached the TGWU's agreements with employers, and the obligations of the union and its members under the Dock Labour Scheme. Second, membership of the unofficial committee – which continued in existence after July 1949 as the Port Workers' Defence Committee – was incompatible with membership of the TGWU. In pursuit of the latter point, the example of an unofficially convened meeting at Canning Town Hall on 7 August 1949 was offered, 'at which the Union and certain of its officers had been vilified and the

policy of the Union held up to ridicule'. The officials were especially
critical of Dickens, Constable and Saunders, whose involvement
in the strike contradicted an assurance which all 17 men had
apparently given to the February 1949 investigation, that in future
they would not associate themselves with unofficial activity.

In their defence, the three argued that this earlier assurance had
been falsely given on their behalf by a spokesman who had misrepresented their views. In answering the other charges, Dickens
restated the unofficial movement's insistence that the Canadian-
related stoppage had not been a strike, but a lock-out on the part
of the employers, with the lock-out committee being formed to
maintain organisation in lieu of official recognition. In giving
further evidence of their defiance, four of the 'accused' illuminated
the essentially industrial character of the unofficial movement
which was discussed in the previous chapter. Constable, Marney
and Dash, along with Dickens, 'openly stated that their actions in
relation to any particular issue arising in dockland must be governed
by the circumstances therewith'. As practical men concerned with
defending what they perceived to be the interests of their fellow
dockers, they consequently refused to offer any assurances as to
their future conduct and observation of the union's rules and constitution. In the words of Dickens, apparently the unofficial leader
of the unofficial leaders, 'he would continue to support the Port
Workers Defence Committee while it was doing its best, in his
opinion, to further the fundamental principles of trade unionism'.
Only Cronin dissociated himself from the movement and its
activities.

The Committee of Inquiry reported on 7 March, and reminded
the General Executive of the union's warning in 1949 that 'serious
notice' would be taken of members who persisted with unofficial
activity. Given the appearance of Dickens, Constable and Saunders
at the previous Executive investigation, and their recurrent 'complete
disregard for the obligations resting upon them as Members', it was
recommended that all three be immediately expelled from the
TGWU. The Committee was also highly critical of Dash and
Marney, but as their actions had not been the subject of any earlier
inquiry, they – along with Blomberg and Kirby – were only to be
debarred from holding union office. The Committee advocated that
Cronin, who had apologised for his unofficial activities, simply be
given a warning as to his future conduct. One further recommen-
dation was added, namely that the Executive declare the Port
Workers' Defence Committee to be, 'a subversive body created and
fostered with the object of sabotaging the constitutional procedure
and policy of the Union'.[9]

The General Executive accepted these recommendations on 7
March. Duly chastened, Tom Cronin went on to earn a reputation

as one of the TGWU's ablest officers in the docks,[10] but the personal implications for the disciplined men were, and indeed remained, unclear. Noting that he and his six comrades were all communists, Jack Dash believed the Inquiry to have been part of the union's general anti-communist campaign. As this had already involved the 1949 ban on communists from lay and delegate office, all seven were in any case ineligible for office. Thus, the punishments exacted on himself, Blomberg, Marney and Kirby, were of symbolic rather than practical importance.[11] For the three expelled men, however, there did appear to be an immediate practical problem. At unofficial meetings held in the ensuing period, the fear was frequently expressed that without a union card, Dickens, Constable and Saunders would be unable to find work in the docks.[12] These three, along with Blomberg, therefore appealed against the Executive's decision, and set about developing support for their position in the docks.

Considerable support for the seven had already taken shape, in the form of an unofficially organised ban on overtime held to coincide with the TGWU Inquiry on 26 and 27 January. Of 4331 men required to put in overtime on 26 January, 2872 refused to do so. In the Royal Docks, where the seven men worked, more than 2000 men supported the ban, against 519 who did not.[13]

With the appeals of the four due to be heard on 14 April, the tense enough situation in the London docks was suddenly complicated by an unexpected dispute between the port's other main union, the 7000 member National Amalgamated Stevedores and Dockers (NASD), and a large ship-owning firm, the Shaw Savill and Albion Company. In general terms, despite having failed to secure a review of the Scheme in August 1949, port employers still remained committed to an overhaul of the Scheme and other changes in working practices. At the Annual General Meeting of the National Association of Port Employers on 31 March, the Executive's yearly report was presented by the Liverpool shipowner, J.R. Hobhouse, who has already been singled out as one of the employers most hostile to the Scheme. The preceding year had, he said, 'shown few notable achievements', with the industry's central problem being the workforce's lack of discipline. Only greater discipline would ensure a quicker turn-round of shipping, but for this end employers would have to fight: 'They should not hesitate to insist upon an important matter of principle, even if it led to a stoppage, because every stoppage where the employer could be proved right meant less stoppages in future.'[14] In seeking a restoration of discipline, Hobhouse was particularly concerned that the unions should withdraw from the National Dock Labour Board (NDLB). But in extracting greater efficiency from the workforce, one of his London colleagues, Sir Basil Sanderson, had a more practical solution.

On Wednesday 12 April Sanderson announced that his company, Shaw Savill and Albion, intended from Monday 17 April to engage an unspecified number of dock workers on weekly rather than daily terms, and that these workers would be recruited inside rather than outside the dock gates. For a number of reasons this proposal was highly controversial. Shaw Savill's existing recruitment policy reflected traditional occupational divisions, with NASD members employed to load and pack cargoes, and TGWU men employed for unloading. Elsewhere in the port many TGWU men were already weekly employees, and some TGWU members indicated that they were willing to accept weekly terms from Shaw Savill. But the NASD, which had never accepted weekly terms, regarded the plan as an unacceptable alteration of established working customs. Since the end of the nineteenth century stevedores had claimed the right to undertake the most skilled aspects of dock work, the loading and packing of cargoes on board ships. An additional claim, the right to be engaged outside the dock gates and not on employers' premises, also dated from this period, and stevedores had resisted previous attempts to revoke it, most recently in March 1945. Stevedores apparently believed that the loss of these 'rights' would substantially dilute their union's independent status. Accepting a greater regularity of employment, as the TGWU had done, would be tantamount to accepting 'dockers' terms', and would invite a strengthening of the TGWU's position at the NASD's expense. These difficulties were aggravated by the particular position of Sanderson's company. According to the *Manchester Guardian*'s labour correspondent, the NASD had 'provided workers for Shaw Savill and Albion for generations'.[15] The NASD suspected that if Shaw Savill – one of the largest employers in the Royal Docks – was prepared to review practices which had prevailed for so long, then other employers would certainly attempt to revise their employment arrangements. Ministry of Labour officials who were monitoring the situation concluded that in these circumstances a dispute between Shaw Savill and the NASD would be entirely of Sir Basil's making.[16]

With such a dispute looking increasingly inevitable, on 11 April Arthur Bird, the TGWU Docks Group Secretary, told the Ministry of Labour that the unofficial leaders' appeals against expulsion from the TGWU had 'no chance of success'. The combined impact of these two disputes, he added, made an unofficial stoppage in the docks extremely likely.[17] Bird's prognosis proved to be entirely accurate. On Friday 14 April the Shaw Savill scheme was rejected by the NASD Executive, which hinted that an official strike would take place if the company carried out its threat to operate the plan on the Monday. In the event, the company postponed the scheme's introduction, submitting it for further discussions with the union, which were to be chaired by the Ministry of Labour. However, instead of going on official strike, during the following week many NASD members found themselves taking unofficial action in support of the expelled TGWU men. On the same day that the NASD rejected the Shaw Savill scheme, 14 April, the TGWU's Rank and File Appeals Committee was convened to hear an appeal lodged by the three expelled men, Dickens, Constable and Saunders. There were no dockers on this Committee, which consisted of six rank and file members elected by the union's Biennial Delegate Conference. On the first day of the hearing, the appellants presented a petition which had been signed by several thousand dockers, calling for their punishments to be revoked.[18] The petition and the appeal which it supported were both in vain, however, and on the following Tuesday, 18 April, the Executive Council's original verdicts were upheld.[19] Early on the following morning the unofficial movement held a meeting at Connaught Fields in East London's Canning Town. Attended by around 3000 dock workers, this gathering strongly condemned the TGWU Executive and voted for strike action.[20] As Bird had anticipated, the unofficial movement – which again comprised members of both unions – used the Shaw Savill problem to maximise trouble arising from the TGWU disciplinary tribunal. As well as Ted Dickens, the meeting was addressed by Albert Timothy, member of the NASD and chairman of the 1949 Lock-out Committee. On 21 April at a further unofficial meeting in Victoria Park, Dickens explicitly linked the NASD's dispute with Shaw Savill to his own expulsion from the TGWU, arguing, 'the attack on the stevedores and the attack by Deakin on his members are one and the same thing. Both are aimed at worsening port workers' conditions.' The meeting passed a resolution demanding a ballot of 'all port workers' on the question of whether the expulsions should be ratified or overturned.[21]

In the face of this renewed unofficial pressure, Deakin was characteristically defiant. Drawing attention to his personal determination to see through the campaign against the unofficial movement, he told the his Docks Group Committee that there was no question of the expulsions being reversed. 'He had had to suffer a good deal of abuse,' he added, 'but his work over a very long period for this Union would speak for itself.'[22] As support for the strike gathered momentum, with the total of 6000 strikers on 20 April increasing to around 12,500 on Monday 24 April,[23] Deakin reiterated his attack on the unofficial movement. On 23 April strike leaders gathered outside Transport House and demanded an audience with Deakin who was not, in fact, inside the building. Following this somewhat farcical incident, he issued a statement condemning 'this indefensible strike' as contrary to the national interests and extremely damaging to food supplies and exports. He also described it as 'a challenge to those principles upon which trade unionism rests, to the right of trade unions to make their own rules and constitution. Those who advise trade unionists to defy their own union are guilty of reckless and irresponsible conduct.' He added that in favouring a ballot on the expulsions – which clearly had no place under TGWU rules – the strike leaders were seeking to save face. No such compromise was possible, however, and the dispute would only end with the men going back to work, the expulsions and the union's authority intact.[24]

The strike ended on 29 April, six days later, after the London Dock Labour Board had issued an ultimatum to the men on strike: those not at work on Monday 1 May would be summarily dismissed from the Scheme. In Victoria Park an unofficial meeting resolved to resume work 'after ten days powerful protest', and pledged that the fight to reinstate the expelled three to the TGWU would continue in union branch meetings. The ultimate futility of this campaign was tacitly conceded by the expelled three, however, with Constable, Dickens and Saunders all declaring their intention to apply for NASD membership.[25]

The strike's important related feature, the dispute between the Shaw Savill shipping company and the NASD, was apparently also resolved during the first week of May. Faced with the NASD's united and determined opposition, on 2 May Shaw Savill agreed to postpone its new recruitment scheme indefinitely.[26]

Aneurin Bevan's 'wholesome deterrent'

The ten day unofficial strike had cost the industry 93,750 working days and freshly damaged the TGWU's already tarnished reputation in the docks.[27] In noting that Deakin had described the unofficial leaders as 'reckless and irresponsible', *The Times* correspondent pointed out that the strikers strongly supported these men and had little time for their official leaders: 'Rightly or wrongly, the men on strike had for a long time felt little loyalty towards the elected representatives, but regarded the "reckless and irresponsible" leaders as vigilant in their interests.'[28]

This latest dispute confirmed the government's growing belief that the TGWU was unable to command a satisfactory level of authority in the docks. Throughout the strike Deakin continued to enjoy the loyal support of his former TUC colleague, George Isaacs, who told the House of Commons that the stoppage was a 'communist inspired' attack on the TGWU's democratic and constitutional position.[29] Insisting as ever that the TGWU be allowed to restore order itself, on 21 April Isaacs urged Cabinet colleagues to avoid any action – particularly the introduction of troops – that would prejudice developments.[30] Such caution had characterised the government's response to previous strikes, but fewer Ministers were willing to support Isaacs on this occasion. On 20 April Maurice Webb, the Minister of Food, told the Cabinet Emergencies Committee that – negligible quantities of eggs and bananas aside – there was no danger of losing perishable items before 27 April. Nevertheless, the Committee decided that matters should not be allowed to slide: if the strike had not ended by Monday 24 April, troops would be deployed immediately to discharge non-food and food cargoes.[31] When troops duly began work in the Royal Docks on 24 April, many more dockers stopped work in protest. Undeterred by this, the Cabinet ordered that tented accommodation be made available in London parks so that, if necessary, up to 20,000 soldiers could be employed in the docks.[32]

This would have been the largest single post-war commitment of troops in the London docks, exceeding by several thousand the total of 12,792 which was deployed in July 1949. But the government's tough response involved more than the use of troops. At the Emergencies Committee meeting on 20 April, consideration had been given to the question of whether criminal proceedings could be taken against the strikers. Sir Hartley Shawcross, the Attorney General, contended that this would not be possible under the 1940 emergency regulation that was still in force, Order 1305. This provided for the compulsory arbitration of trade disputes and forbade strikes and lock-outs in connection with trade disputes, but in his view the stoppage was not strictly a 'trade dispute'. However, there was still the possibility of civil action against the strikers for breach of contract or, for that matter, criminal action against the 'ring leaders' for conspiring to procure a breach of contract. Despite the numbers involved, civil proceedings were strongly supported by Aneurin Bevan. Echoing the tough line which he had taken during the 1948 and 1949 strikes, Bevan stated that for the striking dockers, 'the mere fact of having to attend court, and of having financial penalties imposed would constitute a wholesome long-term deterrent'.[33]

This discussion constituted a significant departure from the informal 'rules' which governed the relationship between the Labour party and the trade unions. Wherever possible, the party was expected to leave the responsibility for dealing with trades disputes to the movement's 'industrial' wing, the trade unions.[34] Previously these 'rules' had largely determined the 1945 government's attitude to the docks: while using troops to protect the wider community from the effects of unofficial action, Ministers had left the job of restoring workplace discipline to the TGWU. However, the 1950 strike demonstrated that the union's internal disciplinary mechanisms had palpably failed to restore order, and in considering the prospect of legal proceedings against unofficial strikers, Ministers were showing a new disposition to take disciplinary matters out of the union's hands. In fact, on 21 April the Cabinet decided to defer legal action. If successful this would have required the London Dock Labour Board to dismiss thousands of strikers for breaching their obligations under the Scheme.[35] Nevertheless, in expounding their views, Shawcross and Bevan anticipated the unprecedented legal action which the government was to take under Order 1305 against seven dockers less than twelve months later.

In the meantime, the government did initiate a breach of the labour movement's informal 'rules'. In the Cabinet on 24 April it was finally – and remarkably – conceded that, 'quite apart from Communist agitation', the recurrent unofficial action in the docks suggested wider industrial problems: 'It was said that dockers were not clear who was their employer and with whom authority rested: there seemed to be a considerable element of ambiguity about the respective positions of the Dock Labour Board and of the employers who used dock labour.'[36] On 1 May, as the workforce voted to resume work, there was general Cabinet agreement that the stoppage had raised a sufficient number of complex industrial matters to merit a thorough and formal inquiry into the causes of unrest in the docks.[37] Such an investigation would inevitably draw attention to the Scheme's defects, and the fact that the workforce was recurrently willing to strike in defiance of its union leaders. Yet Ministers apparently failed to realise that its decision would certainly draw the wrath of the TGWU, the troubled guardian of both the Dock Labour Scheme and the restive workforce. Perhaps believing that there had been an outbreak of collective Cabinet insensitivity, on 2 May the Cabinet Secretary, Norman Brook, briefed Attlee on the delicacy of the situation. He pointed out that when a review of the Scheme had previously been suggested, by Alfred Barnes in July 1949, Bevin had been adamantly opposed. 'In these circumstances,' Brook doubted the wisdom of appointing a formal inquiry with wide terms of reference, recommending a private Ministerial investigation instead.[38]

Thus advised, and indeed in the company of Brook, on 5 May Attlee met Isaacs and Barnes to discuss the proposed inquiry. Barnes gave a new emphasis to the problem of joint control of the Scheme. Whereas in July 1949 he had spoken of the need to bolster dock boards with independent representatives, he now spoke explicitly about the TGWU's conflicting priorities. The primary function of a trade union official was to safeguard the interests of his members, but officials who administered the Scheme, particularly its disciplinary functions, had become estranged from their members. Adding that the dock labour boards obscured the relationship between worker and employer, making it difficult for the latter to take responsible action when trouble arose, Barnes argued in favour of a 'searching inquiry into the working of the Dock Labour Scheme'. This would be undertaken by the Ministries of Labour and Transport in consultation with the dock labour boards, employers, trade unions, the British Transport Commission and port authorities. Isaacs was strongly opposed to such an inquiry, which would give the impression that the Dock Labour Scheme had collapsed throughout the country, and cause grave offence to Arthur Deakin, who had already stated his opposition. In its place, Isaacs favoured a 'survey' into the causes of industrial unrest in the London docks alone. With counsel divided, Attlee concluded the meeting in characteristic fashion. Leaning, it would seem, slightly towards Isaacs, he tactfully advised his two colleagues to pursue the idea of a 'survey' with Bevin, and make recommendations in the light of the latter's views.[39]

A meeting between the three Ministers was held later on the same day, 5 May. Bevin naturally rejected the type of inquiry envisaged by Barnes, but was only marginally less annoyed by Isaacs's proposal. His disapproval was based on the fact that any kind of inquiry would ill reward his beloved TGWU after its strenuous efforts to support the government. Bevin seldom wrote to other Ministers about dock matters, presumably preferring to buttonhole colleagues for an informal chat between meetings. On this occasion, however, he did set out his objections to an inquiry in a formal letter to Isaacs, which suggests that he viewed the situation as being particularly serious. He told Isaacs that subsequent to their meeting with Barnes, he had spoken to Arthur Deakin (mysteriously referred to as 'our mutual friend'), who bitterly resented the imminent appointment of an inquiry into the docks. Deakin had battled against the employers to win the Dock Labour Scheme, which was a vital weapon in the government's strategy for economic recovery. He had also courted the unpopularity of his members by throwing the TGWU's full weight behind other measures designed to support the government, most notably the wage freeze and the anti-communist campaign. According to Bevin, Deakin's consequent anger with the government was fully understandable: 'after the Unions have fought the Communists and struggled with the employers, the Government now seems to be siding with the latter, and in fact, however much it may be covered up, advantage is being taken to interfere with the basic principles of the scheme, and in this the employers are supported by the Ministry of Transport'. In apparently supporting this attack on the Scheme by sanctioning an inquiry, Bevin informed Isaacs that the government was jeopardising its relationship with the TGWU. 'I see in this problem', he noted,

'all the elements of a first-class difference between the Union and
the Government, which will reflect itself in the industry and be very
awkward indeed.' Given the immense bitterness felt by the TGWU
officials, Bevin urged Isaacs to limit the damage by confining the
inquiry's terms of reference to the causes of unofficial strikes in the
Port of London.[40]

In the House of Commons on 11 May Isaacs announced that a
formal inquiry would be held, but in accordance with Bevin's
suggestion the Committee of Inquiry appointed under Sir Frederick
Leggett was commissioned on a narrower basis than that requested
by Alfred Barnes. It was only to investigate the 'problem' of
unofficial stoppages in the London docks, 'with a view to reporting
what steps can be taken to avoid further unofficial action of the
type that has taken place during the last three years and has proved
so injurious to the trade of the country'.[41]

Deakin was publicly relaxed about this development, telling
journalists that as the TGWU had been given prior notice of the
committee's terms of reference, he had never held any objection
to its appointment.[42] The narrowing of the Inquiry's terms of
reference had not, however, appreciably diminished the TGWU's
bitterness. The leadership feared that the investigation would
undermine the union and strengthen the unofficial movement. On
15 May the TGWU Finance and General Purposes Committee
agreed that the union would give evidence to the Inquiry, but only
on the strict understanding that 'there would be no question of the
unofficial element being given a status in the hearings'. Having subsequently given evidence to the Inquiry for the first time, Deakin
assured colleagues that he had done so, having 'definitely laid
down the principle that the Union did not regard itself as being on
trial'.[43] In the meantime Deakin contributed a lengthy article to
the *Transport and General Workers' Record*, entitled, 'Docks and the
Nation; Our Problem – We Can Find the Answer'. This strongly
affirmed the union's right to put its own house in order. Deakin
implied that the government had been sorely mistaken in appointing
the Leggett Committee, with Ministers swayed by the unjustified
'critical atmosphere' which guided present analysis of the Scheme.
In restating the commitment of the workforce and the union to the
Scheme, he attempted also to ward off critics by emphasising the
inestimable value of joint control: 'The unions stood for joint
control. This is where we still stand and we shall remain in that
position. Time has long passed when workers in industry are
prepared to accept the idea that they are not entitled to have a "say"
in the conditions under which their employment is regulated.'[44]

Deakin's principal anxiety, which Bevin had voiced in his representation on the union's behalf to Isaacs, was that the employers
would exploit the 'critical atmosphere' in which the Leggett hearings

were being conducted to secure government support for the termination of joint control. The employers indeed took great satisfaction from Leggett's appointment. In pursuing increasingly confident overtures to the government, the employers secured the support of Sir John Anderson, the former Conservative Cabinet Minister who in 1950 was Chairman of the Port of London Authority. As if to illustrate Victor Allen's argument that the interests of port authorities and port employers were effectively synonymous, on 15 May Anderson led a deputation of employers to discuss the Scheme's future with Attlee. Anderson envisaged the encounter as a chance for port employers to set forth their ideas on how improved industrial relations in the docks could best be effected.[45] It would appear that Anderson approached this task in a spirit of confrontation rather than conciliation, for he included in his delegation Sir Basil Sanderson, the Shaw Savill Company Chairman whose most recent attempt to 'improve' industrial relations had been the dispute which he had initiated with the NASD. Anderson and Sanderson were joined by C.E. Wurtzburg of the British Chamber of Shipping and Sir William Currie of the P&O Steam Navigation Company, and Attlee was accompanied by Barnes and Isaacs.

Anderson spoke first, arguing that without an immediate restoration of the discipline which had collapsed in the docks, the Scheme would continue to operate ineffectively. As remedial action he recommended three revisions to the Scheme: firstly, that the system of joint control be terminated; secondly, that the government assume powers – by an Act of Parliament if necessary – to deal effectively with 'known agitators' in the docks, by imposing heavy fines or even imprisoning them; thirdly, that the legislation which framed the 1947 Scheme be amended so that men withholding their labour in an unofficial strike would be automatically expelled from the industry. Attlee replied by attempting to defuse the employers' anger. Stating that the matter was one of great delicacy, given the communists' determination to exploit the differences between the respective sides of industry, he added that Anderson's observations would be fully considered by the Leggett Committee. Isaacs was less emollient, restating his belief that problems in the docks owed little to specific failings of either the Scheme or the TGWU, but to the communists' undoubted determination to 'break the authority of the TGWU'. In referring to Anderson's proposals, he admitted the possibility of adding to the NDLB's independent representation, but dismissed the idea of ending joint control. He questioned also the efficacy of prosecuting or dismissing the thousands of men who were generally involved in an unofficial strike. Anderson responded by urging that the government should at least be able to remove the 'ringleaders' from the Scheme. The meeting ended there, with only one item subject to agreement: in view of the Inquiry already under way, neither side would make a statement to the press.[46]

In limiting the scope of the Leggett Inquiry to unofficial strikes in London, and continuing to offer the type of strong support for the TGWU which he voiced in this meeting with Anderson, Isaacs was trying to mend the government's fences with Deakin. But the TGWU continued to resent the Leggett investigation, which necessarily drew attention to its weaknesses in the docks. When the report eventually appeared in May 1951, as a Command Paper, the TGWU was indirectly criticised on several points, most notably that the association of union officials with discipline had damaged their standing with the workforce.[47]

In linking criticism of the TGWU to the incidence of unofficial strikes, the report added weight to the employers' argument about the consequences of the union's dual functions under the Scheme. This greatly infuriated the TGWU; yet at the same time its leaders saw the opportunity to bolster joint control's popularity by appealing to their members' adversarial attitude to employers. Delivering his quarterly report to the Docks Trade Group in September 1951, Bird observed that the employers' response to the Leggett report had, predictably enough, been to emphasise its suggestion that joint control was the main cause of trouble. He urged union officers to remind dock members that the employers were firmly opposed to joint control, and were seeking to 'force a change of the Scheme in their favour. It must be understood by all Officers and Members the Employers do not like the Scheme.'[48]

While the Leggett Committee's appointment – and subsequent report – simply intensified bitterness in the port transport industry, wider developments in the second half of 1950 appeared to assuage the government's difficulties with the TGWU. Renewed international tension, stemming from the outbreak of war in Korea, was accompanied by a revival of the government's pre-Leggett assumptions about the political character of unofficial strikes. This ostensibly restored the unity of the government and the TGWU with regard to the causes of the docks unrest.

Korea and the Renaissance of Subversion

On 25 June 1950 North Korean forces invaded South Korea. The Labour government condemned the invasion as an unwarranted act of aggression, and on 27 June strongly supported the United Nations Security Resolution – passed in the temporary absence of the Soviet delegate – which urged the repulsion by force of the North Korean troops. The government believed that the Korean war signalled a genuine threat to international peace and Britain's own security, with Attlee fearing that the Soviet Union would exploit the diversion of British and American troops to the Far East in order forcibly to press claims elsewhere in the world. Nevertheless, Britain committed troops to Korea on the basis that the UN had to be given the teeth which had been lacking in the League of Nations. After a trebling of defence estimates on 3 August, the government ordered the landing in Korea of the first British battalions on 29 August.[49]

With British troops committed in a war that aggravated existing fears about the perceived international communist threat, the government regarded domestic industrial developments with increasing suspicion. In August Philip Noel-Baker, the Minister of Fuel and Power, drew Attlee's attention to the activities of Frank Foulkes, the communist who led the Electricians' Trade Union. According to Noel-Baker, along with other ETU leaders Foulkes had gone on a trip to Moscow, 'no doubt to get instructions'. Noel-Baker urged Attlee to remove 'active and suspected' communists from important positions in power stations.[50] The government viewed industrial unrest in the docks with even more vigilance. An explosion in Portsmouth docks aboard a barge loaded with ammunition bound for Korea, which Royal Navy scientists found in 1952 to have been a complete accident,[51] was characterised by Attlee on 24 July in the House of Commons as a probable act of industrial sabotage.[52] At the end of August unofficial pamphlets appeared in the London and Liverpool docks demanding the implementation of the TGWU's 'Dockers' Charter'. This was the package of unrealised demands for improved pay and conditions which the TGWU had voted for in August 1945, and which had under-pinned the huge unofficial strike of October 1945. National Dock Board officials believed that Ted Dickens and Albert Timothy were planning to travel from London to drum up wider unofficial pressure for the Charter in Glasgow, Grimsby and other northern ports.[53] This information was conveyed to the Ministry of Labour, and as Parliament re-convened in the middle of September to discuss the Korean crisis, Isaacs advised Cabinet colleagues that communist-inspired strikes in the London docks were probably imminent. He based this assessment on the coincidence of unofficial agitation for improved pay and conditions with a trip which Timothy and two other communist dock workers, Cowley and Copland, had recently made to Poland. Estimating this venture in identical terms to Noel-Baker's evaluation of the Electricians' journey to Moscow, Isaacs said that the visitors to Warsaw, 'doubtless had been given a plan of campaign'.[54] The three men had indeed been to Poland, but their visit had hardly been the covert exercise which Isaacs's conspiracy-laden remarks implied. Rather it appears to have been a typical Communist Party-organised trip, designed to instil in members a conviction of the general superiority of life in the 'Popular Democracies'. Thus did the three write in glowing terms about their Polish experiences in the unofficial journal, *Port Workers' News*. Albert Timothy, for example, who was a Catholic as well as a communist, recorded that in Poland religious freedom was absolute.[55]

Having consulted Cabinet colleagues, on 15 September Isaacs took his accusations to Parliament. Despite the almost certain innocence of the dockers' Polish trip, he cited it, 'at a time when our men are facing serious risks in Korea', as evidence that the unofficial movement was planning to interfere with military supplies.[56] For this effort Isaacs was damned with faint praise from his press critics, with *The Times* interpreting his statement as evidence, 'that the Government are for once making ready to meet the threat instead of waiting until a serious stoppage has again been engineered by the agitators'.[57]

The government's response to the Korean crisis and the renewal of unofficial activity in the docks enjoyed the TGWU's full support. In August its General Executive Council resolved, 'that we must stand right up to aggression from whatever quarter it comes and not allow the United Nations Organisation to fall by the wayside'. Such were the circumstances surrounding the initiation of hostilities by 'Communist Imperialism', that the government's 'great scheme of re-armament', regrettable though it was, would enjoy the union's full support.[58] The debate about unofficial activity and political subversion which Isaacs began on 15 September was intensified by Deakin on the following day. When Harry Pollitt, the Communist Party's General Secretary, issued a statement calling for a change in the TGWU's leadership, Deakin said that the government should introduce legislation to ban the Communist Party. He described the CP as 'a conspiracy against the country and the British people'.[59] In the union journal he added that the demands being put forward in the docks for the Dockers' Charter were part of this conspiracy, and were a front for agitation which was actually designed to disrupt the supply of war materials to Malaya as well as Korea.[60]

In calling for a ban on the CP, Deakin took a harder line than the government, with Ministers deciding at the end of September that British public opinion would not tolerate such a move.[61] Yet coming hard on the heels of Isaacs's speech, Deakin's pugnacity indicated that the TGWU and the government once again shared a public determination to characterise unofficial activists in the docks as subversive individuals. It thus appeared that the difficulties between Labour's political and industrial partners, arising from the establishment of the Leggett Committee, had been resolved.

However, the general concurrence of opinion that the agitation for the 'Dockers' Charter' in September 1950 was politically-motivated, in the longer term actually increased pressure on government–TGWU relations. This renewal of tension arose from the government's growing conviction that the docks posed a political problem which required a political solution.

Among the Attlee governments' literally dozens of ad-hoc committees, in July 1950 a Ministerial group was established to draft a bill entitled Overseas Operations (Security of Forces). The purpose of this intended legislation was spelt out in a paper which Chuter Ede presented at the Committee's second meeting on 31 July. This proposed to criminalise all industrial acts – whether sabotage of the type supposedly witnessed at Portsmouth, unofficial strikes or incitement to strike – deemed prejudicial to the conduct of the war effort.[62] In being so largely inspired by an act of sabotage which had not – as it later transpired – actually taken place, the intended Bill was clearly ill-conceived. This the Committee acknowledged at its next meeting, two months later, with one Minister pointing out that since the outbreak of hostilities in Korea, there had been no further attempt to prevent supplies from being dispatched in support of military operations. However, given the unsettled nature of international developments and the likelihood of prolonged UN operations 'against aggression', the Committee remained tied to the idea of taking out some form of legal insurance against unofficial action. Thus, while ruling out the suppression of the Communist Party, Shawcross and Isaacs both wondered whether a viable alternative might be to enlist TUC support for a permanent measure, based on Order 1305, which would outlaw unofficial strikes.[63]

The continued existence of the 1940 regulation represented a vexing problem for the government. On 16 October Sir Hartley Shawcross pointed to trouble ahead, informing the Cabinet that so long as the Order remained in operation, he would find it increasingly difficult to refrain from using it. An inconclusive discussion followed, with Bevin arguing against maintaining compulsory arbitration in the longer term.[64]

This indecision on unofficial strikes reflected the government's general inability to take effective legal action against opponents of the war in Korea. On 6 November Shawcross told Cabinet that the only way to suppress the *Daily Worker*'s regular anti-war propaganda would be to institute a prosecution for treason. As this offence carried a mandatory death sentence, Ministers naturally concurred that it was far too heavy a weapon to use.[65] The possibility that the *Daily Worker* might be prosecuted under new legislation had already been eliminated, when the relevant Cabinet Committee had decided not to proceed with the Overseas Operations

Bill on 3 November. In ruling out tougher measures against anti-war propaganda, the Committee nevertheless reiterated its insistence that the continuation of unofficial action was not permissible.[66] These Ministers regarded the attitude of their trade union partners on unofficial strikes as unacceptably complacent. In September Shawcross had written to Morrison in order to qualify Isaacs's recent remarks on politically-motivated unofficial industrial action. According to Shawcross, most of communism's industrial initiatives since 1945 had only been possible because of the TGWU's inactivity. He had added that the maintenance of unofficial committees beyond the span of strikes was, 'a most dangerous situation requiring the Union to take really stringent steps'.[67]

For Shawcross and others, frustration caused by the TGWU's inactivity continued to mount. In lieu of an agreed strategy to counter unofficial strikes, on 16 October Cabinet had decided to open up discussions with the TUC on two questions: first, how were further communist-inspired strikes to be prevented; and second, how was machinery for long-term negotiation of industrial settlements to be developed.[68] Isaacs and Morrison duly discussed these matters with TUC leaders over an informal dinner in a London restaurant on 22 November, but no new proposals were produced. This confirmed the government's growing suspicion that the unions were either unable or unwilling to initiate action against unofficial strikes.[69]

In precipitating a fresh debate on the nature of unofficial action, the Korean crisis had thus reinforced the government's conviction, evident during the 1950 dock strike, that the TGWU could no longer be relied upon to prevent unofficial stoppages and enforce effective discipline in the docks. These were matters for which the government, it was increasingly felt, would have to assume responsibility. In November Shawcross gave notice of the means by which the government would eventually seek to improve discipline in the docks, by carrying out his October threat to institute legal proceedings under Order 1305. Following a ten-day unofficial strike by North Thames Gas Board workers in London gas stations, ten men were prosecuted and sentenced to a month's imprisonment, which was reduced on appeal to a £50 fine. According to Ministry of Labour officials, these original prison sentences were a great shock both to trade unionists and the general public.[70] In December, following a dispute between members of the Electricians' Trade Union and the airline company BOAC, the Cabinet considered additional prosecutions. An unofficial strike had begun after BOAC had attempted to force electricians to work alongside two non-union members, and the Cabinet was aware that the criminal prosecution of trade unionists who refused to work with non-trade unionists would jeopardise relations with the trade unions. During a second Cabinet discussion of the subject, which rejected prosecutions, the wider difficulties of enforcing Order 1305 were raised.[71] These had long been recognised. Shortly after the Order's introduction in 1940, Sir Frederick Leggett – then Chief Industrial Commissioner at the Ministry of Labour – had warned Bevin that it would be virtually impossible to enforce the legal ban on strikes and lock-outs. The Order would have to serve as a 'substantial deterrent' only: 'A large number of workpeople cannot be sent to prison and it is undesirable to make martyrs by selecting a few for prosecution.'[72] Leggett's initial misgivings had been borne out by the Coalition Government's futile 1942 attempt to prosecute 1200 miners who struck work at Betteshanger Colliery in Kent. Thwarted in their attempts to collect fines which the miners refused to pay, local magistrates had also been unable to imprison the men for lack of gaol accommodation.[73]

With Shawcross insisting that he would have to enforce the Order again sooner or later so long as it remained law, in January 1951 Cabinet considered the regulation's future. In the absence of any other instrument for dealing with unofficial strikes, Herbert Morrison's influential Private Secretary, E.M. Nicholson, urged that it be retained. Nicholson, who regarded industrial unrest as 'a kind of social disease', told Morrison on 13 January that a permanent anti-strike settlement was plainly indispensable: 'In modern social and economic conditions a strike is just as anti-social and almost as obsolete a method of settling disputes as a duel between two individuals.' The Ministry of Labour had to emphasise that strikes and lock-outs were not part of a rational future, 'and any implication that compulsory arbitration is an exceptional and temporary measure pending the restoration of the right to strike should be firmly resisted'.[74] With Morrison dominating discussion of the issue two days later, Cabinet broadly favoured maintaining a permanent system of arbitration machinery, emphasising that it, 'would be undesirable to delete the provisions of the Order relating to the prohibition of strikes and lock-outs'. However, in the wake of the BOAC and gas disputes, it was conceded that disputes relating to recognition or non-unionism ought to be excluded from the Order's scope, and that breaches of the Order would be punishable only by fines and not by prison sentences.[75]

With Cabinet coming round to the position held by the Attorney General, that the law would have to be used against strikers, the government had effectively decided that unofficial strikes could no longer be regarded as matters of internal union discipline. On 17 January Isaacs was moved to the Ministry of Pensions and replaced as Minister of Labour by Aneurin Bevan. This marked another significant departure from the 'separate spheres' approach. In contrast to his predecessor, Bevan had recurrently demonstrated his impatience with the TGWU's attempts to impose discipline among recalcitrant dock workers. As recently as the previous April he had argued that legal action against several thousand striking men in London would prove to be a 'wholesome long-term deterrent'. Attlee's biographer has suggested that Bevan was appointed Minister of Labour for three related reasons. He would have to support the Government's economic policy; he would thus confront rather than lead its left-wing critics; and in this new defensive role he would be confirmed through having 'to come to terms with the powerful right-wing trade union leaders'.[76] In fact, Bevan's three-month career as Minister of Labour hardly fulfilled any of these criteria, the most patent departure from Attlee's plan being his resignation from the government on 21 April over the NHS spending cuts. However, Bevan's one significant act as Labour Minister did owe something to Attlee's intention that the Ministry's new occupant would absorb left-wing criticism of the government. Paradoxically, however, it also revived the tension between the government and the TGWU that had first clearly emerged in May 1950 with the row over the establishment of the Leggett Inquiry into the causes of industrial unrest in the London docks.

The Failure of Legal Sanctions

Bevan's arrival at the Ministry of Labour coincided with the conclusion by the National Joint Council for the Port Transport Industry of a new pay agreement. With TUC support for the wage freeze collapsing in September 1950, on 16 November Arthur Bird notified employers' representatives that the TGWU wished to open negotiations for a pay increase. He observed that the present agreement had lasted for five years, and had been greatly overtaken by a 21 per cent increase in the cost of living. The employers responded by suggesting that Bird's request had been directly influenced by the recent unofficial agitation for the Dockers' Charter, a charge which Bird explicitly denied.[77] Despite the employers' initial resistance, negotiations did proceed, and in January the NJC reached agreement on a flat-rate increase of 2s per day, thus increasing the guaranteed daily minimum to 21s. On 31 January a special meeting of the TGWU National Docks Trade Group Committee recommended that the award be accepted, and the agreement was adopted by a National Docks Delegate Conference on 1 February.[78]

With the settlement again falling short of the Dockers' Charter's central tenet, a daily guarantee of 25s, dockers on the Mersey staged an unofficial protest strike. Although relatively prolonged, support for this stoppage was much thinner than when the Charter had previously been invoked, in October 1945. The 17-day affair cost the industry more than 100,000 days, but this figure suggests that only approximately one-fifth of the Mersey's 18,000 or so workers supported it.[79] Attempts to give the strike a national footing comparable to 1945 were also unsuccessful. According to Jack Dash, the Birkenhead strike committee contacted members of the London Port Workers' Committee by telephone, and asked for support. The London committee were fairly sure that few local men were interested in striking over the settlement, but in a spirit of loyalty to their Mersey comrades they organised a mass meeting on 6 February. The London committee's reservations were fully justified, as only 500 men attended the meeting and only a few hundred more supported the unofficial strike which began in the Royal Docks, also on 6 February. Indeed, Dash emphasised that the general lack of support for the six day strike was unprecedented,[80] and only 16,000 working days were lost. Additional unofficial action against the new wage agreement began on 5 February in Manchester; lasting eight days, this strike cost the industry a further 16,500 days.

The Cabinet's Ministerial Emergencies Committee discussed these developments at 9.30 a.m. on Wednesday 7 February. Five Ministers were present: Chuter Ede, Bevan, Shawcross, Barnes and Hector McNeil, the Secretary of State for Scotland. While Shawcross indicated that there was sufficient evidence to allow criminal proceedings against the London and Liverpool strike leaders under Order 1305, Chuter Ede reported that their attempts to spread the strikes had failed. Nevertheless, the Ministers concluded that the very fragility of the unofficial movement meant that, for once, prosecutions would weaken rather than strengthen its position with the rank and file. Shawcross was authorised to institute prosecutions against the appropriate individuals in the event of the respective unofficial committees' failing to terminate their strikes that afternoon.[81]

Both of Bevan's distinguished biographers have explicitly distanced Bevan from this decision to prosecute the strike leaders. In refuting Bessie Braddock's assertion that during the meeting of 7 February Bevan had stated, 'the strikers are on their knees, now is the time to strike them', Michael Foot noted, 'No one knew better than Bevan what might be the dangers for the Labour Government of the involvement of other Ministers in the decision about a prosecution which rested solely with the Attorney-General.' Foot added that it was actually Hector McNeil who argued in favour of delivering a knock out blow to the strikers. John Campbell's version of events simply has Shawcross ordering the prosecutions, apparently without consulting any of his Ministerial colleagues.[82] Each of these biographers have dismissed too readily the support which Bevan surely gave – and there is nothing in the minutes of the meeting to suggest that he did otherwise – to the case for prosecutions in the Emergencies Committee. Moreover, his compliance with Chuter Ede and Shawcross in accepting that the TGWU was incapable of dealing with the problem, was markedly different from the line usually adopted by Isaacs. On frequent occasions during unofficial strikes the latter had restrained colleagues from premature action, urging that the union be given the maximum opportunity to reassert its own authority.

As the Labour government's leading socialist, Bevan at first sight might appear to be an unlikely supporter of tough strike-breaking measures. But the man who had been expelled from the Labour Party in 1939 for sponsoring a Popular Front with communists was now operating in a very different post-war world. It was as a passionate defender of democratic socialism that he urged the dispatch of land troops to break the communist blockade of Berlin in June 1948;[83] and his frequent advocacy of tough measures against unofficial strikers was couched in similar terms. There was no contradiction between Bevan's socialist convictions and his opposition to unofficial strike action, as his remarks about the 'sectionalism' of the unofficial dockers' movement indicated. Those who threatened the unity of the labour movement, he argued when criticising the London dock strike in July 1949, jeopardised the security of its future, and allowed the Tories the prospect of regaining power. In 1951, with the Labour majority in the House of Commons reduced to only five, the threat which unofficial action posed to the government, and therefore to the continuing project of establishing a democratic socialist Britain, was all the more pervasive. In further explaining Bevan's determination to confront the unofficial movement, a useful parallel might be drawn with the White Paper introduced by a subsequent Labour government in January 1969, *In Place of Strife*. Widely perceived as limiting trade union freedoms, the White Paper's author was Barbara Castle, the one-time Bevanite and herself one of the few prominent left-wingers in Harold Wilson's administration. Castle shared Bevan's determination to eliminate unofficial strikes which, they both believed, advanced sectional aims with two consequences: first, they disrupted the Labour movement's unity; and second, they threw any attempts at strategic economic planning by a Labour government into chaos. More notoriously than Bevan, however, Castle provoked intense opposition from union leaders who believed that it was not for the government to arm itself against unofficial strikes, which they continued to regard as a matter of internal union discipline. Deprived of support from Cabinet colleagues in the face of such stiff TUC opposition – the most notable defector being the 'Keeper of the Cloth Cap', James Callaghan – Castle's proposals fell to the ground in June 1969.[84] In 1951 Bevan and his government colleagues experienced nothing like the hostility which Castle endured in 1969. However, the prosecutions which followed the Emergencies Committee meeting on 7 February did greatly antagonise the TGWU leadership which, like the TUC in 1969, strongly believed that the government had no proper place in imposing industrial discipline upon union members.

With the unofficial stoppages continuing on 7 February, Shawcross ordered the arrests of seven alleged ringleaders. Three of the men – Robert Crosbie, Joseph Harrison and William Johnson – were from the Mersey ports. The other four were familiar names from the London unofficial movement: the two expelled TGWU men, Harry Constable and Ted Dickens; Joseph Cowley, reprimanded in February 1949 by the TGWU Executive for his role in the 1948 strike, and a visitor to Poland several months previously; and Cowley's fellow traveller to Poland, Albert Timothy, the NASD member who had chaired the 1949 lock-out committee. On the evening of 8 February these seven were arrested at the White Hart pub in Stepney, taken to Bow Street Police Station, and charged under Order 1305 with illegally conspiring to incite strike action in connection with a trade dispute.[85] The men were held overnight, but released the next morning on bail, pending an appearance at Bow Street Police Court on 20 February.

Far from weakening the relationship between the unofficial movement and the workforce as Ministers had intended, the arrests actually increased support for the original strike which had been petering out. On 9 February Ministers found that virtually nobody was working in London's Royal Docks, where 10,000 men were usually employed.[86] Workers in all ports except Birkenhead and Liverpool went back to work on or around 13 February, but the London unofficial committee resolved to take a further course of one-day strikes to coincide with the accused men's court appearances. Thus on 20 February, when the seven appeared briefly at the Bow Street Police Court, one-day strikes affected work in London, Manchester, Glasgow and Greenock. With the London committee adhering to its slogan, 'When They're in the Dock, We're out of the Dock!', subsequent hearings of the case were accompanied by strikes in London on 27 February, 16 March, 9 and 16–19 April. While the general Mersey stoppages were called off after 20 February, dockers at Birkenhead came out for one day on 16 April. Taking into account the time lost during the initial Mersey stoppage, the strikes over the pay agreement and in protest at the arrest and prosecution of the seven men cost the industry a total of 230,000 working days in all ports.[87]

Given the obvious relationship between the case of the seven and the renewed incidence of unofficial activity, the TGWU viewed the government's initiative with great hostility. While the government's previous intrusion into internal union disciplinary matters, the appointment of the Leggett Committee of Inquiry, had only taken place after Bevin had attempted to smooth the ground with Deakin, the arrests on 8 February had taken the TGWU completely by surprise. Deakin told colleagues that his first intimation of the legal initiative had not come from labour movement colleagues in government, but when he had read about it in the newspapers on 9 February.[88] At a tense meeting of the Parliamentary Labour Party on 14 February, the TGWU-sponsored MP Bob Mellish protested strongly against the arrests. Mellish said that the police action had precipitated a strike which would otherwise have been avoided, and – like Deakin – demanded to know why he and other dockers' MPs had not been consulted beforehand.[89]

In November 1950, Deakin had argued that the TGWU was facing a war on two fronts. Not only was it targeted by communists who saw it as the major obstacle to increased communist influence in the TUC, but in supporting the Labour government the union also faced heavy criticism from Beaverbrook's Tory press.[90] This had, of course, been the basis of Deakin's disappointment over the Leggett Inquiry. Having fought successfully against two of the Labour government's principal opponents, the communists and the port employers, the TGWU had not expected Ministers to draw attention to the union's alleged shortcomings. Now, in March 1951, Deakin was again angered by the opportunities which the government had presented to both opposition groups. Deakin rightly insisted in the TGWU's Executive meeting of 8 March that, without the arrests, there would have been no serious trouble. Thus the government had inadvertently aided the unofficial movement's attack on the union leadership. Deakin evidently viewed this attack with great bitterness, stating, 'I know the drive is against me personally.' While the communist and unofficial elements had drawn comfort from the on-going court proceedings, Deakin added that the trial had allowed employers to reopen debate about the joint administration of the Dock Labour Scheme. He implied that members of the government who believed joint control to be a source of trouble in the docks were actively supporting the port employers against the union.[91]

Meanwhile, the case of the seven accused dock workers was lurching towards its conclusion. The final hearings began at the Old Bailey on 9 April under Lord Chief Justice Goddard, with Shawcross prosecuting. Shawcross disingenuously opened by asking the jurors not to be swayed by the possibility that sinister communist forces were at work in the docks, for no doubt 'the accused men had a deep and sincere belief in the justice of their demands'. However, in pursuit of these demands, they had been 'prepared to hold the nation to ransom and defy the law of the land'.[92] The seven faced two main charges: first, that they had conspired to incite dock workers to strike in connection with a trade dispute, contrary to the law under Order 1305; and second, that 'otherwise than in contemplation or furtherance of a trade dispute', they had conspired to induce men to break their obligations under the Dock Labour Scheme by absenting themselves from work without the permission of their employers. On 18 April the jury declared that the seven were guilty on this second count. However, apparently uncertain that the strike had actually involved a 'trade dispute' – and for a successful prosecution under Order 1305 this definition was absolutely essential – the jurors were unable to agree on the first one. Stating the impossibility of reconciling a disagreement on the first charge with the verdict on the second charge, Shawcross had to discontinue proceedings. He entered a *nolle prosequi*, and the men were acquitted. Pressed on this subject by Anthony Howard in 1992, Shawcross said that the jury's 'perverse verdict' was greeted with considerable relief by some of his government colleagues, who had held 'mixed feelings' about prosecuting the men. He added that the outcome was welcomed 'with great triumph by the dissident trade unionists who were gathered outside'.[93] Led by a jubilant Jack Dash, several hundred dockers carried the acquitted men shoulder high through the streets of London, and the Ministry of Labour's London industrial relations officer gloomily recorded that the case's 'damp squib' conclusion had been interpreted by dockers as 'a victory for "collective action"'.[94]

Bevan, who had been discussing Order 1305's future with representatives from both sides of industry on the Ministry of Labour-sponsored Joint Consultative Committee,[95] decided that the regulation would have to be abolished. This was duly accomplished by his successor as Minister of Labour, Alfred Robens. In June 1951 Robens informed Frank Soskice, who had become Attorney General after Shawcross was appointed President of the Board of Trade on 24 April, that the Order was no longer operable, as the unions were no longer prepared to support it. Together Robens and Soskice compiled a replacement, Order 1376, which made provision for legally-enforceable arbitration in disputes, without prohibiting strikes and lock-outs. This new regulation was approved by Cabinet on 26 July.[96]

The decision to prosecute the seven dockers had backfired. Where the unofficial movement had been facing its first serious defeat, with very few dockers interested in a strike over the new wage agreement, the trial ultimately brought it a highly publicised victory. This victory caused great unease within the TGWU. So shaken were Deakin and Bird by events, that on 19 April they felt moved to secure a vote of confidence from the union's Docks Trade Group Committee.[97] In drawing renewed public attention to the TGWU's problems in the docks, the trial had also placed fresh pressure on the government's relationship with the union at an extremely inopportune moment. It was a bitter coda to Ernest Bevin's life that at the time of his death – Saturday, 14 April 1951 – members of the union which he had created and led for 20 years were being prosecuted by the Labour government. On 21 April the government was further shaken by the resignation of the Minister of Labour, Aneurin Bevan. Bevan's opposition to the rearmament package had, as Kenneth Morgan demonstrates, been privately stated as early as 1 August 1950. But Morgan also believes that the unaccustomed criticism from the left which Bevan encountered as a result of the dockers' prosecutions, 'had a direct bearing on his later response to the issue of National Health Service charges'.[98] Indeed, it was at a meeting in Bermondsey on 3 April – primarily attended by dockers – that Bevan dropped the first public hint of his impending resignation. Responding to a heckler he said, 'I will never be a member of a Government which makes charges on the National Health Service.'[99] This suggests then, that in addition to straining the patience of the TGWU leadership, the government-instigated crisis in the docks had also significantly influenced Bevan's eventual resignation. With Gaitskell's chief critics, Bevan and Wilson, no longer in Cabinet, there was little further resistance to the over-inflated rearmament package that proved to be the government's ultimate undoing.

Conclusion: The Great Alliance

This book has focused on events in the docks essentially in order to re-emphasise the general observations which were made about the 1945 Labour government in the opening chapter. To recap, Attlee's first administration was not simply concerned – as conservative historians like Correlli Barnett have contended – with constructing a costly and enterprise-sapping 'New Jerusalem'. Its two central tasks, in fact, were economic recovery and the international containment of communism. In pursuing these goals it was greatly supported by the TUC, which, given the labour alliance's informal 'rules' of behaviour, accepted responsibility for marshalling working-class support behind both the wage freeze and anti-communism. Of course, as the first chapter acknowledged, historians who sympathise with the 1945–51 governments' achievements have broadly recognised the labour alliance's contribution to the successes of the period. Peter Hennessy, for instance, describes the TUC's support for the wage freeze as, 'a measure of the never-to-be-repeated unity of the labour movement'.[1] However, the subsequent chapters also demonstrated that even these historians have been slow to acknowledge the tension between the 1950 government and its largest union ally, the Transport and General Workers' Union. This slow build up of tension arose not so much from the 1945 strike – when the government's response to the largest stoppage was relatively relaxed – but from subsequent strikes in the 1945–50 period, with disruption in this vital area of the industrial economy complicating the government's increasingly urgent economic and international priorities.

The government characterised these later strikes as communist conspiracies, but they actually had nothing to do with political subversion. The real causes of the strikes – direct and indirect – were industrial in character. This book has looked in detail at the five largest strikes of the period. Each of these – in 1945, 1948, 1949, 1950 and 1951 – directly arose from a difference of opinion between the TGWU and some of its dock members on a specifically industrial issue. The table below demonstrates that between them, these five single *industrial* disputes absorbed the vast bulk – some 70 per cent – of the 2.89 million days lost to dock strikes during the 1945–51 period as a whole.

Table 6.1: Days Lost to the Five Main Disputes, 1945–51

Dispute	Days Lost	(% of total)
Dockers' Charter, October 1945 (various ports)	1 107 000	(38.3%)
'Zinc Oxide', June 1948 (London)	200 000	(6.92%)
Canadian Seamen, April–July 1949 (various ports)	400 000	(13.84%)
Expulsions, April–May 1950 (London)	93 750	(3.24%)
Wage claim/protest at prosecution of seven dockers, Feb–April 1951 (various)	230 000	(7.96%)
Aggregate of 5 Disputes	2 030 750	(70.26)[2]

As has been shown, the underlying causes of the strikes were also industrial in character: poor amenities, the persistence of casual recruitment, the workforce's antipathy to the new discipline introduced by the Dock Labour Scheme, the TGWU's unpopular association with this discipline, and the particular working culture of the docks, where workers traditionally relied on each other rather than the union. Yet the governments' wider priorities were such that Ministers expended little sympathy on dockers who went on strike. In disrupting economic activity, the strikes seemed to delay the process of Western European economic stabilisation which, in concert with American and Western European allies, the government perceived as the first step to halting communism's post-war progress. In a prospering Europe, it was believed, the ground would be cut from underneath communism's feet.[3] The government duly regarded the unofficial movement with great hostility, and viewed the TGWU's inability to maintain discipline amongst its docks membership with mounting frustration. It was this frustration which persuaded the 1950 government to establish an inquiry into the London unofficial strikes in 1950, and then to order the prosecution of the seven dockers in 1951. These actions blatantly contradicted the labour alliance's 'rules', and although predictable, the TGWU leadership's ensuing anger was immensely significant. The docks-related developments certainly qualify the conventional historical understanding of the general relationship between the 1945–51 governments and the unions.

At the same time, however, it should be noted that these strains were largely self-inflicted. In disregarding the industrial origins of the unofficial strikes, and instead emphasising their allegedly political characteristics, the government created trouble for itself. George Isaacs continually sought to excuse the TGWU for failing to maintain order in the docks by arguing that the trouble was inspired by Arthur Deakin's communist opponents in the docks. Yet by drawing attention to the union's internal weaknesses, this only served to convince Isaacs's Cabinet colleagues that they themselves would have to take action against the strikers. That Ministers would have to intervene in a more active manner than simply deploying troops to maintain supplies, was also in some ways made inevitable by the government's increasingly strident public attitude to the strikes. Eventually, and following some particularly reckless Ministerial statements which were made after the outbreak of war in Korea, the government was obliged to take action commensurate with the assertion that dock strikes were a political rather than an industrial challenge.

The government caused the TGWU a great deal of embarrassment by establishing the Leggett Inquiry and taking the seven dockers to court, for both of these developments brought public attention to the union's problems in the docks. The TGWU was anxious to divert attention from its inability to command authority in the docks, especially as its critics cited the TGWU's assumption of managerial responsibilities under the Dock Labour Scheme as being the hub of the problem. Having fought long and hard for the Scheme, Deakin and his colleagues were understandably sensitive to attacks upon it, particularly as much of the criticism came from the port employers. This criticism of the union's role in the Scheme was, in any case, misplaced. The port employers' position, shared by the Ministry of Transport, was that industrial relations in the docks had deteriorated as a result of the Scheme. Yet such indiscipline was not simply a mechanical consequence of the union's participation in the Scheme's managerial or disciplinary functions, however unpopular this was with dockers. The deeper explanation – the real cause of the trouble – was the TGWU's long-term inability to put down solid organisational roots in the docks. History always counted for much in the closed world of the docks, and history was always working against the TGWU.[4]

This real situation was no less damning for the union, and its persistent attempts to deflect attention from its historical weakness meant that although the government's actions in 1950 and 1951 were insensitive, the later tension was largely of the TGWU's own making. It is possible that Attlee and other Ministers were put under pressure by the British secret services to accept that the strikes were communist conspiracies. The obvious absence of documentary evidence means that this can neither be established nor ruled out, but it is significant that police and government law officers generally dismissed evidence of political involvement in the strikes. However, one source of red plot rumours can be positively identified: the TGWU itself. The union's dock officials, and indeed Deakin, continually encouraged the public and the government to believe that there was an important political dimension to the unofficial strikes. In insisting that the dockers' unofficial movement was politically motivated, Deakin inadvertently induced the government to respond in a 'political' manner. Given that Deakin took this position in order to ease the pressure on his union, and given the strain which the government's eventual response placed the labour alliance under, this was an ironic, and ultimately unfortunate situation.

Having rocked the stability of the labour alliance during a crucial period in the troubled history of the 1950 government, events in the docks also fuelled Labour's bitter internal divisions of the 1950s. Firstly, the government's decision to prosecute the seven dockers' leaders in February 1951 indirectly encouraged Aneurin Bevan to resign from the government, and bring into the public domain his private disdain for Hugh Gaitskell. Secondly, Bevan's growing impatience with the 'sectionalist' unofficial movement from 1948 onwards set him – ironically, perhaps – at growing loggerheads with Deakin and the TGWU official leadership. Increasingly insistent that the government's socialist duty was to assume the TGWU's responsibility for maintaining discipline in the docks, Bevan earned Deakin's undying enmity. In the vicious infighting between Labour 'loyalists' and Bevanite 'rebels' which followed the electoral defeat of October 1951, Deakin was to emerge as Bevan's chief – and most vitriolic – TUC opponent.

This tension notwithstanding, the relationship between Labour and the unions was plainly invaluable between 1945 and 1951. A clear community of interests existed and the link was also seen as an electoral advantage rather than a handicap. When Attlee spoke of Labour being the only genuinely 'national' party during the 1945 General Election, the unions were seen as central to Labour's uniquely representative character, setting it apart from the Conservative party of 'property and privilege'. Moreover, Labour's determination to encompass a 'national' interest was genuine, as the controversies arising from events in the docks indicated. The 'sectional' interests of the dockers' unofficial strikes were not allowed to prevail; and nor were the interests of Deakin and the TGWU allowed to take precedent over the government's wider priorities. On this point a useful comparison can be made with events which took place once the Conservatives had regained power in 1951. In the later 1930s Bevin had increasingly felt that he was able to hold meaningful discussions with the Tories, and a full working relationship between the Tories and the unions had developed during the war. This relationship proved immensely profitable for the unions after 1951, so much so that at times Deakin actually enjoyed more influence with Tory Ministers than he had done with their Labour predecessors. In the interests of political expediency and industrial peace, Churchill's Minister of Labour, Sir Walter Monckton, was certainly much softer on unofficial strikes and union officials who failed to resolve unofficial strikes than George Isaacs and Nye Bevan. In October 1954 Monckton faced a huge dock strike – partly resulting from an inter-union dispute between the TGWU and the National Amalgamated Stevedores and Dockers – which seriously disrupted work in London, Liverpool and several other ports. Conservative Ministers considered breaking this strike with service labour, as Labour had done on several occasions between 1945 and 1951. However, after Deakin had advised Monckton that this would be undesirable for it would cause the strike to spread, Churchill's Cabinet decided against using troops. During a subsequent dock strike in 1955, Monckton and his colleagues displayed an identical reluctance to go against the wishes of the TGWU by sending troops in to the ports.[5] This, it should be added, was part of a wider trend: between 1951 and 1964 the Conservative governments used service personnel to break industrial disputes on only three occasions.[6]

The character and benefits of the labour alliance in the 1940s can be further appraised by looking at the 1960s, when Labour regained office with Harold Wilson as Prime Minister. As in 1945, Wilson's government was beset by great economic difficulties and hence heavily reliant on trade union support. With the National Plan of 1965 the government duly attempted to construct a voluntary compact with unions and employers that would guarantee prolonged economic growth. Attlee's government had largely retained union support by observing the unwritten rules of the labour alliance, but at great political cost the Wilson government departed from these rules on two notable occasions, offending its union partners greatly on wages policy and industrial relations law. In 1965 the TUC had accepted voluntary wage restraint as part of an overall strategy for phased economic growth, but in July 1966 the government placed this policy on a statutory footing and announced an absolute freeze on wage increases for six months. In assuming a statutory and explicitly deflationary character, the 1966 freeze was a new departure, disrupting the rules and spirit of the labour alliance. Relations with the TGWU, still the TUC's largest affiliate, were particularly damaged, for its lower-paid members were disproportionately affected by the freeze and further deflationary measures which the government imposed in 1967 and 1968. By the end of 1966, in Robert Taylor's words, much of the government's 'moral credit' with the unions had been used up.[7] Hence the scale of trade union opposition encountered by Wilson's Employment Secretary, Barbara Castle, when she introduced *In Place of Strife*, a White Paper on industrial relations reform in January 1969. In emphasising the manner in which her White Paper sought to strengthen organised labour – including a clause that guaranteed the right of union membership – Castle always insisted that it was 'first and foremost a charter of trade union rights'.[8] *In Place of Strife* is best remembered, however, for its so-called 'penal clauses'. These proposed giving the government the statutory power to declare a 'conciliation pause' and delay an unofficial strike, to order a ballot in advance of an official strike, and to impose a settlement in the case of a demarcation dispute. Workers who refused to observe the conciliation pause would be liable for fines, and on ballots and demarcation disputes recalcitrant unions open to financial penalties.[9] In attempting to give the government responsibility for problems which trade unions regarded as matters of internal union discipline, Castle's policy was bitterly opposed by millions of trade unionists. Representing as significant a breach of the 'rules' of the union–party relationship as any Labour government had proposed, the policy was dropped after concerted pressure from the TUC General Council and trade union-sponsored MPs.[10]

Britain's social and political landscape has changed a great deal since the 1940s and 1960s. Yet in the 1990s the experiences of the Attlee and Wilson governments stand as valuable lessons for 'New Labour'. Attlee and his colleagues were committed to providing the unions with a range of positive benefits: comprehensive social insurance, the NHS, limited common ownership of utilities and industries, price subsidies and full employment. In return the unions made significant concessions on wages and productivity and, working closely in partnership, Labour and the unions guided Britain through immense difficulties. Labour governments in the 1960s and 1970s were unable to recreate this spirit of partnership, and hence failed to emulate the Attlee governments' achievements. Attlee and other Labour leaders in the middle of the century unambiguously accepted trade unions for what they were and remain, popular and democratic institutions representing millions of working people. Only through sharing the Attlee government's appraisal of the positive value of trade unionism, and by seeking to engage the active and voluntary co-operation of the trade union movement, can a future Labour government hope to survive and flourish.

Notes

Preface

1. Ralph Miliband, *Parliamentary Socialism*, pp. 272–317; John Saville, *The Labour Movement in Britain*, pp. 82–121.
2. Correlli Barnett, *The Audit of War*.
3. Kenneth O. Morgan, *Labour in Power 1945–1951*, p. 45; Peter Hennessy, *Never Again: Britain 1945–1951*.
4. Seamus Milne, 'To bury the axe or split the pact?', The *Guardian*, 18 April 1995.

Chapter 1: Labour in Power, 1945–50

1. Michael Foot, *Aneurin Bevan II 1945–60*, p. 17.
2. *The Times*, 27 July 1945.
3. Lewis Minkin, *The Contentious Alliance*, p. xii.
4. Ralph Miliband, *Parliamentary Socialism*; John Saville, *The Labour Movement in Britain*.
5. Minkin, *Contentious Alliance*, pp. 9–15.
6. Minkin, *Contentious Alliance*, pp. 27–39.
7. Alan Bullock, *The Life and Times of Ernest Bevin, Volume One*, pp. 243–4.
8. Paul Davies, *A.J. Cook*, pp. 169–71.
9. Minkin, *Contentious Alliance*, pp. 39–40.
10. Ernest Mandel, *The Meaning of the Second World War*.
11. Paul Addison, *The Road to 1945*, pp. 127–64; Angus Calder, *The People's War*, p. 158.
12. Minkin, *Contentious Alliance*, p. 54.
13. Keith Middlemas, *Politics in Industrial Society*, pp. 271–7; Minkin, *Contentious Alliance*, p. 57.
14. Addison, *Road to 1945*, p. 234; Minkin, *Contentious Alliance*, p. 60.
15. Alan Bullock, *The Life and Times of Ernest Bevin Volume Two*, pp. 230–4.
16. Michael Foot, *Aneurin Bevan I 1898–1945*, pp. 460–1.
17. *Parliamentary Debates*, Vol. 399, 1072, 1144, 28 April 1944.
18. Kenneth Harris, *Attlee*, pp. 256–7.
19. Henry Pelling, *The Labour Governments 1945–51*, p. 43; Kenneth O. Morgan, *Labour in Power*, p. 60.
20. Kevin Jefferys (ed.), *Labour and the Wartime Coalition. From the Diary of James Chuter Ede 1941–1945*, p. 229.
21. Francis Williams, *A Prime Minister Remembers*, p. 84.
22. Alan Bullock, *Ernest Bevin, Foreign Secretary 1945–51*, p. 98.
23. Alec Cairncross, *Years of Recovery*, pp. 6–9.

24. Peter Hennessy, *Never Again: Britain 1945–1951*, p. 90.
25. Hennessy, *Never Again*, p. 214.
26. Morgan, *Labour in Power*, p. 331.
27. Kenneth O. Morgan, *Labour People*, p. 164.
28. Hennessy, *Never Again*, p. 214.
29. Cairncross, *Years of Recovery*, p. 65.
30. Hennessy, *Never Again*, pp. 299–302.
31. Cairncross, *Years of Recovery*, p. 121.
32. Cabinet Conclusions, 17 August 1947, CAB 128.
33. Bullock, *Foreign Secretary*, pp. 706–18; Cairncross, *Years of Recovery*, pp. 66–86.
34. Quoted in Russell Jones, *Wages and Employment Policy 1936–1985*, p. 30.
35. Middlemas, *Politics in Industrial Society*.
36. *Transport and General Workers' Record*, September 1945.
37. Cabinet Conclusions, 13 November 1947, CAB 128.
38. Jones, *Wages and Employment Policy*, p. 154.
39. *Statement on Personal Incomes, Prices and Profits* (Cmd. 7321 February 1948).
40. Cairncross, *Years of Recovery*, pp. 405–6.
41. Cairncross, *Years of Recovery*, pp. 18–19.
42. Kenneth O. Morgan, *The People's Peace*, pp. 126–7.
43. Bullock, *Foreign Secretary*, pp. 368–70.
44. Henry Pelling, *Britain and the Marshall Plan*, p. 13.
45. Hennessy, *Never Again*, p. 294.
46. M. Adereth, *The French Communist Party*, pp. 145–54.
47. Bullock, *Foreign Secretary*, pp. 417–22.
48. 'Third Period' of modern epoch, with capitalism allegedly in dying throes; was said to have been reached after the 1914–20 imperialist war and revolutionary sequels and 1920–27 partial stabilisation of capitalism.
49. 'Two Camps' thesis and Moscow broadcast extensively quoted in *The Times*, 6 October 1947.
50. Isaac Deutscher, *Stalin: A Political Biography*, pp. 570–1.
51. Minkin, *Contentious Alliance*, p. 64.
52. Lenin's (often misquoted) remarks from '*Left Wing' Communism: An Infantile Disorder*, pp. 90–1.
53. Willie Thompson, *The Good Old Cause: British Communism 1920–1991*, p. 37.
54. Francis King and George Matthews (eds), *About Turn*, is a verbatim account of the 24 September–3 October 1939 Central Committee sessions which discussed the new position.
55. Sam Bornstein and Al Richardson, *Two Steps Back*, is an interesting Trotskyist account of the CP in wartime.
56. Denis MacShane, 'Workers of the World Unite?', *History Today*, September 1990.
57. V.L. Allen, *Trade Union Leadership*, p. 290.
58. Bullock, *Foreign Secretary*, p. 499.
59. Pelling, *Marshall Plan*, pp. 62–3.

60. Allen, *Trade Union Leadership*, pp. 295–6; Pelling, *Marshall Plan*, pp. 62–3.
61. Allen, *Trade Union Leadership*, pp. 306–12.
62. *The Times*, 9 February 1948.
63. H.A. Clegg, *General Union*, pp. 117–22.
64. In being elected General Secretary, Deakin polled 203,314 votes to Papworth's 47,378; but 620,370 ballot papers were returned unused; *Transport and General Workers' Record*, December 1945.
65. *The Times*, 10 February 1948.
66. Deakin to Tewson 26 October 1948, MSS.292/20/33.
67. TUC Circular, 'Trade Unions and Democracy', 27 October 1948, MSS.292/23.1/27.
68. Eric Silver, *Victor Feather, TUC*, p. 97.
69. TUC, *Defend Democracy*, 24 November 1948, MSS.292/23.1/27.
70. Correspondence between John Eddington & Co. Ltd and TUC General Council, 28 October to 1 November 1948, MSS.292/777.5/1.
71. TUC, *The Tactics of Disruption*, January 1949, MSS.292/777.5/1. Subtitled *Communist Methods Exposed*, the pamphlet cost 2d, compared to the slightly bulkier *Defend Democracy*, which cost 3d.
72. *Transport and General Workers' Record*, January and July 1949.
73. *Daily Worker*, 12 July 1949.
74. TUC General Council, 9 September 1949, MSS.292/20/33.
75. TUC General Council, 22 February 1950, MSS.292/20/34.

Chapter 2: On the Waterfront

1. Kenneth O. Morgan, *Labour in Power 1945–1951, p. 499.*
2. Trade Disputes (All Industries) 1945–51, LAB 34/60–67.
3. Steve Peak, *Troops in Strikes*, pp. 83–98.
4. Fernand Braudel, *The Mediterranean and the Mediterranean in the Age of Philip II*, p. 664.
5. Jonathan Schneer, 'The War, The State and the Workplace: British Dockers During 1914–1918', in J.E. Cronin and J. Schneer (eds.), *Social Conflict and the Political Order in Modern Britain*, p. 97.
6. Gordon Phillips and Noel Whiteside, *Casual Labour: The Unemployment Question in the Port Transport Industry 1880–1970*, pp. 55–7.
7. John Lovell, *Stevedores and Dockers*, pp. 59–91.
8. Lovell, *Stevedores and Dockers*, p. 31.
9. Phillips and Whiteside, *Casual Labour*, pp. 77–85.
10. Ken Coates and Tony Topham, *The Making of the Labour Movement*, p. 350.
11. Lovell, *Stevedores and Dockers*, pp. 180–213.
12. Phillips and Whiteside, *Casual Labour*, pp. 93–4.
13. Schneer, 'The War, The State and the Workplace', p. 97.
14. Alan Bullock, *The Life and Times of Ernest Bevin, Volume One: Trade Union Leader 1881–1940*, pp. 117–18.
15. Phillips and Whiteside, *Casual Labour*, p. 36.
16. Lovell, *Stevedores and Dockers*, p. 31.
17. Lovell, *Stevedores and Dockers*, p. 36.

18. Denis Delay, *Myths about the Origins and Effects of the National Dock Labour Scheme*, TUC paper July 1986. I owe this reference to Mr Bob Aspinall of The Museum of London Library.
19. Ross McKibbin, *The Ideologies of Class*, p.156.
20. Phillips and Whiteside, *Casual Labour*, p. 121.
21. Lovell, *Stevedores and Dockers*, chapters 3–7.
22. Coates and Topham, *Making of the Labour Movement*, p. 436.
23. Bullock, *Bevin, Volume One*, pp. 122–30.
24. Stephen Hill, *The Dockers*, pp. 127–49.
25. V.L. Allen, *Trade Union Leadership*, p. 224.
26. Bullock, *Bevin, Volume One*, p. 520, p. 613.
27. Phillips and Whiteside, *Casual Labour*, p. 169.
28. Phillips and Whiteside, *Casual Labour*, p. 226.
29. Allen, *Trade Union Leadership*, pp. 60–3.
30. Angus Calder, *The People's War*, p. 269.
31. Alan Bullock, *The Life and Times of Ernest Bevin, Volume Two: Minister of Labour 1940–1945*, pp. 30–1. The ports of the North Western Approaches were Liverpool, Birkenhead, Garston, Manchester, Preston, Bromborough, Ellesmere Port, Partington, Widnes, Runcorn and Western Point.
32. Allen, *Trade Union Leadership*, pp. 174–6.
33. *Parliamentary Debates*, Vol. 376, 1340, 4 December 1941.
34. *Transport and General Workers' Record*, October 1941.
35. Quoted in Lewis Minkin, *The Contentious Alliance*, p. 55.
36. *Transport and General Workers' Record*, October 1941.
37. *Parliamentary Debates*, Vol. 376, 1340, 4 December 1941.
38. Allen, *Trade Union Leadership*, p. 185.
39. *Parliamentary Debates*, Vol. 399, 1591–2 and 1662–5, 5 May 1944.
40. *Report of a Commission of Inquiry into the London Dock Dispute, March 1945. Ministry of Labour and National Service*, 1945 (copy in LAB 10/580).
41. Lovell, *Stevedores and Dockers*, pp. 134–5.
42. Allen, *Trade Union Leadership*, p. 186.
43. Isaacs to Ammon, 10 August 1945, BK 1/57.
44. Dock Workers (Regulation of Employment) Bill, *Parliamentary Papers 1945–46*, Vol. I.
45. *Parliamentary Debates*, Vol. 415, 1756–9, 1816–17, 12 November 1945.
46. Dock Workers (Regulation of Employment) Act 1946, *Public General Statutes 1946*.
47. NAPE EC, 19 November 1945.
48. Bevin to Isaacs, 12 November 1945, FO 800/491.
49. TGWU GEC Report, 1945–46, MSS.126 T&G/4/1/25; NAPE EC meeting, 10 December 1945.
50. NAPE EC, 25 October 1945.
51. Macdonald to Donovan, 8 July 1946, MT 81/16.
52. NJC Decasualisation Sub–Committee, 20 March 1946, BK 1/57.
53. Robert Letch (PLA) to Aubrey Clark (MoT), 26 June 1946, MT 81/16.
54. *Transport and General Workers' Record*, September 1946.

55. TGWU GEC Report, 1945–46, MSS.126 T&G/4/1/25.
56. *Port Transport Industry: Report of a Committee of Inquiry* (Cmd. 9813, 1956).
57. Delay, *Myths*. Original emphasis.
58. *Transport and General Workers' Record*, January 1947.
59. Macdonald to Saunders, 12 April 1947, MT 81/16.
60. BK 1/61.
61. 'Comments on draft scheme', 15 February 1947, MT 81/16.
62. Clark to Page, 15 July 1947, MT 63/408.
63. James Callaghan, *Time and Chance*, p. 95.
64. Clark to Page, 15 July 1947, MT 63/408.
65. National Portworkers' Defence Committee, *The Enquiry and YOU!*, May 1947, MSS.15B/40.
66. NASD Stevedores' Sectional Committee Minutes, 13 May 1947.
67. P. 60.
68. NASD Joint Executive Council Minutes, 15 May and 11 June 1947.
69. *Fairplay Weekly Shipping Journal*, 15 May 1947, clipping in T 228/168.
70. Jack Dash, *Good Morning, Brothers!*, p. 60.
71. NJC Decasualisation Sub–Committee, 20 March 1946, BK 1/57.
72. Chairman's speech to the NDLC's sixth AGM, 27 June 1946, BK 1/151.
73. Ammon and Bevin speeches to the NDLC's seventh AGM, 5 June 1947, BK 1/153.
74. *Transport and General Workers' Record*, November 1947.

Chapter 3: The 1945 Government and Unofficial Dock Strikes

1. Trade Disputes (All Industries), 1945–49, LAB 34/60–64.
2. Keith Jeffery and Peter Hennessy, *States of Emergency*, pp. 154–60, 198–208; Kenneth O. Morgan, *Labour in Power 1945–1951*, pp. 373–8; Peter Weiler, *British Labour and the Cold War*, p. 230.
3. *Transport and General Workers' Record*, July 1945.
4. DNTGC, 30 October 1945.
5. NAPE Executive Committee, 4 October 1945.
6. *The Times*, 4 October 1945.
7. *Manchester Guardian*, 5 October 1945.
8. *The Times*, 9–12 October 1945.
9. Trade Disputes (All Industries), 1945, LAB 34/60.
10. London Central Strike Committee, *Mandate*, October 1945, BK 1/105.
11. *The Times*, 15 October 1945.
12. London Central Strike Committee, *Why Strike?*, October 1945, BK 1/105.
13. DNTGC, 12 October 1945.
14. *The Times*, 13 October 1945.
15. *Manchester Guardian*, 13 October 1945.
16. *World News and Views*, 4 August 1945.

17. *Daily Worker*, 12 and 26 October 1945.
18. Bristol port authorities to NDLC, 22 October 1945, BK 1/105.
19. *The Times*, 18 October 1945.
20. DNTGC, 22 October 1945. This meeting probably took place over the weekend of 21–22 October.
21. *Transport and General Workers' Record*, November 1945.
22. *Daily Herald*, 25 October 1945.
23. TGWU GEC, 9 November 1945, MSS.126/T&G/1/1/23.
24. *Manchester Guardian*, 3 November 1945.
25. TGWU GEC Report, 1945–46, MSS.126 T&G/4/1/25.
26. *Daily Herald*, 31 October 1945.
27. *Daily Herald*, 11 October 1945.
28. Jeffery and Hennessy, *States of Emergency*, p. 155.
29. *Parliamentary Debates*, Vol. 414, 229–30, 10 October 1945.
30. Cabinet Conclusions, 15 October 1945, CAB 128.
31. *Parliamentary Debates*, Vol. 414, 698, 15 October 1945.
32. *Daily Herald*, 31 October 1945.
33. Cabinet Conclusions, 26 October 1945, CAB 128.
34. Jeffery and Hennessy, *States of Emergency*, p. 160.
35. Jack Dash, *Good Morning, Brothers!*, p. 59.
36. *Transport and General Workers' Record*, November 1945.
37. DNTGC, 30 October 1945.
38. *The Times*, 2 November 1945.
39. Trade Disputes (All Industries), 1948, LAB 34/63.
40. NDLB press statement, 23 June 1948, BK 2/72.
41. *Unofficial Stoppages in the London Docks* (Cmd. 8236, 1951), para. 36.
42. Port Workers Strike Committee, *The Men's Own Case*, BK 2/72.
43. NASD Joint Executive Council Minutes, 18 August 1948. The leadership of the National Amalgamated Stevedores and Dockers comprised two Sectional Committees – the Stevedores and the Dockers – which were subordinate to the Joint Executive Council.
44. *Transport and General Workers' Record*, February 1947.
45. *Daily Herald*, 19 June 1948.
46. Minutes of meeting between Saunders (LDLB) and Platt and Harvey (TGWU), 19 June, BK 2/72. The officer favouring compromise was Harvey.
47. *Transport and General Workers' Record*, July 1948.
48. Cabinet Conclusions, 24 June 1948, CAB 128.
49. *The Times*, 23 June 1948.
50. *Parliamentary Debates*, Vol. 452, 1364, 23 June 1948.
51. Jeffery and Hennessy, *States of Emergency*, p. 148.
52. Newsam's report, 'Dock Strike', CAB 21/2653.
53. EC, 21 June 1948, CAB 134. The Ministers present were Ede (Home Office), Alexander (Defence), Strachey, Woodburn (Scottish Secretary), Shawcross (Attorney General) and Edwards (Labour, deputising for Isaacs).
54. *Manchester Guardian*, 24 June 1948.
55. *The Times*, 25 June 1948.
56. *The Times*, 26 June 1948.
57. EC, 21 June 1948, CAB 134.

58. Alan Bullock, *Ernest Bevin, Foreign Secretary, 1945–1951*, p. 575.
59. Ministerial meeting, 24 June 1948, CAB 130/38.
60. Peter Hennessy, *Never Again*, p. 199.
61. *The Times*, 29 June 1948.
62. *The Times*, 28 June 1948.
63. Cabinet Conclusions, 28 June 1948, CAB 128.
64. Jeffery and Hennessy, *States of Emergency*, p. 192.
65. Cabinet Conclusions, 16 January 1947, CAB 128.
66. Cabinet Conclusions, 28 June 1948, CAB 128.
67. Jeffery and Hennessy, *States of Emergency*, p. 150.
68. EC, 28 June 1948, CAB 134.
69. 'Points Agreed Upon by Cabinet for the PM's Broadcast', 28 June 1948, PREM 8/1086,
70. 'Brothers', BBC Radio 4, 5 January 1993.
71. Full text of Attlee's speech, which was broadcast at 9 p.m. on 28 June 1948 and again at 7 a.m. and 8 a.m. on 29 June 1948, in *Daily Herald*, 29 June 1948.
72. *Manchester Guardian*, 30 June 1948.
73. Cabinet Conclusions, 29 June 1948, CAB 128.
74. The *Manchester Guardian* and the *Daily Telegraph*, 30 June 1948; the *Daily Mail*, 2 July 1948, *Daily Worker*, 29–30 June 1948.
75. *Transport and General Workers' Record*, July 1948.
76. *Manchester Guardian*, 30 June 1948.
77. Whitlock's account of the strike, LAB 10/783.
78. John Lovell, *Stevedores and Dockers*, pp. 214–18.
79. Whitlock to Tennant, 29 June 1948, LAB 10/783.
80. LAB 34/64.
81. For a varied selection, see Jeffery and Hennessy, *States of Emergency*, pp. 154–60, 198–208; Morgan, *Labour in Power*, pp. 375–8; Weiler, *British Labour and the Cold War*, p. 230.
82. TGWU GEC, 28 February 1949, MSS.126/T&G/1/1/27.
83. NASD Joint Executive Council, 11 April 1949.
84. W.E. Thomas notes, 12 and 13 April 1949, LAB 10/831.
85. Shawcross to Attlee, 13 April 1949, LAB 10/831.
86. W.E. Thomas's note of conversation with Hogger of the NDLB, 12 April 1949, LAB 10/831.
87. *Review of the British Dock Strikes* (Cmd. 7851, 1949), Appendix VI.
88. Bristol RIRO report, 18 May 1949, LAB 10/833.
89. Scottish RIRO notes, 21 May and 3 June 1949, LAB 10/832.
90. Cmd. 7851, p.14.
91. Ministerial meeting, 23 May 1949, PREM 8/1081.
92. EC, 30 May 1949, CAB 134.
93. Whitlock note, 26 May 1949, LAB 10/832.
94. Cabinet Conclusions, 2 June 1949, CAB 128.
95. Ammon to Attlee, 7 June 1949, BK 2/75.
96. Ministerial meeting, 10 June 1949, CAB 130/46.
97. EC, 30 May and 1 June 1949, CAB 134.
98. Ministerial broadcast, 11 June 1949, LAB 43/150.
99. Cmd. 7851, pp.12–14.
100. NASD Joint Executive Council, 21 June 1949.

101. Port Employers in London, 22 June 1949, LWA 73.
102. Whitlock to Diack, 29 June 1949, LAB 10/904.
103. London Central Lock–out Committee, *We Want Work*, 30 June 1949, BK 2/76.
104. *Transport and General Workers' Record*, July 1949.
105. Cmd. 7851, Appendix XIII.
106. *Parliamentary Debates*, Vol. 466, 982, 28 June 1949.
107. EC, 4 July 1949, CAB 134.
108. *Manchester Guardian*, 7 July 1949.
109. Cabinet Conclusions, 7 July 1949, CAB 128.
110. *Manchester Guardian*, 12 July 1949.
111. Cabinet Conclusions, 11 July 1949, CAB 128.
112. Cmd. 7851, Appendix XIII.
113. Ministerial broadcast, 13 July 1949, LAB 10/904.
114. *Manchester Guardian*, 18 July 1949.
115. TGWU Biennial Delegate Conference 1949 Report, para. 54, MSS. 126/T&G/1/4/13.
116. Port Emergency Committee meeting with Lord Ammon, 19 July 1949, BK 2/76.
117. Ammon to Attlee, 19 July 1949, PREM 8/1081.
118. *The Times*, 20 July 1949.
119. Bevin to Ammon, 3 September 1945, FO 800/491.
120. *The Times*, 22 July 1949.
121. Cmd. 7851, pp. 25–6.
122. *The Times*, 23 July 1949.
123. *House of Lords*, Vol. 164, 557–65, 27 July 1949.
124. Port Employers in London, 22 July 1949, LWA 73.
125. DNTGC, 21 July 1949.

Chapter 4: Communist Conspiracies? The Allegations and the Reality

1. *The Times*, 13 October 1945.
2. *The Times*, 25 June 1948.
3. *Daily Herald*, 29 June 1948.
4. EC, 12 April 1949, CAB 134.
5. Cabinet Conclusions, 13 April 1949, CAB 128.
6. Ministerial Meeting, 23 May 1949, PREM 8/1081.
7. Cabinet Conclusions, 26 May 1949, CAB 128.
8. Memo by Andrews, 9 June 1949, LAB 10/832.
9. *Manchester Guardian*, 4 July 1949.
10. *Daily Worker*, 5 July 1949.
11. EC, 4 July 1949, CAB 134.
12. *Parliamentary Debates*, Vol. 466, 2596, 8 July 1949.
13. *Review of the British Dock Strikes, 1949*, (Cmd. 7851, December 1949).
14. *The Times* and *Manchester Guardian*, both 16 December 1949.
15. Morrison's speech in Lewisham, 24 March 1950, CAB 124/4; extended extracts in *The Times*, 25 March 1950.
16. John Callaghan, *British Trotskyism*, pp. 27–9.

17. Bevin to Isaacs, 21 November 1945, FO 800/491.
18. DNTGC, 22 October 1945.
19. DNTGC, 12 October 1945.
20. EC, 21 June 1948, CAB 134.
21. Port Workers' Strike Committee, *The Men's Own Case*, BK 2/72.
22. *The Times*, 19 June 1948.
23. Harrison to Gould, 31 October 1949, LAB 16/97.
24. Shawcross to Harrison, 29 November 1949, LAB 16/97.
25. Ministerial meeting, 23 May 1949, PREM 8/1081.
26. *Western Daily Press*, 7 May 1949, clipping in LAB 10/783.
27. Whitlock to Barnes, 25 May 1949, LAB 10/833.
28. EC, 25 May 1949, CAB 134.
29. EC, 30 May 1949, CAB 134.
30. Andrews memo, 9 June 1949, LAB 10/832.
31. Jack and Bessie Braddock, *The Braddocks*, p. 203.
32. Wilson to Isaacs, 13 June 1949, LAB 10/832.
33. Ministerial meeting, 10 June 1949, CAB 130/46.
34. Copy of full text of Isaacs's broadcast, 11 June 1949, LAB 43/150.
35. Keith Jeffery and Peter Hennessy, *States of Emergency*, p. 202.
36. Central Lock–out Committee, *To All Portworkers*, July 1949, LAB 16/201 (original emphasis).
37. Hull to Diack, 5 July 1949, LAB 10/904.
38. Cabinet Conclusions, 7 July 1949, CAB 128.
39. Shawcross to Isaacs, 7 July 1949, LAB 10/904.
40. Cabinet Conclusions, 8 July 1949, CAB 128.
41. *Parliamentary Debates*, Vol. 466, 2596, 8 July.
42. Ministerial Broadcast, 13 July 1949, LAB 10/904.
43. *Manchester Guardian*, 12 July 1949.
44. Isaacs to Lord Ammon, 6 August 1948; Thomas to Isaacs, 25 February 1949, BK 2/149.
45. NDLB report, 'Docks Amenities', March 1949, CAB 124/602.
46. Isaacs to Morrison, 25 March 1949, CAB 124/602.
47. LP, 1 April 1949, CAB 132.
48. LP, 28 October 1949, CAB 132.
49. Alec Cairncross, *Years of Recovery*, p. 33.
50. Thomas to Isaacs, 13 January 1950, BK 2/150.
51. *Unofficial Stoppages in the London Docks: Report of a Committee of Inquiry* (Cmd. 8236, May 1951), p. 30.
52. LP, 11 May 1951, CAB 132.
53. Cmd. 8236, p. 12.
54. *Port Transport Industry: Report of a Committee of Inquiry* (Cmd. 9813, 1956), p. 29.
55. National Portworkers' Defence Committee, *The Enquiry and You!*, May 1947, MSS.15B/40.
56. Fred Lindop, 'Unofficial Militancy in the Royal Group of Docks 1945–67', *Oral History*, Volume 11 Number 2, Autumn 1983, p. 27.
57. Cmd. 8236, p. 7; Bevin to Ede, 11 July 1949, FO 800/519.
58. Cmd. 8236, p. 5.
59. Denis Delay, *Myths About the Origins and Effects of the National Dock Labour Scheme*, TUC paper, 1986.

60. V.L. Allen, *Trade Union Leadership*, p. 186.
61. Port Workers' Strike Committee, *The Men's Own Case*, June 1948, BK 2/72.
62. London Port Workers' Strike Committee, *Reflections on the Strike*, July 1948, BK 2/72.
63. Cmd. 9813, p. 17.
64. Cmd. 8236, p. 7.
65. Cmd. 8236, p. 8; Cmd. 9813, p. 17.
66. Industrial Disputes, 1947–1951, BK 2/71.
67. Lindop, 'Unofficial Militancy in the Royal Group of Docks', p. 27.
68. Port Workers' Strike Committee, *The Men's Own Case*.
69. *Daily Worker*, 26 June 1948.
70. *Manchester Guardian*, 26 June 1948.
71. *Manchester Guardian*, 28 June 1948.
72. David F. Wilson, *Dockers: The Impact of Industrial Change*, pp. 196–8.
73. *Observer*, 17 July 1949.
74. Macdonald to Saunders, 12 April 1947, MT 81/16.
75. Clark to Page, 15 July 1947, MT 63/408.
76. Port Employers in London, 29 June 1948, LWA 73.
77. NAPE, 8 July 1948, LWA 57.
78. Hobhouse to Macdonald, 8 August 1949, BPA 244.
79. Hobhouse to Barnes, 11 August 1949, BPA 244.
80. Barnes to Hobhouse, 22 August 1949, BPA 244.
81. Cabinet Conclusions, 18 July 1949, CAB 128.
82. Lord Callaghan, letter to author, 3 September 1992.
83. Callaghan to Attlee, 15 July 1949, FO 800/519.
84. Bevin–Callaghan correspondence, 19–20 July 1949, FO 800/519.
85. Allen, *Trade Union Leadership*, p. 180.
86. Lord Callaghan, letter to author, 3 September 1992.
87. London Port Workers' Strike Committee, *Reflections on the Strike*.
88. Lindop, 'Unofficial Militancy in the Royal Group of Docks', p. 30.
89. LDLB list, 4 August 1949, BK 2/76.
90. Raphael Samuel, 'The Lost World of British Communism', *New Left Review*, No. 154, November–December 1985, p. 46.
91. Lindop, 'Unofficial Militancy in the Royal Group of Docks', p. 30.
92. Cyril Smith, conversation with author, 5 August 1992.
93. Bill Hunter, *They Knew Why They Fought*, p. 23.
94. *Manchester Guardian*, 28 June 1948.
95. Field Survey Group of the British Institute of Management, 'Research in the London Docks', Interim Report 31 December 1948, CAB 21/2653.
96. NJC, 12 May 1950, BK 2/283; Attlee to Morrison, 3 May 1950, PREM 8/1534.
97. Cmd. 8236, p. 13.
98. Cmd. 9813, pp. 16–19.
99. DNTGC, 21 July 1949.

Chapter 5: The Alliance Under Strain: The 1950–51 Labour Government and the Docks

1. Cabinet Conclusions, 25 February 1950, CAB 128.
2. Kenneth O. Morgan, *Labour in Power 1945–1951*, p. 462.
3. Charles Webster, *The Health Services Since The War, Volume I*, pp. 133–77.
4. *Parliamentary Debates*, Vol. 487, 228, 24 April 1951.
5. Morgan, *Labour in Power*, p. 477.
6. Alec Cairncross, *Years of Recovery*, p. 233.
7. DNTGC, 21 July 1949.
8. TGWU GEC, 15 December 1949, MSS.126/T&G/1/1/27.
9. TGWU GEC, 6–10 March 1950, MSS.126/T&G/1/1/28.
10. David F. Wilson, *Dockers*, p. 193.
11. Daniel Ballard and David E. Martin, 'Jack Dash', *Dictionary of Labour Biography*, Volume IX (1993), p. 60.
12. *The Times*, 27 April 1950.
13. London RIRO memo, 26 January 1950, LAB 10/940.
14. NAPE, 5th AGM, 31 March 1950, LWA 57.
15. *Manchester Guardian*, 14 April 1950.
16. A.S. Andrews to J.A. Diack, 11 April 1950, LAB 10/955.
17. Ibid.
18. *The Times*, 15 April 1950.
19. DNTGC, 20 April 1950.
20. Stillwell to Whitlock, 19 April 1950, LAB 10/955.
21. London RIRO memo, 21 April 1950, LAB 10/955.
22. DNTGC, 20 April 1950.
23. *The Times*, 21 and 25 April 1950.
24. *The Times*, 24 April 1950.
25. London RIRO memo, 29 April 1950, LAB 10/955.
26. *The Times*, 3 May 1950.
27. Industrial Disputes, 1950, BK 2/71.
28. *The Times*, 24 April 1950.
29. *Parliamentary Debates*, Vol. 474, 331, 20 April 1950.
30. Cabinet Conclusions, 21 April 1950, CAB 128.
31. EC, 20 April 1950, CAB 134.
32. Cabinet Conclusions, 25 April 1950, CAB 128.
33. EC, 20 April 1950, CAB 134.
34. Lewis Minkin, *The Contentious Alliance*, pp. 27–40.
35. Cabinet Conclusions, 21 April 1950, CAB 128.
36. Cabinet Conclusions, 24 April 1950, CAB 128.
37. Cabinet Conclusions, 1 May 1950, CAB 128.
38. Brook to Attlee, 2 May 1950, PREM 8/1534.
39. Brook's notes of meeting, 5 May 1950, PREM 8/1534.
40. Bevin to Isaacs, 6 May 1950, FO 800/495.
41. *Parliamentary Debates*, Vol. 475, 581, 11 May 1950.
42. *The Times*, 12 May 1950.
43. TGWU FGPC, 15 May and 29 June 1950, MSS.126/T&G/1/1/28.
44. *Transport and General Workers' Record*, June 1950.
45. Anderson to Rickett, 8 May 1950, PREM 8/1289.

46. Prime Minister's Office note of meeting, 15 May 1950, PREM 8/1289.
47. *Unofficial Stoppages in the London Docks: Report of a Committee of Inquiry*, (Cmd. 8236, May 1951), p. 13.
48. DNTGC, Bird's Quarterly Report, 30 September 1951.
49. Kenneth Harris, *Attlee*, pp. 454–5; Peter Hennessy, *Never Again: Britain 1945–1951*, p. 466.
50. Morgan, *Labour in Power*, p. 437.
51. Justin Davis–Smith, *The Attlee and Churchill Administrations and Industrial Unrest 1945–1955*, p. 17.
52. *Parliamentary Debates*, Vol. 478, 35–37, 24 July 1950.
53. Parkin to Gould, 28 August 1950, BK 2/79.
54. Cabinet Conclusions, 14 September 1950, CAB 128.
55. *Port Workers' News*, October 1950, copy in BK 2/79.
56. *Parliamentary Debates*, Vol. 478, 1405, 15 September 1950.
57· *The Times*, 16 September 1950.
58. TGWU GEC Quarterly Report, 21 August 1950, MSS.126/T&G/1/1/28.
59. *The Times*, 18 September 1950.
60. *Transport and General Workers' Record*, October–November 1950.
61. GPC, 29 September 1950, CAB 130/63.
62. GPC, 31 July 1950, CAB 130/63.
63. GPC, 29 September 1950, CAB 130/63.
64. Cabinet Conclusions, 16 October 1950, CAB 128.
65. Cabinet Conclusions, 6 November 1950, CAB 128.
66. GPC, 3 November 1950, CAB 130/63.
67. Shawcross to Morrison, 15 September 1950, CAB 124/1196.
68. Cabinet Conclusions, 16 October 1950, CAB 128.
69. Isaacs to Morrison, 28 November 1950, LAB 43/152.
70. Memo on Order 1305, 24 January 1951, LAB 10/1006.
71. Cabinet Conclusions, 7 and 11 December 1950, CAB 128.
72. Leggett to Bevin, 8 September 1940, LAB 10/116.
73. Henry Phelps Brown, *The Origins of Trade Union Power*, pp. 98–9.
74. Nicholson to Morrison, 13 January 1951, CAB 124/1195.
75. Cabinet Conclusions, 15 January 1951, CAB 128.
76. Harris, *Attlee*, p. 470.
77. NJC, 16 November 1950, BK 2/283.
78. TGWU FGPC, 15 February 1951, MSS.126/T&G/1/1/29.
79. Industrial Disputes 1951, BK 2/71.
80. Jack Dash, *Good Morning, Brothers!*, pp. 80–2.
81. EC, 7 February 1951, CAB 134.
82. Michael Foot, *Aneurin Bevan II 1945–60*, pp. 318–19; John Campbell, *Nye Bevan and the Mirage of British Socialism*, p. 224.
83. Foot, *Bevan II*, p. 230.
84. This characterisation of Callaghan was provided by Peter Jenkins; Lewis Minkin, *The Contentious Alliance*, pp. 112.
85· Dash, *Good Morning, Brothers!*, p. 77.
86. EC, 9 February 1951, CAB 134.
87. Trade Disputes, 1951, LAB 34/67.

88. TGWU General Executive Council, General Secretary's Quarterly Report, 5 March 1951, MSS.126/T&G/1/1/29.
89. Tony Benn, *Years of Hope: Diaries 1940–1962*, p. 140.
90. *Transport and General Workers' Record,* October–November 1950.
91. TGWU GEC, 8 March 1951, MSS.126/T&G/1/1/29.
92. *The Times*, 10 April 1951.
93. 'Brothers', broadcast BBC Radio 4, 5 January 1993.
94. Dash, *Good Morning, Brothers!*, p. 81; London RIRO memo, 18 April 1951, LAB 10/1039.
95. Joint Consultative Committee, 24 January and 4 April 1951, LAB 10/1006.
96. Cabinet Conclusions, 26 July 1951, CAB 128.
97. DNTGC, 19 April 1951.
98. Kenneth O. Morgan, *Labour People*, p. 214; *Labour in Power*, p. 440.
99. Foot, *Bevan II*, p. 320.

Chapter 6: Conclusion: The Great Alliance

1. Peter Hennessy, *Never Again: Britain 1945–1951*, p. 382.
2. Trade Disputes (All Industries) 1945–51, LAB 34/60–67.
3. David W. Ellwood, *Rebuilding Europe: Western Europe, America and Postwar Reconstruction*, p. 92.
4. John Lovell, *Stevedores and Dockers*, especially pp. 214–18.
5. Cabinet Conclusions, 14 and 20 October 1954; 14 June 1955, CAB 128.
6. Steve Peak, *Troops in Strikes*, pp. 105–6.
7. Robert Taylor, *The Trade Union Question in British Politics*, p. 139.
8. Barbara Castle, *The Castle Diaries 1964–1976*, p. 281.
9. *In Place of Strife: A Policy For Industrial Relations* (Cmnd. 3888, January 1969), p. 20, pp. 29–30.
10. Lewis Minkin, *The Contentious Alliance*, p. 114.

Bibliography

A. Unpublished Primary Sources

1. Government Papers, Public Records Office, Kew

BK 1	National Dock Labour Corporation.
BK 2	National Dock Labour Board.
CAB 21	Registered files, Prime Ministerial correspondence and briefing papers.
CAB 128	Cabinet Minutes and Conclusions
CAB 129	Cabinet Papers.
CAB 130	Ad–hoc Cabinet Committees.
CAB 132	Lord President's Committee.
CAB 134	Cabinet Emergencies Committee.
FO 800	Private Papers of Foreign Secretary.
LAB 10	Ministry of Labour & National Service. Industrial Relations Department.
LAB 16	Ministry of Labour & National Service. Solicitor's Department.
LAB 34	Ministry of Labour & National Service. Records of Industrial Disputes.
LAB 43	Minister of Labour's Private Papers.
MT 63	Ministry of Transport. Port Transit Files.
MT 81	Ministry of Transport. Ports: Registered Files.
PREM 8	Prime Minister's Office.
T 228	Treasury. Trade Department file.

2. Papers of Employers' Organisations and Trade Unions

London Museum Library:

BPA	National Association of Port Employers working files.
LWA	London Wharfingers' Association working files.
	National Association of Port Employers, Executive Committee.
	Port Employers in London (London Ten) files.

Modern Records' Centre, University of Warwick:

MSS.15 B/40	Frank Maitland (ILP journalist and activist) deposit.
MSS.126	Transport and General Workers' Union.
MSS.292	Trades Union Congress.

National Museum of Labour History, Manchester:
National Amalgamated Stevedores and Dockers.

Transport House, London:
Transport and General Workers' Union, Docks National Trade Group
Committee.

B. Printed Primary Sources

1. Newspapers

Daily Herald
Daily Worker
Manchester Guardian
Scotsman
The Times

BBC Press Clippings Collection, Edinburgh University Library.

Communist Party of Great Britain Archive, Wallis Road, London (now
in National Museum of Labour History, Manchester):   *World News and
Views.*

2. Official Reports

Parliamentary Debates, Fifth Series, Volumes 376–487.
House of Lords Debates, Fifth Series, Volume 164.
Statement on Personal Incomes, Costs and Prices (Cmd. 7321, February
1948).
Review of the British Dock Strikes (Cmd. 7851, December 1949).
Unofficial Stoppages in the London Docks. Report of a Committee of Inquiry
(Cmd. 8236, May 1951).
Port Transport Industry. Report of a Committee of Inquiry (Cmd. 9813, July
1956).
In Place of Strife. A Policy For Industrial Relations (Cmnd. 3888, January
1969).

3. Trade Union Publications

Trades Union Congress, *Defend Democracy*, November 1948.
Trades Union Congress, *The Tactics of Disruption*, March 1949.
Denis Delay, *Myths About the Origins and Effects of the National Dock
Labour Scheme*, Trades Union Congress, 1986.
Transport and General Workers' Record, 1940–51.

4. Unofficial Pamphlets

Modern Records Centre:
MSS.15B/M/3/D/1/31 National Docks Strike Committee, *To You The Public
We Present Our Case*, November 1945.

Public Records Office:

BK 1/105 London Central Strike Committee, *Why Strike?*, October 1945.

BK 1/60 National Portworkers' Defence Committee, *The Enquiry and YOU!*, May 1947.

BK 2/72 London Portworkers' Strike Committee, *The Men's Own Case*, June 1948.

Ibid. London Portworkers' Strike Committee, *Reflections on the Strike*, July 1948.

BK 2/76 London Central Lock-out Committee, *We Want Work*, June 1949.

LAB 16/201 London Central Lock-out Committee, *To All Port Workers*, June 1949.

BK 2/79 Birkenhead Portworkers' Committee, Untitled, September 1950.

Ibid. London Portworkers' Committee, Untitled, September 1950.

C. Secondary Sources

Place of publication London unless otherwise stated.

1. Articles

Kenneth Knowles, 'The Post–War Dock Strikes', *Political Quarterly* Volume XXVII (1951).

Fred Lindop, 'Unofficial Militancy in the Royal Group of Docks 1945–67', *Oral History*, Volume 11 Number 2, Autumn 1983.

Dennis MacShane, 'Workers of the World Unite', *History Today*, September 1990.

Raphael Samuel, 'The Lost World of British Communism', *New Left Review* No. 154, November–December 1985.

– 'Staying Power: The Lost World of British Communism, Part Two', *New Left Review* No. 156, March–April 1986.

2. Books

Paul Addison, *The Road to 1945* (Jonathan Cape, 1975).

M. Adereth, *The French Communist Party: A Critical History* (Manchester University Press, 1984).

V.L. Allen, *Trade Union Leadership* (Longman, 1957).

– *Trade Unions and the Government* (Longman, 1960).

Correlli Barnett, *The Audit of War* (Macmillan, 1986).

Tony Benn, *Years of Hope: Diaries, Papers and Letters, 1940–1962* (Hutchinson, 1994).

Sam Bornstein and Al Richardson, *Two Steps Back: Communists and the Wider Labour Movement, 1935–45* (Socialist Platform Ltd, 1982).

Jack and Bessie Braddock, *The Braddocks* (MacDonald, 1963).

Fernand Braudel, *The Mediterranean and the Mediterranean in the Age of Philip II* (Harper Collins, 1992).

Alan Bullock, *The Life and Times of Ernest Bevin, Volume One: Trade Union Leader 1881–1940* (Heinemann, 1960).

– *Volume Two: Minister of Labour* (Heinemann, 1975).

– *Ernest Bevin, Foreign Secretary, 1945–51* (Heinemann, 1983).

Alec Cairncross, *Years of Recovery: British Economic Policy 1945–51* (Cambridge University Press, 1985).

Angus Calder, *The People's War* (Jonathan Cape, 1969).

James Callaghan, *Time and Chance* (Collins, 1987).

John Callaghan, *British Trotskyism. Theory and Practice* (Blackwell, 1984).

John Campbell, *Nye Bevan and the Mirage of British Socialism* (Weidenfeld and Nicolson, 1987).

Barbara Castle, *The Castle Diaries 1964–1976* (Macmillan, 1990).

– *Fighting All the Way* (Macmillan, 1993).

H.A. Clegg, *General Union: A Study of the National Union of General and Municipal Workers* (Oxford University Press, 1954).

– *A History of British Trade Unions since 1889. Volume III 1934–1951* (Oxford University Press, 1994).

Ken Coates and Tony Topham, *The Making of the Labour Movement: The Formation of the Transport and General Workers' Union 1870–1922* (Spokesman, 1994).

J.E. Cronin and J. Schneer (eds), *Social Conflict and the Political Order in Modern Britain* (Croom Helm, 1982).

Jack Dash, *Good Morning, Brothers!* (Lawrence and Wishart, 1969).

Paul Davies, *A.J. Cook* (Manchester University Press, 1987).

Justin Davis-Smith, *The Attlee and Churchill Administrations and Industrial Unrest 1945–55* (Pinter, 1990).

Isaac Deutscher, *Stalin: A Political Biography* (Oxford University Press, 1966).

G.G. Eastwood, *George Isaacs* (John Gardiner, 1952).

David W. Ellwood, *Rebuilding Europe: Western Europe, America and Postwar Reconstruction* (Longman, 1992).

Michael Foot, *Aneurin Bevan I 1897–1945* (MacGibbon and Kee, 1962).

– *Aneurin Bevan II 1945–60* (Davis Poynter, 1973).

Kenneth Harris, *Attlee* (Weidenfeld and Nicolson, 1982).

Peter Hennessy, *Never Again: Britain 1945–51* (Jonathan Cape, 1992).

Stephen Hill, *The Dockers: Class and Tradition in London* (Heinemann, 1976).

Bill Hunter, *They Knew Why They Fought: Unofficial Struggles and Leadership on the Docks 1945–1989* (Index, 1994).

Keith Jeffery and Peter Hennessy, *States of Emergency* (Routledge and Kegan Paul, 1983).

Kevin Jefferys (ed.), *Labour and the Wartime Coalition. From the Diaries of James Chuter Ede 1941–1945* (Historians' Press, 1987).

Russell Jones, *Wages and Employment Policy 1936–1985* (Allen and Unwin, 1987).

Francis King and George Matthews (eds), *About Turn: The Communist Party and the Outbreak of the Second World War* (Lawrence and Wishart, 1990).

V.I. Lenin, *'Left Wing' Communism: An Infantile Disorder* (Foreign Languages Press, 1975).

John Lovell, *Stevedores and Dockers* (Macmillan, 1969).

Ross McKibbin, *The Ideologies of Class: Social Relations in Britain 1880–1950.* (Oxford University Press, 1990).

Ernest Mandel, *The Meaning of the Second World War* (Verso, 1986).

Keith Middlemas, *Politics in Industrial Society* (Andre Deutsch, 1979).

Ralph Miliband, *Parliamentary Socialism* (Merlin, 1973).

Lewis Minkin, *The Contentious Alliance: Trade Unions and the Labour Party* (Edinburgh University Press, 1992).

Kenneth O. Morgan, *Labour in Power 1945–1951* (Oxford University Press, 1984).

– *Labour People* (Oxford University Press, 1992).

– *The People's Peace: British History 1945–1987* (Oxford University Press, 1990).

Steve Peak, *Troops in Strikes* (Russell Press, 1984).

Henry Pelling, *Britain and the Marshall Plan* (Macmillan, 1988).

– *A History of British Trade Unions* (Penguin, 1963).

– *The Labour Governments, 1945–51* (Macmillan, 1984).

Henry Phelps Brown, *The Origins of Trade Union Power* (Oxford University Press, 1986).

Gordon Phillips and Noel Whiteside, *Casual Labour: The Unemployment Question in the Port Transport Industry 1880–1970* (Oxford University Press, 1985).

Ben Pimlott, *Harold Wilson* (HarperCollins, 1992).

Guy Routh, *Occupation and Pay in Britain, 1906–79* (Macmillan, 1980).

Victor Rothwell, *Britain and the Cold War* (Jonathan Cape, 1982).

John Saville, *The Labour Movement in Britain* (Faber and Faber, 1987).

Eric Silver, *Victor Feather, TUC* (Victor Gollancz, 1973).

John Stevenson and Chris Cook, *The Slump* (Jonathan Cape, 1977).

A.J.P. Taylor, *English History 1914–45* (Oxford University Press, 1965).

Robert Taylor, *The Trade Union Question in British Politics* (Blackwell, 1993).

Willie Thompson, *The Good Old Cause: British Communism 1920–1991* (Pluto Press, 1992).

Nick Tiratsoo (ed.), *The Attlee Years* (Pinter, 1991).

Charles Webster, *The Health Services Since the War, Volume I, Problems of Health Care: The National Health Service Before 1957* (HMSO, 1988).

Peter Weiler, *British Labour and the Cold War* (Stanford University Press, 1988).

Francis Williams, *A Prime Minister Remembers* (Heinemann, 1961).

David F. Wilson, *Dockers: The Impact of Industrial Change* (Fontana, 1972).

3. Additional Biographical Information

Dictionary of Labour Biography (Macmillan, 1975–1993).

Dictionary of National Biography (Oxford University Press, 1941–50, 1951–60).

Who Was Who (various volumes).

M. Stenton and S. Lees (eds), *Who's Who of British Members of Parliament. Vol. IV 1945–1979* (Harvester Press, 1981).

Index